SPORTS ANALYTICS

As the analysis of big datasets in sports performance becomes a more entrenched part of the sporting landscape, so the value of sport scientists and analysts with formal training in data analytics grows. *Sports Analytics* provides the most authoritative and comprehensive guide to the use of analytics in sports and its application in sports performance, coaching, talent identification and sports medicine available.

Employing an approach-based structure and integrating problem-based learning throughout the text, the book clearly defines the difference between analytics and analysis and goes on to explain and illustrate methods including:

- Interactive visualisation
- Simulation and modelling
- Geospatial data analysis
- Spatiotemporal analysis
- Machine learning
- Genomic data analysis
- Social network analysis

Offering a mixed-methods case study chapter, no other book offers the same level of scientific grounding or practical application in sports data analytics. *Sports Analytics* is essential reading for all students of sports analytics, and useful supplementary reading for students and professionals in talent identification and development, sports performance analysis, sports medicine and applied computer science.

Ambikesh Jayal is a Senior Lecturer in Computing and Information Systems at Cardiff Metropolitan University, UK.

Allistair McRobert is a Senior Lecturer of Performance Analysis at Liverpool John Moores University, UK.

Giles Oatley is a Senior Lecturer at Federation University, Australia.

Peter O'Donoghue is a Reader in Sports Performance Analysis in Cardiff School of Sport at Cardiff Metropolitan University, UK.

Routledge Studies in Sports Performance Analysis

Series Editor
Peter O'Donoghue
Cardiff Metropolitan University

Routledge Studies in Sports Performance Analysis is designed to support students, lecturers and practitioners in all areas of this important and rapidly developing discipline. Books in the series are written by leading international experts in sports performance analysis and cover topics including match analysis, analysis of individual sports and team sports, technique analysis, data analytics, performance analysis for high-performance management, and various methodological areas. Drawing on the latest research, and introducing key concepts and best practice, the series meets a need for accessible, up-to-date texts at all levels of study and work in performance analysis.

Available in this series:

Data Analysis in Sport
Peter O'Donoghue and Lucy Holmes

Performance Analysis in Team Sports
Pedro Passos, Duarte Araújo and Anna Volossovitch

Doing a Research Project in Sport Performance Analysis
Peter O'Donoghue, Lucy Holmes and Gemma Robinson

Sports Analytics
Analysis, Visualisation and Decision Making in Sports Performance
Ambikesh Jayal, Allistair McRobert, Giles Oatley and Peter O'Donoghue

For more information about this series, please visit: www.routledge.com/Routledge-Studies-in-Sports-Performance-Analysis/book-series/RSSPA

Routledge Studies in Sports Performance Analysis

Series Editor

Peter O'Donoghue

Cardiff Metropolitan University

SPORTS ANALYTICS

ANALYSIS, VISUALISATION
AND DECISION MAKING IN
SPORTS PERFORMANCE

**AMBIKESH JAYAL, ALLISTAIR McROBERT,
GILES OATLEY AND PETER O'DONOGHUE**

Routledge
Taylor & Francis Group

LONDON AND NEW YORK

Abhikash Jayal

I would like to dedicate my contribution in this book to my parents, especially to my father Kaushal Anand, and my beloved wife Aavia for their love and encouragement.

Alistair McRobert

I dedicate this work to my wife, Gliona, for her love, support and understanding.

Giles Oatley

I would like to dedicate my contributions in this book to my dearly beloved wife Cristina.

Peter O'Donoghue

I dedicate the work I contributed to the book to Professor Richard Bhaig Ahan of the Cardiff School of Sport for his unstinting support to me.

CONTENTS

FIGURES

xii

TABLES

PREFACE

The terms *analytics*, *data science*, *big data* and *Data Age* have come to prominence in recent years. Analytics is now applied within business, banking, medicine and security sectors as well as sports. The benefits of using data during player recruitment and talent development processes have been well recognised since Michael Lewis (2003) wrote the book *Moneyball* (New York, NY: W.W. Norton and Co.) and Brad Pitt starred in a film of the same name. Moneyball is the nonfictional story of how general manager Billy Beane used sabermetrics to recruit undervalued players, helping the Oakland A's compete with wealthier baseball teams.

Recent developments in information technology have increased our ability to record and store large volumes of data. Developments in data capture technology, storage capacity, system portability and output devices have been exploited by the field of sports performance analysis as described by Mike Hughes and Ian Franks during a keynote address at the World Congress of Science and Football III (1995, 'Computerised notational analysis of football', Cardiff, UK). Since this keynote address, there have been further developments in data capture and storage technology within sports performance analysis. Player tracking systems can collect large volumes of data during training and competition. This is just one source of data available to performance analysts who are increasingly working in a multidisciplinary role dealing with various scientific data.

The opportunities presented by large volumes of high-quality data have been recognised by sports organisations, with marketing decisions increasingly justified by analytic approaches. Textbooks by Harrison and Bukstein (2017) and Fried and Mumcu (2017) provide excellent examples of such analytic processes within chapters written by an array of academic and practicing experts. Alamar's (2013) book is more relevant to the coaching context and is heavily referred to in the current book as a result. However, a gap remains with respect to analytics opportunities arising from specific advances within the area of sports performance analysis. Sports analytics modules and, indeed, programmes can now be taken within universities and this book provides background material on analytic principles and approaches.

The book commences with an introductory chapter describing analytics. The term has been widely used and, in some cases, misused. Some work described as "analytics" applies the same methods that would typically have been previously referred to as "analysis" methods. The distinction between "analytics" and more routine traditional "analysis" is not a black and white distinction. However, the first chapter provides a framework allowing readers to consider whether approaches can be described as analytics. Chapter 2 discusses different types of data used in sports performance analysis and charts the progress in data processing from the hand notation era through the present, summarising the "Data Age 2025" report in the context of sports.

Chapters 3 to 10 discuss different analytics approaches that can be used in sports performance analysis. Chapter 3, "Interactive visualisation", uses the decathlon in track and field athletics to describe how data can be analysed and presented to inform decathletes and their coaches of the areas to concentrate on to increase their points. Chapter 4, "Simulation and modelling", uses the 2019 Rugby World Cup as an example of tournament prediction for target setting purposes. Chapters 5 and 6 cover the related areas of geospatial data and spatiotemporal analysis. Chapter 5 provides a background to geospatial data technology followed by Chapter 6 discussing the analysis of player movement in team games in detail. Chapter 7, "Machine learning and sports", covers the primary statistical, text processing, rule-based and artificial intelligence methods used to analyse data within data mining activities. Chapter 10 provides a macroscopic view of broad knowledge discovery in data bases (KDD) and data mining approaches that utilise the analysis techniques covered in Chapter 7. Chapter 8 discusses the possibilities of genomics in sports, which has potential uses within talent development programmes. The chapter includes details of genes and genomic analysis services that are relevant to sports performance. Chapter 9 on social network analysis explores how it can be used to examine transfer activity between clubs as well as interaction between players in team games.

Chapter 11 considers the logistical challenges presented by analytic processes, especially where multiple methods are applied to data. In particular, the experience of analysing decathlon data from Chapter 3 is discussed as rationale for data management environments and analytics infrastructure. The final chapter of the book is a case study on sports analytics applications in soccer. The chapter commences by covering common analysis requirements in soccer coaching and management. Having established this background, the chapter describes an analytics approach developed through a collaboration of academics and practitioners.

REFERENCES

Alamar, B.C. (2013) *Sports analytics: A guide for coaches, managers and other decision makers*, New York, NY: Columbia University Press.
Fried, G. and Mumcu, C. (2017) *Sport analytics: A data-driven approach to sport business and management*, London: Routledge.
Harrison, C.K. and Bukstein, S. (2017) *Sports business analytics: Using data to increase revenue and improve operational efficiency*, London: Routledge.

CHAPTER 1

WHAT IS ANALYTICS?

INTRODUCTION

The purpose of this first chapter is to distinguish between analytics and other forms of data analyses activities. The term *analytics* has been frequently used and, in some cases, misused in recent years. "Analytics" is not just another label for methods that have been traditionally referred to as "analysis". There is a school of thought that the term analytics applies when data are analysed in a way that supports decision making. In our view, however, this alone does not mean that the term analytics should be used. There are many forms of routine data analyses activities that inform decision making within management information systems (MIS) and other important application areas. Changes have occurred in recent years that fundamentally differ from the way data have been previously analysed. Graduates who earlier would have run a mile from any form of quantitative analysis now aspire to follow careers in "data science" and "analytics" and are up-skilling in packages and programming languages such as R, Tableau and Python. This is not because some relabeling of quantitative analysis has made it sexy or trendy – there has been a genuine change in the type, volume and format of data available, how the data are captured, how they are analysed and how resulting information is used. Statistics and data mining, which have developed separately from visualisation and interactive techniques (Keim et al., 2010: 3), have recently begun integrating with visualisation.

The volume of data created is increasing; in 2013, reports indicated that 90% of the world's data had been created in the preceding two years

(Science Daily, 2013; IBM, no date). Many readers will not remember the days before mobile phones, tablets, the Internet and social media. Photographs used to be taken with cameras and were not viewable as photographic prints or slides until the film had been developed (by the way, we do not mean the slides presented in Microsoft PowerPoint). This usually required that a person send or take the film to a film processing business and, perhaps, receive their prints and/or slides a week later. Nowadays, a photograph can be taken, checked, edited and placed on social media websites for viewing by a wide audience in a matter of seconds. There have been similar advances in video. In the 1970s, the British Broadcasting Corporation (BBC) showed highlights of two matches on its "Match of the Day" programme; these were the only two matches they filmed that weekend. Today, all professional soccer matches as well as many local semi-professional soccer matches are filmed. Individual amateur clubs in many sports can film their games in full. Individuals can make video recordings, edit these and upload them onto social media within seconds. However, the widespread use of video has not been without problems. Parents can routinely be seen filming their children competing in sports using mobile phones and tablets. Event organisers seem to have lost control of who films at events. Child protection policies typically require anyone filming at sports venues to register with the venue, provide identification details and disclose what they are filming and the purpose of the recordings being made. These policies are becoming increasingly harder to enforce; just about everyone in the audience has a mobile phone capable of recording video.

Marr (2015) predicted that the volume of data created would continue to grow until 2020 in a blog post that discussed the growth in video data, photographs and data gathered from smart devices. However, he also stated that less than 1% of the data created up to the time of his blog post were actually analysed. Indeed, there is agreement from other sources that data are being generated faster than they can be analysed (Keim et al., 2010: 1). Thus, there is great potential for exploiting "big data"; for instance, Marr (2015) suggested that the integrated use of "big data" could reduce healthcare costs and increase operating margins of retail businesses. It is essential to avoid using data for irrelevant tasks and to avoid processing and presenting data in inappropriate ways (Keim et al., 2010: 1). A further challenge is to provide the right information at the right time for decision support. This requires an understanding of the context of the data, the business processes and interactions with

2

customers to determine where data can be exploited most beneficially. This could involve creating models of major organisational entities or of customer behaviour (Keim et al., 2010: 24). For example, supermarkets may have a store card that has benefits for the customer while also allowing purchase data to be gathered in a straightforward manner every time the customer uses the supermarket card. This data can then be used to model customer purchasing patterns both at the individual level and in terms of broader customer groupings and trends.

The volumes of data that can now be exploited, technological advances, the need of businesses to effectively use these data and the constraints of time and cost have all led to the current era of data analytics. Businesses can use data to achieve an information edge over their competitors (Alamar, 2013: 2–4). The emergence of data analytics has been driven by business needs, opportunities created by new and growing data sources, medical research and intelligence work by government agencies. Many of these developments have been quite independent but have created opportunities for data science/analytics businesses to develop and form partnerships with major corporations. There are now international conferences and webinars on data analytics. However, there is no single professional body for data analytics and thus there is no uniform definition of analytics. Therefore, we have considered the main texts in the areas of sports data analytics (Alamar, 2013; Miller, 2016) and knowledge of data analytics used in other domains (Keim et al., 2010) to form what we feel is a consensus on an accepted analytics definition.

A good starting point is Alamar's (2013: 5) sports analytics framework, which recognises the roles of data management, analytic models and information systems in supporting decisions. Data management is necessary so that data can be captured and stored in a useable form. The analytic models describe how these data can be processed to answer queries of interest to the decision makers. The role of information systems is to ensure that resulting information is presented in an understandable form that makes decision making efficient. An important fourth component discussed by Alamar, but not explicitly shown in his framework diagram, is leadership. Initiating any change within organisations requires leadership and the introduction of analytic systems is no exception. Organisations can be reluctant to change current practices even when there are clear benefits to such change. Management needs to fully support and drive such changes to capitalise on their investment in analytics. Developing an analytics system requires an understanding of how data and information are used in decision making within the business and how this decision-making process can be enhanced (Alamar, 2013: 79). Alamar (2013: 81–82) used an example of a magnet board for discussing tactics in sports and the opportunities and concerns with replacing this with a fully automated display and supporting database.

Figure 1.1 represents Keim et al.'s (2010: 10) visual analytics process. Data can be transformed by cleaning, normalising or grouping. The visualisation tools available can be selected interactively by users. This requires infrastructure (Keim et al., 2010: 12) to integrate the different elements of the analytics process as well as an effective interface that can be used by decision makers who have a transparent view of the undertaken analyses. For example, visual tools could be applied first to help explore data and develop hypotheses. Once working hypotheses are established, quantitative techniques can be applied.

Selling analytics is important, as there are costs to create data management systems, purchase analytics packages, introduce information systems and staff these. The benefits to decision makers need to outweigh the costs. Decision makers have time to use high-quality well-presented information in decision making but they may not have time to gather the data. Prior to the introduction of an analytics system, decision makers may have spent time gathering the data they need, thus saving costs in paying other staff to do it, but this may not have been the best use of the

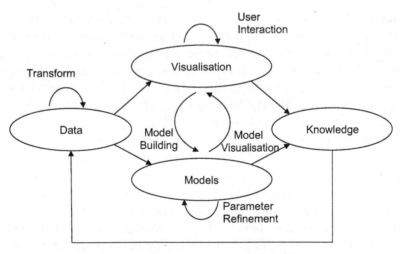

Figure 1.1 Visual analytics process (Keim et al., 2010)

4

decision makers' time and involved a lost opportunity cost. One way to sell analytics to businesses is to justify its cost as less than the lost opportunity cost of not having an analytics system.

The challenge of selling data analytics to sports bodies comes against a backdrop of reluctancy to invest in sports science support services. Sports performance analysis has been provided, in some cases in high levels of a sport, using unpaid interns and volunteers. This challenge was covered in the Sportdata & Performance Forum, held in Dublin in November 2016:

> Directors within elite sporting organisations cannot be expected to sanction spending on new data analytics and associated technologies without a credible assessment of what the return on such investments might be. Sportdata & Performance Forum shows you how to overcome this challenge!
>
> (SDPF, 2016)

This forum was an opportunity to discuss how to optimise the use of sports analytics to gain a competitive advantage.

The main criterion that distinguishes analytics from more routine data analysis activities is the integrated use of computerised data analysis techniques with human expertise (Keim et al., 2010: 149). There are things that computers can do well and other things in which human experts are better (Miller, 2016: 23). Analytics makes complementary use of both types of analysis. This requires decision makers to have some understanding of the data, where they came from and how they are analysed. The following section provides some examples of integrated use of computer technology and human expertise in decision-making contexts.

ANALYTICS IN NON-SPORTS DOMAINS

Credit card and fraud detection

Data analytics is relevant in all fields where the exploitation of large volumes of data can be beneficial to organisational success. Areas where analytics is relevant include physics, astronomy, climate, emergency management, epidemiology and terrorism informatics (Keim et al., 2010: 8).

One way in which analytics goes beyond routine data analysis is in the use of "business intelligence". Intelligence provides the ability to predict events or recommend courses of action using available information. Business intelligence includes identifying recurring situations, forecasting trends and detecting events (Keim et al., 2010: 9).

Credit card fraud detection is a branch of business intelligence. Many readers may, at some time, have been contacted by their banks about suspected credit card fraud. The banks have fraud detection systems that are triggered as soon as a suspicious transaction takes place. These systems use information about the customer and the types of transactions for which they use their credit card together with details of the suspicious transaction that has just been made. Typically, the bank's fraud detection unit will contact the customer to query the transaction. If it was a legitimate transaction made by the customer, the customer's profile information can be updated to prevent further unwarranted flagging, especially if this type of transaction may be more frequent in the future. If, on the other hand, the transaction was not made by the customer, action can be taken to protect the customer's account and investigate the fraud further. O'Donoghue (2016) commented on the occasional legitimate transactions he has made that appear unusual but had not been flagged by his bank's fraud detection system. In considering some fraudulent transactions attempted on his credit card account that may not appear so unusual, O'Donoghue commented that his bank knows more about his personality than he does! The banks' fraud detection units are good at what they do. Their processes certainly fall under the umbrella of data analytics because they are dealing with transaction data that are constantly streaming in, transactions are monitored by the detection systems in real time and the customer and bank staff are involved in decision making.

Transport

Transport is another field in which analytics plays a vital role. Consider a rail network made up of multiple interconnected rail lines. If a train is delayed, it may cause delays to other trains travelling behind it on the same line. Passengers on the train may also be inconvenienced if they miss connections at the stations. The rail network is constantly monitored to not only identify where trains are delayed but to alert the rail

6

company to serious consequences of some delayed trains. Staff equipped with this information need to make real-time decisions to manage the situation. For example, consider a train travelling from station J to K to L and then station M. It may be decided that a train currently travelling between stations J and K will not make its usual stop at station L but will pass directly through the station on route to stop M. When this decision is made, it needs to be communicated to the relevant platform at station K as well as to the train. Passengers at station K will need to be advised not to board the train if they plan to get off the train at station L because the train will not stop there. Instead, they need to board a later train that travels from station K to station L. Passengers who are already on the train need to be advised that the train will not be stopping at station L before the train reaches station K. Any passengers currently on the train who are travelling to station L need to leave the train at station K and wait for the next train service travelling between stations K and L. Computerised systems can analyse the situation with respect to delayed trains and make suggestions about potential courses of action such as the one just described. It is up to human decision makers facilitated with this information to make the decisions and communicate them in sufficient time to avoid unnecessary inconvenience to passengers. There may be situations where making the right decision inconveniences tens of passengers but making the wrong decision could inconvenience thousands of passengers. This is all happening in real time; the world is not going to stop to allow the decision makers to consider the problem over a prolonged period. The large volume of data involved are updating constantly, complex algorithms are highlighting problems and potential solutions and decisions need to be made and implemented under time pressures. This clearly goes beyond a routine data analysis task and is instead an example of data analytics.

Meteorology

Weather has an impact on many areas of life (Stockton, 2016), including military activity, transport, business and entertainment. Weather forecasting has existed since ancient times and is of interest to the general public, who are provided with weather forecasts through the media. The accuracy of weather forecasting has been helped by the increase in sensors and satellites used to record the raw data as well as the increase in data processing power provided by modern computer systems. The potential damage and losses that can be caused by failing to forecast adverse weather conditions have motivated the use of big data in meteorology (Hamm, 2013). IBM has been developing the Deep Thunder system since 2016, which claims to forecast the weather 2.5 days sooner that other technologies (Gallagher, 2012). Modelling weather is extremely challenging and uses vast volumes of data. The way in which data are presented also influences human decision making within forecasting; Gallagher (2012) describes more visually informative presentations of weather data than the traditionally used weather maps. Whereas government agencies are prepared to fund some weather forecasting analytics that are of clear national benefit (Hamm, 2013), other weather analytics systems may be provided commercially. For example, wind farms may be prepared to pay for such services. More general apps may be marketable to mobile phone users who make decisions about what to wear when travelling to work or for leisure (Stockton, 2016).

DIFFERENCES BETWEEN SPORTS AND OTHER BUSINESSES

There are many similarities between the use of analytics in sports and other areas of business and industry. Sports businesses seek to make money through their various activities the same way any other business does. Like other businesses, sports businesses aim to generate revenue, develop marketing strategies and optimise pricing. Pricing needs to consider what Miller (2016: 126) refers to as the three Cs: costs, customers and competition. An example of analytics in sports contexts is predicting game day attendances (Miller, 2016: 106–109). If such predictions underestimate attendances, caterers may not make provisions for the needs of the fans. If the predictions overestimate attendances, too much raw material used in catering may go unused and wasted. The consequences of underestimating and overestimating attendances need to be considered when making decisions about catering and other services and products related to attendance.

A fundamental difference between businesses within sports and other fields is that sports businesses co-operate within leagues and tournaments (Miller, 2016: 1). The "on-field" competition between sports businesses is essential to maintaining interest from consumers, whether fans attending at stadia or television audiences. All sports businesses benefit individually from this co-operation within leagues and tournaments.

8

FRAMEWORK FOR COMPARING ANALYTICS
AND ROUTINE ANALYSIS

Methods can be compared in terms of different aspects. A good example of this is the comparison of qualitative and quantitative data analysis presented in a table by Thomas and Nelson (1996: 367–368). This chapter explains what the authors consider to be analytics by contrasting analytics with more routine traditional analyses using the aspects shown in Table 1.1. However, the distinction between analytics and traditional analysis is not as clear as the difference between quantitative and qualitative data analysis. Thomas and Nelson were able to list six aspects that each clearly distinguished between qualitative and quantitative methods; the use of research design, use of hypotheses, types of sample, setting, role of the researcher in data gathering and data analysis methods. There is such a variety of data analytics techniques that we cannot simply say that all the properties listed under the analytics column of Table 1.1 need to be in place for a method to be considered data analytics. For example, if a system monitors data that streams in, providing visual summary information to assist decision makers in real time, we can make a strong case for this being an example of analytics even though the system may not possess any of the other properties listed in this column. It is simply not a black and white distinction. We

Table 1.1 Framework for comparing analytics with traditional analysis

Aspect	Traditional analysis	Analytics
Data types and sources	Relatively simple, centralised	Complex, heterogeneous, distributed
Data quality	Complete, clean	Incomplete, inconsistent, updating (streaming)
Data format	Consistent	Variable
Analysis methods	Small number of methods	Large array of analysis tools
Decision makers' view of data processing	Opaque	Transparent
Relation between analysis and decision making tasks	Sequential, lapse time	Concurrent, real time
Output	Fixed report	Interactive, dynamic presentation, visualisation
Data querying	Standard process, some ad hoc queries	Interactive, flexible exploratory querying

cannot even say there is a minimum number of the properties listed in the analytics column that are required for a system to be considered a data analytics system. Whether we describe a system as a data analytics system depends on both the number of these properties that it possesses as well as the extent to which they are present in the system.

DATA TYPES AND DATA SOURCES

In sports, data and information are used to represent different things (O'Donoghue, 2015: 62–63). Data are input into a process that produces summary information. Where there is a pipeline of processes, the information produced by one process may be the raw data that are entered into a further process in the pipeline. Thus, data and information are considered with respect to particular processes. This use of the terms "data" and "information" comes from computer programming lessons in the 1980s using third generation programming languages (Chandor, 1980: 106). Simple data processing systems input data from a single file, processing it to produce standardised output information. Some of this output information was standardised and printed on stationery. During the early days of "office automation", this saved printing time because only case-specific information needed to be added to the form.

Analytics approaches are not so simple and use data of multiple types that may include sound, video, images, written reports, other qualitative data, quotes, numerical information and categorical facts that are either unstructured or of various structures. Alamar (2013: 25–32) discusses data about baseball players, including box score data and video clips. Unstructured data such as scout reports and interviews can also be included within the array of data maintained on players. Later in his book, Alamar (2013: 47) considers intangible elements within analytic processes; these include qualities such as leadership and coachability. Effort is needed to ensure these multiple types of relevant data are stored effectively. This can involve video clipping and imposing a degree of structure on originally unstructured data. Cross referencing between video and event data is possible in standard video analysis packages. We should never discard the full match video, as we can afford certain volumes of data duplication. The various types of data may come from multiple repositories that may be physically stored at different sites and accessed over distributed networks of data stores.

10

Metrics are combinations of existing variables that can be used more efficiently than multiple raw variables by analytic systems. These metrics can be tuned over time and new metrics can be developed. Alamar (2013: 66–75) described four stages of metric creation: opportunity, survey, analysis and communication. The raw data that are stored within data management systems provide the opportunity to develop metrics that can be used more efficiently by decision makers than current forms of provided information. Existing ways of summarising the data, including previous attempts to create metrics, can be surveyed. The process of pilot testing and refining metrics involves an analysis of data to determine whether the proposed metric is associated with aspects of business success of interest to decision makers. Once the metric is finalised, it needs to be communicated to decision makers to allow them to use it. This involves providing the measurement scale for the metric and how it can be interpreted by decision makers.

DATA SOURCES

There are challenges to using data from distributed sources; in analytic systems created without the use of pre-existing data stores, Alamar (2013: 9) recommends the use of centralised systems because of the advantage of having "one version of the truth". Centralised systems can store data more consistently in a way that is easier to access than distributed and hybrid systems (Alamar, 2013: 41–42). Integrated data can be used more synergetically than segregated data from distributed sources. The data to be stored also need to be considered carefully because large datasets are slower to process (Keim et al., 2010: 25). However, there is a balance between having smaller pre-processed datasets that are quicker to process and having more complete data that include rich contextual information important in decision making. For example, Alamar (2013: 35) described the problem of overreliance on previous performance data about an opponent in wrestling without considering whether that opponent's matches were against left- or right-handed wrestlers.

DATA QUALITY

There are two ways of looking at data quality. First, we can exclude any data from an analysis process that fails to demonstrate the necessary qualities of reliability and validity. Alamar (2013: 15) states that good information cannot be produced from bad data. There are seven desirable qualities that measurements should have (Miller, 2016: 30). They should be:

- Reliable: the process of measurement should be consistent and repeatable.
- Valid: the measurement should measure the concept of interest.
- Explicit: there should be an objective process for measurement with operational definitions of any terms used.
- Accessible: the data source for the measurement must be feasible and available.
- Tractable: the method can be used easily within wider analysis processes.
- Comprehensible: the measure must be as simple to understand as possible and have a means of interpreting its values.
- Transparent: the measurement procedure should not only be objectively applied but must also be documented for decision makers so they understand the measurement fully.

The second way of looking at data quality is to accept that the quality of some data might be limited. The data may be compromised by limited reliability but may still represent an important aspect of interest to decision makers. It may be the best data available despite the known problems. This means that we need to manage data quality issues within analytic processes. For example, when exit polls are used to predict the result of the UK general election, a margin of error is typically quoted. Managing inconsistent and incomplete data is a challenge for computerised systems. Data entry routines need to identify formatting errors and illogical inputs, prompting users to re-enter these data. An example of an illogical input occurs when someone is booking a return flight and enters a date that is before the date of departure. Many readers have experienced situations where they have had to re-enter data into systems and may find this frustrating. However, it is better that such errors are recognised and rectified early and that the data are entered correctly. The more important point to understand within this chapter is that although we may be used to online systems making these checks, they are not performed by magic. Someone had to implement these within system interfaces, with some systems needing to check input data with stored data during the validation process. This can require more than double the lines of code in a computerised system but it is necessary for commercially used software to have this level of robustness. Simpler systems for individual programmers may be used privately and require the user (system programmer) to ensure that all data are complete and correct before running the system. Error tolerance has become import-ant in real-time systems with the Ada and C++ programming languages including exception handling constructs. One property that may char-acterise a system as analytic is its ability to deal with incomplete and inconsistent data. Streaming data is never complete because more data (whether social media messages, transactions or other data) are continu-ally added. There may be inconsistencies within individual data records or between related data records. An example of a data record that con-tains inconsistent data regards a tennis match in which the server player is recorded to have won the point and a winner with an even number of shots played in the point. If there were an even number of shots, the last player to play the ball is the receiving player. If the serving player did win the point, it must have been because the receiving player made an error by playing the ball into the net or out of court. In a situation like this, the error can be flagged to be dealt with later, the system can insist on the data being corrected before it is stored or the error can be left as the user entered it. An inconsistency between two data records occurs when the scores recorded for two points indicate they were consecu-tive points within the match but the score at the start of the point and the recorded outcome of the first point are inconsistent with the score recorded at the start of the second point. Again, this error can be flagged for immediate or later correction. Alternatively, data records that fail to satisfy consistency and completeness checks can be excluded from some analyses. Uncertainty within some data may be considered a property of the data to be reasoned about during analysis. This means that stochastic variables will be included to represent uncertainty within and between records. For example, in relational databases, links between records may have a likelihood weighting associated with them.

DATA FORMATS

Data files used in simple analysis processes store the data in a uniform format. This does not prevent variant records from being stored when necessary, which can be facilitated by programming languages, spread-sheet packages and database systems. Alamar (2013: 41–42) stated that

13

analytic systems should also aim to store data in uniform formats. The authors agree with this when a management information system is being set up for the first time with little to no pre-existing data stores that need to be integrated. However, very often, there are pre-existing and valuable data repositories that systems need to exploit. These may have differing formats and it may be necessary to develop protocols to transform data into some single uniform structure that can be dealt with by system functions. This avoids duplication of processing functions for different formats of the same data. For example, a spatiotemporal analysis system may be used to generate tactical information about performances in game sports using player movement data. Such data can come from a variety of player tracking technologies and are stored in formats developed for the data gathering systems. A spatiotemporal analysis system needs to analyse such data from a variety of sources; therefore, data will need to be transformed into a common format suitable for analysis. This common format improves the portability of the analysis system.

There are data management challenges arising from formatting issues. Systems often expand in terms of the data types used and so they need to be developed in a way that allows extension to the sets of variables used and volumes of data that can be stored. Traditional databases have structures that allow such expansion through the use of metadata. Once further data are included within data management systems, we also need flexibility to use changed information formats to show the results of newer analyses processes.

ANALYSIS METHODS

There are many different types of data and established ways of processing these data. Statistical analysis is well established, featuring procedures for difference testing, correlation, regression analysis and multivariate techniques implemented within commercially available statistical analysis packages such as SPSS (SPSS, an IBM company, Armonk, NY), Minitab (Minitab, State College, PA) and SAS (SAS Institute, Carly, NC). These packages typically employ a Windows-based user-friendly interface in which menus are used to navigate to popup windows where tests can be selected, applied to chosen variables and tailored with options. When analyses need to be repeated, going through the menus and selecting the necessary options for each occasion involves considerable duplication of

14

effort. This has spurred the advent of statistical programming languages, such as R (Free Publisher Foundation, Boston, MA), in which the analyses steps can be stored and reused on different datasets. This is similar to the stored program concept in computing that saves instructions having to be re-specified every time they are executed. Some statistical techniques come under the wider umbrella of machine learning, which will be discussed in Chapter 7. Other analysis methods include operational research used in logistics planning, scheduling of resources and optimisation problems. Qualitative data are analysed using interpretive content analyses methods. There are specialist economic analysis techniques that consider opportunities and costs in monetary terms. Genomic analysis is specialised in DNA, which is discussed in Chapter 8. Artificial intelligence techniques are used to process complex pattern-like data; this will be discussed further in Chapter 7. Data analysis systems could use one of these techniques to process relevant data. However, one criterion that could allow us to classify a system as analytic is that it uses more than one of the analysis methods listed here. As Miller (2016: 51) puts it, data scientists need to be methodological eclectics.

DECISION MAKERS' ROLE

A contrast between analytics and routine data analysis is that decision makers are not merely consumers of information but have a role in the analysis. Analytics fully integrates computerised data processing with expert human decision making. Alamar (2013: 55–63) discussed the role of decision makers within the analysis by considering the following five points:

1   The thought process that led to the analysis.
2   The context of the information.
3   The degree of uncertainty within the analysis.
4   How information informs the decision-making process.
5   How uncertainty can be further reduced.

The first point requires decision makers to ask relevant questions of the data. The context of any information used in decision making is important, as information may have been derived from previous situations that do not fully reflect the current one. There are three sources of uncertainty. First, there is genuine uncertainty due to inherent variability within the application. Second, there is uncertainty due to measurement issues relating to variables used. Third, there is uncertainty due to factors that have not been included within the analysis. The fourth point is concerned with how information produced by computers and other quantitative analyses techniques is used along with the experience and expertise of decision makers. The final point is addressed by having a cyclic process of improving methods and processes with experience. These considerations all require decision makers to have knowledge of data sources, data quality and the broad methods of analysis that have been used to produce the information. This transparency assists decision makers in weighting information appropriately when making decisions.

This contrast between analytics and traditional analysis can be further illustrated by considering sports performance analysis. When coaches use performance analysis support, they have typically played a key role in the development of the system by providing its functional requirements. The main functional requirements identified by coaches are the output variables produced by the system, summary event variables and indications of the types of related video sequences. The input data needed to produce these outputs can be derived by analysts without much further discussion with coaches. The data storage aspects of the system are often dictated by the generic video tagging package that the system uses during implementation; for example, Sportscode (HUDL, Omaha, NE), Dartfish (Dartfish, Fribourg, Switzerland), Nacsports (Las Palmas de Gran Canaria, Spain) and Focus (Dalgety Bay, Scotland). There are other sports analysis packages that do not involve event tagging such as STATS (STATS, Chicago, IL) that also have specific data formats. Once the system has been piloted, tested and accepted by the coaches, it can be used within their coaching practice. Typically, the analyst tags a match, providing summary statistics, video sequences and the whole match video to the coaches. The coaches may be unaware of the process of data entry although they may notice some events that have been tagged incorrectly. This lack of understanding of the analysis process can lead to lack of understanding of the data limitations as well as poor working conditions for analysts. Shared understanding of operational definitions by coaches and analysts helps ensure objectivity of data and further enhances data collection accuracy.

Some coaches have more of a grasp of analysis because they have conducted performance analysis tasks themselves. For example, coaches who are keen to provide quality feedback to players may receive tagged videos from analysts and then do further analysis and prepare highlight videos prior to team briefings. These coaches have a much greater ownership of the analysis and a deeper understanding of the data and its limitations. There may be some events that have been recorded incorrectly; for example, an event attributed to the wrong player. The coach may tolerate such errors made by the analyst during data entry, especially if they require the tagged video before the analyst can feasibly check every event entered. Analysts should make every effort to ensure the most important events are tagged correctly. As soon as a match is completed, the analyst should immediately check as much data as they can before the tagged video is handed over. There are simple consistency checks that can be done on the data; for example, in some team games, possessions alternate between teams. The possession change events can quickly be looked at to ensure that they do indeed alternate and analysts should correct any errors that have been made. Another example of a coding error is incorrect player identification. Events can be quickly reviewed using the interactive video replay facility of the tagging package. When it is done for each player in turn, an error attributed to the player that was committed by another player can be identified and corrected quite quickly. Any remaining coding errors will not have an undue effect on feedback to the players when the coaches are preparing highlights videos from the tagged video. This is because the coaches will see where such a tagging error has been made and not include the given clip within the presentation shown to the players. However, where data are used to monitor trends in performance without coaches inspecting relevant video sequences, it is particularly important to ensure the data are correct.

Coaches who take an active interest in the analysis can often be seen in close proximity to analysts during matches while they are coding the matches live. In such situations, performance information is typically generated live by the system and presented on specific output windows. This requires automatic processing of data as it is entered using features such as statistical windows in Sportscode. A statistical window contains scripts that calculate outputs based on raw data that have been entered and send the resulting information to different areas of the output window. The coach is able to view these outputs live and request to view video sequences of occasional events that have been recorded. Areas of the output window can change colour (from amber to green or red, for example) to highlight if a player is doing particularly well or poorly. These coaches have a much greater appreciation of the analysis process and the demands made upon analysts than coaches who do not engage with analysts during matches. Just as decision makers need to have an appreciation of the data they are using and the analysis methods, the analysts should also have a good understanding of the application context. As Miller (2016: 51) puts it, "data scientists should speak the language of business".

RELATION BETWEEN DATA ANALYSIS AND DECISION-MAKING TASKS

Traditional data analysis produces information that is used by decision makers to form policies and strategies. This is a sequential process in which the analysis is completed having produced all the necessary information for decision-making processes to use. Analysis within analytics processes operates concurrently, permitting back and forth communication between analysts and decision makers. Once initial information is available, decision makers may require further information to inform different elements of the decision.

Franks et al.'s (1983) model of performance analysis within a basic coaching process has stood the test of time, with more recent models adding detail to the original Franks et al. (1983) model as technology develops (O'Donoghue and Mayes, 2013; O'Donoghue, 2015). The Franks et al. (1983) model conveys a sequential approach whereby analysis is done and information is provided for use by coaches to help prepare athletes. The technology available to performance analysts today allows a more concurrent approach, as live analysis is possible during competition and training. The elements of Franks et al.'s (1983) model can be rearranged to reflect this concurrent relationship between analysis and decision making within analytic approaches. The portability of systems allows for information to be provided to coaches much more flexibly than in the 1980s. Video sequences and match statistics can be accessed when coaches are planning training sessions. With the advent of GPS systems, movement during training can be analysed and information used within training sessions. The Dartfish package (Dartfish, Fribourg, Switzerland) provides an "in-the-action" feature, displaying delayed video material of performances on the computer screen. This allows an athlete to perform a skill during training and observe it on a computer screen seconds later along with the coach before continuing with training.

18

An example of concurrent data analysis and decision making is in Formula 1 motor racing. This is a high-profile sport where big data analytics is used at all stages, from developing cars to simulating strategies for races to live race monitoring and decision support. The cars themselves have been described as "big data factories on wheels" (Moore-Colyer, 2015) employing hundreds of sensors monitoring thousands of components that feed telemetry data on wind force, tyre pressure, fuel burn and brake temperature to team engineers at the race venue (Gardiner, 2016). Technical regulations of the sport change regularly and big data plays a role in maximising performance within the constraints of the new regulations (Gardiner, 2016). When a car suffers damage during a race, live data are used to determine further damage if the car continues and the action that needs to be taken in the pits to best rectify the damage, as well as the race strategy that will give the best chance of success under the new circumstances (Bi, 2014). When watching Formula 1 races on television, viewers can see the multiple screens with purpose-designed dashboards presenting information in a manner to assist rapid decision making. During races, decisions need to be made about what instructions to provide to drivers and when to provide those instructions (Moore-Colyer, 2015).

Analytics is also used within the Extreme Sailing series to provide real-time and post-race information to competitors, coaches, spectators at the venues and Internet viewers (Extreme Sailing, 2016). This service has been developed by Extreme Sailing in collaboration with SAP. Wind measuring devices installed on buoys in the water and GPS devices on the competing boats gather data that are transmitted back to the SAP sailing cube where they are combined with geographical data about the venue and tidal information. The SAP sailing cube is a mobile television studio and editing suite that is transported to Extreme Sailing events across the world. Live video from the water is displayed on a giant screen for spectators and broadcast online. The data are presented as 2D and 3D visualisations to enhance the spectator experience. The 2D visualisations of sailing performances are sent to the boats in real time for use in tactical decisions. These tactical decisions may be made between races at an event using data from the preceding races. A coaching app displays a real-time dashboard on tablets used by coaches in non-competing boats on the water. This allows start line biases to be recognised and considered in tactical adjustments between races. The data can also be analysed post event to determine sailor profiles and optimise strategies for future races. The boat images in the 2D visualisations can be clicked on to obtain speed, bearing and wind angle data. There are specific analyses for important elements of races such as the start and winning lanes.

VISUALISATION

Visualisation combines automated analysis with interactive graphical presentations to make sense of large amounts of complex data (Keim et al., 2010: 7; Wong and Thomas, 2004). Visual analytics involves the development and use of tools to detect patterns in data and present these in appropriate ways for different user groups who need different views of the data. Examples of application areas for visualisation include 3D modelling in engineering, molecular structures, cosmology, biology and meteorology. Complex multi-dimensional data cannot be handled by traditional chart types and so alternative innovative presentation methods are required. There are many challenges in visualisation. Data need to be reduced and scaled so as not to overload users with information. Visualisation will be covered in Chapter 3.

DATA QUERYING

Traditional analysis processes involve basic work flows that provide the same information during working situations. For example, sports performance analysis will have a basic analysis process that is repeated for each match. This uses the same variables and provides information in a consistent format. There may be some ad hoc querying that takes place but this would be considered outside the main analysis process.

In analytic approaches, the need for flexible querying is a requirement of the system. Variables may evolve over time as decision makers tune the set of information they use and the way they use it. "What-if" questions can be explored using predictive models (Alamar, 2013: 107; Miller, 2016: 147–168) and simulated adjusting states or parameters to represent alternative decisions that could be taken or scenarios that could be faced. These predictive models can estimate probabilities of different outcomes given different scenarios. These probabilities can then be used together with value assessments of the outcomes, whether those

20

are benefits of a favourable outcome or penalties from less favourable outcomes. Such analyses allow decisions involving opportunities and risks to be much better informed.

Analyses to answer "what-if" ad hoc queries have implications for real-time analysis. There is a trade-off between the accuracy of predictions and the amount of time it takes to simulate alternative scenarios. Analysts can prepare results for anticipated queries in advance of decision makers using the information produced by simulations. Providing an ability to simulate scenarios in a real-time decision-making environment involves tailoring of the simulation system to introduce parameters for alternative scenarios of interest. This requires an easy-to-operate interface to allow these parameters to be entered and adjusted so that simulations can be quickly started. The number of simulation runs of the scenario must be reduced within real-time situations to allow results to be communicated efficiently to decision makers. This may require an effective visual presentation of alternative scenario predictions to allow comparisons to be made by decision makers. There also needs to be an understanding and, preferably, a representation of margins of error in predictions made using lower numbers of simulated runs within decision-making meetings. The increased margin of error is acceptable to decision makers when it promotes real-time analysis of "what-if" queries.

SUMMARY

Data are generated at ever increasing rates and there are opportunities for sports to utilise big data analytics. The distinction between routine analysis and analytics is not clear cut and is a matter of judgement based on the extent to which different aspects of analysis are present in a system. An approach may be considered analytic if one or more of the following are sufficiently present:

- Complex data are from multiple distributed sources.
- Inconsistent and incomplete data are used.
- Streaming data and live updates are involved.
- Data are in varying formats.
- Multiple analysis methods are applied.
- Data processing techniques are transparent to decision makers.

- Data processing and decision making operate concurrently.
- Information is provided interactively.
- Visualisation is used to manage the presentation of complex data.
- Ad hoc querying of data is supported.

REFERENCES

Alamar, B.C. (2013) *Sports analytics: A guide for coaches, managers and other decision makers*, NY: Columbia University Press.

Bi, F. (2014) 'How Formula One teams are using big data to get the inside edge'. www.forbes.com/sites/frankbi/2014/11/13/how-formula-one-teams-are-using-big-data-to-get-the-inside-edge/#2fd101344d6a, accessed 24th October 2016.

Chandor, A. (1980) *The Penguin dictionary of computers*, Harmondsworth, Middlesex, UK: Penguin.

Extreme Sailing (2016) http://ess2016.sapsailing.com/gwt/Home.html, accessed 22nd September 2016.

Franks, I.M., Goodman, D. and Miller, G. (1983) 'Human factors in sports systems: An empirical investigation of events in team games'. Proceedings of the Human Factors Society, 27th annual meeting, pp. 383–386.

Gallagher, S. (2012) 'How IBM's Deep Thunder delivers "hyper-local" forecasts 3–1/2 days out'. http://arstechnica.com/business/2012/03/how-ibms-deep-thunder-delivers-hyper-local-forecasts-3-12-days-out/, accessed 24th October 2016.

Gardiner, B. (2016) 'How big data is driving Formula 1 success'. www.cio.com.au/article/596554/how-big-data-driving-formula-1-success/, accessed 24th October 2016.

Hamm, S. (2013) 'How big data can boost weather forecasting'. www.wired.com/insights/2013/02/how-big-data-can-boost-weather-forecasting/, accessed 24th October 2016.

IBM (no date) 'Bringing big data to the enterprise'. www-01.ibm.com/software/data/bigdata/what-is-big-data.html, accessed 18th October 2016.

Keim, D., Kohlhammer, J., Ellis, G. and Mansmann, F. (2010) *Mastering the information age: Solving problems with visual analytics*, Goslar, Germany: Eurographics Association.

Marr, B. (2015) 'Big Data: 20 mind-boggling facts everyone must read'. www.forbes.com/sites/bernardmarr/2015/09/30/big-data-20-mind-boggling-facts-everyone-must-read/#288753b56c1d, accessed 18th October 2016.

Miller, T.W. (2016) *Sports analytics and data science: Winning the game with methods and models*, Old Tappan, NJ: Pearson.

Moore-Colyer, R. (2015) 'Big data analytics accelerates Williams' Formula One performance'. www.v3.co.uk/v3-uk/feature/2416146/big-data-analytics-accelerates-williams-formula-one-performance, accessed 24th October 2016.

O'Donoghue, P.G. (2015) *An introduction to performance analysis of sport*, London: Routledge.

22

O'Donoghue, P.G. (2016) 'Analytics in sport', Keynote address at the International Society of Performance Analysis of Sport Workshop, 22 March 2016.

O'Donoghue, P.G. and Mayes, A. (2013) 'Performance analysis, feedback and communication in coaching', In T. McGarry, P.G. O'Donoghue and J. Sampaio, J. (eds.), *Routledge handbook of sports performance analysis* (pp. 155–164), London: Routledge.

Science Daily (2013) 'Big Data, for better or worse: 90% of world's data generated over last two years'. www.sciencedaily.com/releases/2013/05/130522085217. htm, accessed 18th October 2016.

SDPF (2016) '3rd Annual Sportdata and Performance Forum, Dublin, 22nd–23rd November 2016'. www.sportdataperformance.com/, accessed 24th October 2016.

Stockton, N. (2016) 'Deep Thunder can forecast the weather – Down to a city block'. www.wired.com/2016/06/deep-thunder-can-forecast-weather-city-block/, accessed 24th October 2016.

Thomas, J.R. and Nelson, J.K. (1996) *Research methods in physical activity*, 3rd edn., Champaign, IL: Human Kinetics.

Wong, P.C. and Thomas, J. (2004) 'Visual analytics', *IEEE Computer Graphics and Applications*, 24(5): 20–21.

CHAPTER 2

COMPLEX DATA AND THE DATA AGE

INTRODUCTION

This chapter distinguishes complex data from basic data, discusses big data and charts the developments towards what we refer to as the "Data Age". The chapter is divided into three sections. The first section covers the basic data types used in computerised systems. Data structures, such as arrays and records, data files and databases are then discussed. The second section discusses complex data, including natural language, multimedia data and knowledge. Whereas the raw data used in natural language processing and multimedia may be thought of as character strings and structured files, respectively, there is additional higher-order linguistic and pattern structure data that need to be maintained that qualify as complex data. The second section finishes by distinguishing between information and intelligence. The third section is a brief history of information technology relevant to sports performance analysis commencing with the pre-computer age and ending with a review of the Data Age 2025 report. This identifies some characteristics of "big data" used in analytic processes and discusses them in a sports performance analysis context.

BASIC DATA

Basic data types

Ultimately, all data processed on computers are in electronic form and typically stored on magnetic media. This means that binary is used to represent all data no matter how simple or complex. Numbers, characters, text, graphics and sound are all represented by strings of binary digits. The ASCII (American Standard Code for Information Interchange) code is used to represent basic characters (letters, digits, punctuation symbols and mathematical operators) as sequences of eight binary digits. Some data can be stored in bytes of 8 bits (binary digits), whereas other data require 32-word, 64-word or multiple-word representations. For example, some readers may be familiar with the RGB (Red Green Blue) format used to represent colour. A value between 0 and 255 is used to represent the contribution of each of these three primary colours of light to the given colour. This is because a number between 0 and 255 can be stored in an 8 bit byte. When the three values are combined, we have potentially 16,777,216 colours that can be represented in this format. Given this understanding that data stored on computer-accessible media are ultimately represented in binary form, the purpose of this section is to briefly describe the basic types of data used in computerised systems.

Boolean data are used to represent the truth of propositions. Boolean expressions are also used in conditional statements of programming languages to select alternative instructions to be executed. Boolean expressions can be combined using operators such as AND, OR and XOR (exclusive OR). Categorical variables can be represented in many programming environments by defining these data types, including the possible nominal or ordinal values. It is also possible to have set variables in which the base sets are categorical variables.

Numeric data are easily represented by transforming numerical values to base 2. Cardinal numbers are positive whereas the set of integers includes all whole numbers, including negative numbers. Real numbers are measured on a continuous scale and so, theoretically, there is an infinite number of values between 1.0 and 2.0, for example. However, there is a limit to the precision with which real numbers can be represented by computers and on magnetic media, which readers need to be aware of. Real numbers are typically represented in two parts using floating point representation. This representation includes a significand (representing the significant digits), which is between 0 and the base used to represent the number (e.g. 2 or 10), and an exponent, which represents the number of places that the decimal point needs to move to give the correct value. For example, when using base 10, we could have 4.5E+09 represent 4.5 billion. Here, the significand is 4.5 and the exponent is 9; that is, we need to move the decimal place 9 places to the right, giving 4,500,000,000.

Very small numbers are represented using negative exponents. Numerical data can be processed using mathematical functions as well as arithmetic operators.

Characters have already been mentioned. These form the basis of character strings that are used to represent names, addresses and other text data. Character strings can be processed using a variety of text commands to search for substrings, save sections of strings and join strings together.

Data structures

Large data structures can be formed using the basic data types described previously. A record or structure is a Cartesian product of data fields that may have differing data types. In some programming languages, these are referred to as structures and in others they are referred to as records. For example, we may have a record that contains a person's name, address, date of birth, telephone number, sex, marital status and credit balance. The name and address are character strings. The telephone number could be a numeric value or character string or a record of three numeric values (country code, area code and local number). The use of a character string might be justified if we did not wish to use a record and need an initial "0" at the beginning of the telephone number. The date of birth could be represented as a record of three numbers for the day, month and year. Hence, it is possible to have records within records. Finally, the credit balance is a numerical quantity. A record type can be fixed or "variant", which contains fields for some data that may not be required for other data. For example, we may store the scores of a two-legged soccer tie and only wish to record the extra time score and penalty shoot-out score if they are required.

An array is a table of elements of the same type. For example, a character string is a special case of an array; it is an array of characters. We can also have arrays of numerical values, records and any other basic data type. It is unlikely that we would store a record about a single customer; typically, we would store the same form of data about all our customers, requiring an array of records. Two-dimensional arrays are also possible and can be used to represent different zones on a game-playing surface so that records of events that took place in those zones could be stored and retrieved. Indeed, we can have multidimensional arrays of data; for example, we may have array dimensions

26

for matches, half a match, time within the half, and players contesting the match. The element of such a record could be a Boolean field indicating whether a player is on the field at the given time and numerical fields for X and Y locations on the playing surface. As well as having arrays of records, we can also have fields of records as arrays of values. Thus, arrays and records can be combined into quite complex data structures storing large volumes of data. This can be done within the main memory when data are processed but it is also essential to store these data structures on magnetic media so that when computers are nonfunctioning, the data are not lost.

Databases

Data files have been used to store data since the advent of computers, although the storage media has changed over time, storage capacities increased and storage devices are more compact and cheaper. Some very modest systems use several data files rather than a single file whereas larger systems maintain more complex file structures. This has led to the development of databases. A database is a collection of files that are interlinked through relationships between key elements of database records. The benefits of using databases are that data can be designed and modelled around application and organisational needs and a consistent approach can be applied to data storage and querying through database management systems and database querying languages, respectively. Today, databases are so commonplace that their use is no longer restricted to commercial organisations and government bodies; instead, private individuals can maintain databases using commercially available packages such as Microsoft Access (Microsoft Inc., Redmond, WA). Databases will be covered more in Chapter 10.

COMPLEX DATA

Natural language

Natural language goes beyond text processing in that it involves understanding of syntax and semantics for computers to recognize the entered text. This is an example of complex data because there are higher-order data about linguistic properties stored as well as the basic text data. There are many applications of natural language processing, including language translation, which is now accomplished by freely available software such as Bing's translator (www.bing.com/translator, accessed 25/10/17). The Google Translate app goes further by translating text that has first been pre-processed from handwritten or audio form (https://translate.google.co.uk/, accessed 25/10/17). The user can simply point their mobile phone at some text on a notice or sign post or handwritten text on paper or a whiteboard and the text is recognised, transforming the optically presented characters into print characters before translating into the user's own language. There are some tasks where natural language processing is not recommended; for example, where recognition, clarification and correction stages may slow down data access (Shneiderman, 1980: 208).

Multimedia data

Multimedia computing developed rapidly in the early 1990s with advances in hardware and software. Specialist graphic and sound features of early multimedia computers are now standard for modern computers, smart phones and tablets. Multimedia is not just the collection of text, image, video, animation and sound processing tools but their aesthetic integration within products (Paulissen and Frater, 1992: 2–3). In the early days of multimedia computing, peripheral devices such as image scanners were needed to input photographs onto computer disks for processing. Similarly, video capture cards were required to record video data onto computer disks before video sequences could be presented on computer screens. Today, the use of multimedia is much more interactive – camera devices built into computers, mobile phones and tablets allow data to be recorded, edited and communicated. Multimedia databases have been used in many fields, including medicine and tourism (Paulissen and Frater, 1992: 9–12). Some of the complexity in multimedia data comes from how they are processed. Consider the "simulcam" feature of the Dartfish package (Dartfish, Fribourg, Switzerland) that shows two separate performances together to allow direct comparison. Dartfish has used gold and silver medal downhill skiing performances to illustrate this form of video presentation (www.youtube.com/watch?v=wZBOJnJM1XA, accessed 26/10/17). The separate videos of the two skiing performances are processed so that the backgrounds match up despite the different use of zooming and panning when the videos were recorded. This is a sophisticated image processing task that requires specific data structures in addition to the raw video to manage the transformation and video merging process. Similarly, where sound or voice data are analysed, more complex data structures are needed than would be the case for simply storing and retrieving audio files.

Knowledge

Knowledge engineering is an area of artificial intelligence concerned with capturing and utilising expert human knowledge within computerised systems. Expert systems have been developed to help solve problems in specialist domains (Lyons, 2015). An expert system stores knowledge derived from multiple experts within a knowledge base. There is a variety of formats in which knowledge can be represented such as facts and rules, predicate calculus and frames. An inference engine is used to deal with queries from users, applying reasoning to the knowledge stored to come to a solution. The chain of reasoning used to answer a query explains how the conclusion was reached. The explanation capability can also clarify why the expert system asks for particular facts from the user while it is processing the query. This is done by gradually building up an explanation envelop around the query, which includes sub-problems considered and knowledge reasoned about to produce the solution (O'Donoghue, 1985). This temporary session knowledge includes facts deduced from reasoning about information provided by users and stored knowledge from the knowledge base. Expert systems also have a learning capability that allows the knowledge base to be refined as new knowledge becomes available from domain experts. Expert systems are particularly useful for diagnosis tasks such as suggesting faults in equipment given a set of symptoms that can be tested.

Intelligence

Our ability to gather data has increased rapidly in recent decades and advances have also been made in the way data are processed to produce information. The types of data that are stored and processed have a range of complexities as has already been mentioned because computerised systems are able to store higher-order knowledge about application domains. The distinction between intelligence and information is that information is considered in context. The Central Intelligence Agency (CIA) described intelligence as follows:

> Reduced to its simplest terms, intelligence is knowledge and fore-knowledge of the world around us – the prelude to decision and action by US policymakers.
>
> (CIA, 1999)

Thus, intelligence involves assessment of capabilities, intentions and trends to predict situations ahead of initiating action; intelligence seeks to be proactive rather than reactive. Sports performance analysis involves gathering and analysing data to make decisions about training and preparation for future matches. We can present information on our own performances, identifying areas requiring attention, or on future opponents, illustrating how they play and tactics they perform particularly well. However, these activities fall short of providing intelligence.

A sports intelligence approach interprets information in context, making connections between pieces of information and knowledge to tell a story. It also explains why the information is important in the given context, identifying opportunities and threats. Intelligence is actionable and, therefore, it is important to undertake intelligence work secretly to avoid opponents being able to anticipate actions to be taken. If we have a forthcoming match against a given opponent, we may consider the players they have available for the fixture, the importance of the match to our opponents and the threats they pose given knowledge of our own strengths and weaknesses. In predicting aspects of the forthcoming match, we may ask ourselves how we would act if we were in the position of our opponents preparing for the fixture and, therefore, how we should prepare to combat such action.

HISTORY OF INFORMATION TECHNOLOGY

Pre-computer age

In October 2017, when this chapter was written, one of the authors (O'Donoghue) watched the film *The Day of the Jackal* based on the novel by Frederick Forsyth (1971). It is worth watching to gain an appreciation of the difficulties managing data prior to the use of computer systems.

30

Consider the fictional situation in which a series of events have led the French security services to believe an assassin they are trying to apprehend is using the identity of a Danish national. They need to apprehend the assassin before he attempts to kill President De Gaulle. There are two critical data analyses tasks that need to be done. First, they need to find out if any Danish nationals had their passports stolen in countries the assassin was known to have visited. This involved requesting information from Danish embassies without compromising their own intelligence efforts to locate and apprehend the assassin. The second task is to search for the names of any Danish nationals who had their passports stolen in the last year and are currently staying in hotels in Paris. The hotels have information cards that they complete for all guests. These are collected and couriered to a central location where a list of several hundred Danish men is compiled, arranged in alphabetical order, typed up and a copy sent to lead detectives working on the case. Consider the task of separating the cards about Danish guests from other guests and sorting them into alphabetical order of surname. Some sorting algorithms involve an order of N^2 comparisons and cards swaps (N is the number of cards dealt with). These are time-consuming tasks to undertake manually. However, completing them does make looking for a name within the sorted list as straightforward as looking up a name in a paper telephone directory. Now imagine how the security services' job today has been helped by information technology. Consider the specific example from Forsyth's (1971) novel of identifying Danish nationals who have had their passports stolen in particular countries and cross referencing these names against male Danish guests currently staying in Paris hotels. Databases of alleged passport thefts can be accessed and filtered by computer querying. Similarly, databases of hotel guests can be filtered by sex and nationality or indeed searched for records containing particular names. The use of computers and communication technology has rapidly improved the efficiency with which security services can use data. There are other examples in Forsyth's novel and the film version of the story in which manual data collection, analysis and transportation processes slow the work of the security services and are exploited by the assassin for the purposes of identity theft and evading the authorities. Many of these potential inefficiencies and risks are reduced by the advent of information technology. However, it should also be recognised that advances in information technology have also been followed by the development of cyber-crime, computer hacking, spyware and malware.

Consider the analysis of a forthcoming opponent during the pre-computer age. Video material was scarce even at the top level of a sport. Scouts might have needed to attend matches of a future opponent and provide a report. This means that the squad was relying on secondhand information. Coaching, in some cases, was done without any supplementary information to assist the coaches' own observations and analysis; or as Hayes (1997) put it, coaching was "unhindered" by notational analysis.

Computerised sports performance analysis

Despite the view expressed by Hayes (1997), manual notation techniques, such as tally charts and shorthand notation, were used to record details from sports performances during the pre-computer era (Hughes and Franks, 2004). The use of computers has provided many benefits to sports performance analysis as it has in numerous other application domains. Performance analysis has progressed from using mainframe computers (Ariel, 2007) to more portable personal computers (Dufour, 1993), laptop computers (Liddle and O'Donoghue, 1998) and iPads (Butterworth, 2016).

The earliest computerised notational analysis systems replaced the use of shorthand notation with keys on a standard keyboard. Advances in data input peripheral devices were exploited by computerised notational analysis systems, including concept keyboards, digitisation tablets, graphical user interfaces and touch-sensitive screens (Hughes and Franks, 1995). Voice recognition has also been used within match analysis systems progressing from the work of Taylor and Hughes (1988) to the voice recognition feature of Focus X2 (Elite Sports Analysis, Delgaty Bay, Scotland, UK), which can be trained to recognise verbally coded events spoken by a human operator. Automatic player tracking is now done using a range of technologies, including GPS devices (Mangan et al., 2017), infrared systems (Leser and Roemer, 2015), ultrasonic systems (Leser and Roemer, 2015) and image processing (Carling et al., 2008). Other technologies exploited for data gathering in sports performance analysis include smart devices, sensors, goniometers, accelerometers and sensors (Baca, 2015), as well as eye movement tracking (Liebermann and Franks, 2004).

Output from computerised match analysis systems has been presented on computer screens before the advent of Windows-based operating systems (Hughes and McGarry, 1989), as well as through Windows interfaces.

32

Multimedia technology has played a major role in integrating video with structured event databases within the main commercial packages used today. These systems allow criteria to be entered so that video clips satisfying those criteria can be played interactively or saved as a standalone highlights movie. These highlights movies can be discussed by players and coaches when displayed using data projectors during team briefings and debriefings. Video sequences accessed and replayed interactively can also be displayed using data projectors. However, there is a growing use of more flexible web-based coaching environments to access video sequences. This allows players to view passages of play on their own phones or tablets in their own time prior to training sessions. These packages also support discussion forums about areas of performance requiring attention. Other advances in the output of sports performance information include virtual reality (Leser and Roemer, 2015) and augmented reality (Wiemeyer and Mueller, 2015).

As well as advances in processing power, portability of computers, input and output peripheral devices, there have been advances in data storage capacity that have benefitted sports performance analysis. Early personal computers had limited main memory; for example, the Acorn BBC model B only had 32 kB of memory and no hard disk. This meant that all program and data files needed to be stored on 100 kB floppy disks. Other early machines like the Commodore Pet used tape as a secondary storage mechanism. The serial access of tape devices made accessing and updating data much less efficient than with random access disks. IBM personal computers and Apple Mac computers had greater processing ability, memory and internal hard disks. These devices saw improvements in secondary storage options with the formerly used 1.44 MB disks replaced by memory sticks and flash drives in the order of gigabytes rather than megabytes. External hard disks are now in the order of terabytes, which is comparable with the storage capacity of servers used in previous eras. Furthermore, the Internet allows personal computers to access cloud storage, which many find more convenient than using memory sticks and external hard drives. For backup purposes, cloud storage overcomes the risks involved in keeping backup disks and personal computers in the same location.

The advances in physical hardware storage have made advances in logical data structures possible. During the early days of computerised performance analysis, sports performance data were stored in basic data files. As the data stored increased in volume and complexity, database systems started to be used to store sports performance data (Lyons, 2015). Multimedia computers used with today's commercial video analysis packages have hard disks that can store match videos in various formats such as AVI and WMV.

The delivery of information about sports is now in real time. Satellite and terrestrial television coverage includes information bars that scroll scores and news headlines. In previous eras, if soccer fans missed a midweek result at the end of the 10 o'clock news, they might not see the result until the next day in the newspaper. Today, it is recognised that data provide sports organisations with an edge to such an extent that there is a market for independent sports data analysis organisations. Online sports data are provided through the official websites of teams, events, venues, tournaments and sports governing bodies (Lorenc and Gonzalez, 2017: 147). Sports organisations use a blend of in-house and public sources of data during their analyses for sports performance and marketing activities (Breedlove, 2017: 112). The Internet provides the platform for independent sports analysis companies to reach their market directly and efficiently. There is now a network of smart devices – referred to as the "Internet of Things" – that provide greater opportunities for data users and data providers than ever before (Dabnichki and Miyaji, 2015).

One major change in sports performance analysis in recent years has been the use of data beyond sports coaching contexts. Fans have become consumers of sports data as sports coverage merges performance information within media coverage to entertain and engage audiences. This merging of information and entertainment in sports has been referred to as "infotainment" (Kirkbride, 2013). Kirkbride (2013) describes how these data can be "pushed" onto television audiences or "pulled" by users of sports data provided on the Internet. Data are often provided in real time in sports such as cricket and Formula 1 motor racing. Sophisticated object and player tracking technology provide large volumes of accurate data that are processed and summarised as graphical images such as flight paths of golf balls, locations of tennis balls at the instant when players return serves and locations of cricket balls as they reach the crease. These data enhance broadcast coverage and can also be used to support the decisions of officials. A further development is the use of video and supporting data to enhance fan experience at sports venues and to increase revenues for sports organisations (Lorenc and Gonzalez, 2017: 148–150). One motivation for developing "smart stadiums" is the recognition that many fans watch sports events at home because of

34

the quality of coverage they are provided with from broadcasters (Intel, 2014). Smart stadiums can be created cost effectively by integrating data provision services with existing "Internet of Things" devices owned by fans. Sports organisers can provide video and additional visualisations to sports fans at events by collaborating with broadcasters when mutually beneficial to do so (Bukstein, 2017: 12).

Data Age 2025 report

The future of the "Data Age" is speculated in the IDC (International Data Corporation) Data Age 2025 white paper sponsored by Seagate (Reinsel et al., 2017). This section discusses the report and its implications for sports performance analysis. The white paper forecasts five key trends that will intensify until 2025:

- The function of data in business and life in general
- Embedded systems and the Internet of Things
- The use of mobile and real-time data
- Artificial intelligence
- Data security

The function of data in business and life in general

The Data Age white paper forecasts a new era in which the way we live will be transformed by smart home devices, intelligent assistant technology and autonomous transport; we will interact with these devices (obviously and consciously or automatically in the background) 4,800 times per day or every 18s on average. There will still be active data gathering by organisations (Farris, 2017: 75–76) as well as the use of data generated by customers (Mathew, 2017: 62–65). We can expect the volume of data gathered and analysed during training and competition to increase as players wear monitoring devices with increasing sampling rates. The Data Age 2025 report predicts that the proportion of standalone devices will decline as devices become more interconnected. The global datasphere will increase from 16.1 ZB to 163 ZB (i.e. 163 trillion gigabytes) with 20% of the datasphere serving critical functions and 10% serving hypercritical functions. Critical functions include data necessary for users to continue their business and social activities whereas hypercritical functions include embedded medical and transport applications. Advances in telemedicine are expected to become more prevalent in sports, as well as in other applications.

Embedded systems and the Internet of Things

As has already been mentioned, the Internet of Things is comprised of devices with embedded systems for creating and communicating data. These include chip cards, security cameras, smart meters, devices within transport and smart buildings and toys. The Data Age 2025 report forecasts the following about the Internet of Things:

■ The number of data-generating devices will grow from less than one per person to more than four per person by 2025.
■ The proportion of data used on personal devices considered productive rather than entertainment will grow. Much of this productive data are typically stored on personal computers and servers.
■ The volume of data generated will continue to outpace our ability to store it. Reinsel et al. (2017) put this into perspective by comparing the 16 billion 12 TB hard drives required to store the forecasted 163 ZB of data expected to be created by 2025 with the 8 billion hard drives produced between 2007 and 2017.

We can expect an increase in the use of embedded systems within training and competition environments. We are already seeing a rapid increase in the use of embedded systems within recreational exercise as people monitor their training using widely available apps. Many of these apps are connected to global databases allowing people to compare their performances on different courses and distances.

The use of mobile and real-time data

The report predicts that data will become increasingly available wherever and whenever anyone needs it, as the growth in data available in real time is 1.5 times the growth of non-real-time data. By 2025, 75% of the world's population will have mobile devices and nearly 25% of data will be available in real time. The report forecasts that 95% of this 25% will be created by the Internet of Things. There is already a wealth of sports data that can be accessed by sports fans live. However, there is still a great scope for further data to be provided to users live. Some data used by coaches and high-performance managers cannot currently be provided live during sports performances. Although this provides technological challenges, it is more important to ensure that any developments in live data provision are high priority and required. This is to avoid the highly publicised issue of data being generated and not used (Ismail, 2017).

Artificial intelligence

Artificial intelligence continues to advance as a branch of computer science and is expected to play a significant role in the analysis of big data in 2025. The report predicts that the amount of data analysed using cognitive systems will grow by a factor of 100 by 2025. The report also credits artificial intelligence with assisting credit card companies detect fraud within 60ms and includes medical, transport, insurance and artistic fields among those in which artificial intelligence can be applied. Much movement data in sports are patterns that can be analysed using artificial intelligence techniques such as neural networks. The wealth of data created during sports performances is a resource that can be exploited within sports performance research. Machine learning techniques can be applied to these data in the search for successful tactics in sports.

Data security

The Data Age 2025 report recognises threats to data security and privacy and a growing percentage of unsecured data. The report identifies five classes of data security:

- Lockdown: for hypercritical and critical data.
- Confidential: for commercially valuable data such as industrial research and development reports and customer lists.
- Custodial: customer information that could be used in identity theft if not secured.
- Compliance-driven: information that must be retained for legal or professional reasons.
- Private: information that is private but not critical; for example, personal emails.

These risks apply to sports performance data just as they do to personal bank details. For example, tactical data falling into the wrong hands could give opponents unfair insider knowledge (Marr, 2017). Marr (2017) also mentions that compromised data related to planned player trades could jeopardize negotiations.

SUMMARY

This chapter discussed various types of data in distinguishing complex data from basic data. The chapter also charted developments in information technology from the pre-computer era to the present and related the Data Age 2025 white paper forecasts to sports. As the volume of data created by the Internet of Things and other systems grows, there will be a gap between the amount of data gathered and the amount analysed. Therefore, it is vitally important that efforts made to provide live data from sports performances focus on data required by coaches, sports science support and customers.

REFERENCES

Ariel, G. (2007) 'Sports technologies from Mexico City Olympics to the future Olympics in Beijing 2008', *6th International Symposium of the International Association of Computer Science in Sport*, Calgary, June 2007.

Baca, A. (2015) 'Data acquisition and processing', In A. Baca (ed.), *Computer science in sport: Research and practice* (pp. 46–81), London: Routledge.

Breedlove, J. (2017) 'Developing and measuring the effectiveness of data driven direct marketing initiatives', In C.K. Harrison and S. Bukstein (eds.), *Sports business analytics: Using data to increase revenue and improve operational efficiency* (pp. 107–129), London: Routledge.

Bukstein, S. (2017) 'Evolution and impact of business analytics in sport', In C.K. Harrison and S. Bukstein (eds.), *Sports business analytics: Using data to increase revenue and improve operational efficiency* (pp. 1–22), London: Routledge.

Butterworth, A. (2016) 'Domestic and international netball performance analysis: A comparative reflection', *World Congress of Performance Analysis of Sport XI*, Alicante, Spain, November 2016.

Carling, C., Bloomfield, J., Nelson, L. and Reilly, T. (2008) 'The role of motion analysis in elite soccer: Contemporary performance measurement techniques and work rate data', *Sports Medicine*, 38: 839–862.

Central Intelligence Agency (Office of Public Affairs) (1999) *A consumer's guide to intelligence* (p. vii), Washington, DC: Central Intelligence Agency.

38

Dabnichki, P. and Miyaji, C. (2015) 'Computers, informatics and sport', In A. Baca (ed.) *Computer science in sport: Research and practice* (pp. 18–32), London: Routledge.

Dufour, W. (1993) 'Computer assisted scouting in soccer', In T. Reilly, J. Clarys and A. Stibbe (eds.), *Science and football II* (pp. 160–166), London: E and FN Spon.

Farris, M. (2017) 'The Aspire Group's ticket marketing, sales and service philosophy', In C.K. Harrison and S. Bukstein (eds.), *Sports business analytics: Using data to increase revenue and improve operational efficiency* (pp. 69–88), London: Routledge.

Forsyth, F. (1971) *The day of the Jackal*, London: Penguin (Hutchinson and Co).

Hayes, M. (1997) 'Notational analysis – The right of reply', *BASES Newsletter*, 7(8): 4–5.

Hughes, M.D. and Franks, I.M. (1995) 'Computerised notational analysis, keynote address', *World Congress of Science and Football II*, Cardiff, UK, April 1995.

Hughes, M.D. and Franks, I.M. (2004) 'How to develop a notation system', In M. Hughes and I.M. Franks (eds.), *Notational analysis of sport: Systems for better coaching and performance in sport* (2nd edn., pp. 118–140), London: Routledge.

Hughes, M.D. and McGarry, T. (1989) 'Computerised notational analysis of squash', In M. Hughes (ed.), *Science in squash* (pp. 156–168), Liverpool, UK: Liverpool Polytechnic.

Intel (2014) 'Smart stadiums take the lead in profitability, fan experience and security'. www.intel.com/content/dam/www/public/us/en/documents/solution-briefs/iot-smart-stadiums-brief.pdf, accessed 26th October 2017.

Ismail, N. (2017) 'Mobility predictions for 2017', *Information Age*. http://www.information-age.com/mobility-predictions-2017-123463851/, accessed 18th March 2018.

Kirkbride, A. (2013) 'Media applications of performance analysis', In T. McGarry, P.G. O'Donoghue and J. Sampaio, J. (eds.), *Routledge handbook of sports performance analysis* (pp. 187–209), London: Routledge.

Leser, R. and Roemer, K. (2015) 'Motion tracking and analysis systems', In A. Baca (ed.) *Computer science in sport: Research and practice* (pp. 82–109), London: Routledge.

Liddle, S.D. and O'Donoghue, P.G. (1998) 'Notational analysis of rallies of European Circuit badminton', In A. Lees, I. Maynard, M. Hughes and T. Reilly (eds.), *Science and racket sports II* (pp. 275–281), London: Routledge.

Liebermann, D. and Franks, I. (2004) 'The use of feedback-based technologies', In M. Hughes and I.M. Franks (eds.), *Notational analysis of sport: Systems for better coaching and performance in sport* (2nd edn., pp. 40–58), London: Routledge.

Lorenc, M. and Gonzalez, A. (2017) 'Leveraging digital marketing to engage customers and drive revenue', In C.K. Harrison and S. Bukstein (eds.), *Sports business analytics: Using data to increase revenue and improve operational efficiency* (pp. 145–156), London: Routledge.

Lyons, K. (2015) 'Databases and expert systems', In A. Baca (ed.), *Computer science in sport: Research and practice* (pp. 33–45), London: Routledge.

Mangan, S., Ryan, M., Devenney, S. and Collins, K. (2017) 'The relationship between technical performance indicators and running performance in elite Gaelic football', *International Journal of Performance Analysis in Sport*, 17. https://doi.org/10.1080/24748668.2017.1387409.

Marr, B. (2017) 'The big risks of big data in sport'. www.forbes.com/sites/bernardmarr/2017/04/28/the-big-risks-of-big-data-in-sports/#319883887c6f, accessed 26th October 2017.

Mathew, R. (2017) 'Customer relation management and fan engagement analytics', In C.K. Harrison and S. Bukstein (eds.), *Sports business analytics: Using data to increase revenue and improve operational efficiency* (pp. 53–68), London: Routledge.

O'Donoghue, P.G. (1985) 'An expert system for prescribing safe exercise training programmes', M.Sc. Dissertation, Jordanstown, UK: University of Ulster.

Paulissen, D. and Frater, H. (1992) *Multimedia-mania: Experiencing the excitement of multimedia computing*, Grand Rapids, MI: Abacus.

Reinsel, D., Gantz, J. and Rydning, J. (2017) '"Data Age 2025: The evolution of data to life-critical don't focus on Big Data; Focus on the data that's big", an IDC White Paper', *Sponsored by Seagate*. www.seagate.com/www-content/our-story/trends/files/Seagate-WP-DataAge2025-March-2017.pdf, accessed 11th April 2017.

Shneiderman, B. (1980) *Software psychology*, Cambridge, MA: Winthrop Publishers.

Taylor, S. and Hughes, M. (1988) 'Computerised notational analysis: A voice interactive system', *Journal of Sports Sciences*, 6: 255.

Wiemeyer, J. and Mueller, F. (2015) 'Information and communication technology-enhanced learning and training', In A. Baca (ed.) *Computer science in sport: Research and practice* (pp. 187–213), London: Routledge.

CHAPTER 3

INTERACTIVE VISUALISATION

INTRODUCTION

The term *visualisation* has been used in sports performance analysis circles as though it is something new. When one reads textbooks on visualisation (Few, 2009; Kirk, 2012; Yau, 2011) and examines examples used on social media, it soon becomes apparent that what is referred to as visualisation has been done for centuries. Visualisation is the summarising of data using visual means of presentation. Kirk (2012: 122–158) provides an excellent taxonomy of data visualisation methods, including standard pie charts, area charts, scatter plots, line graphs, box plots, bar charts and column charts as well as lesser known but useful methods such as tree maps, stream graphs, flow maps, chord diagrams and glyth. Popular word processing, spreadsheet and presentation software packages all provide means of constructing various types of charts. Packages like Tableau (www.tableau.com, accessed 29/11/2017) provide greater flexibility and functionality for visualising data than the chart-drawing facilities in spreadsheet and statistical analysis packages. However, these packages require skill to produce charts that convey data in the most efficient way to enhance viewer understanding. Few (2009: 19–24) lists qualities that analysts should have to visualise data and enhance communication. The analyst needs to be interested in the data for motivation to explore it and discover interesting patterns and comparisons that can be displayed. The analyst also needs to have good problem-solving skills to choose the most appropriate visualisations to represent the analyses results. They need to be methodical to develop data analysis and presentation processes

41

using the tools at their disposal. This also involves creativity and imagination to experiment with different approaches. Data analysis and visualisation skills can improve with experience as analysts encounter problems that require them to use system features and options they may not have used before. Analysts should be sceptical about exploratory results, looking for errors that may have been made. Familiarity with the data and its context helps detect potential analyses errors.

Although many of the chart types are not new, the flexibility with which we can interact with data has changed. Visualisation is more inclusive and no longer a task requiring specialist statisticians (Kirk, 2012: 8, 18–19). Technology allows charts to be sorted by different variables, filtered by case-based or temporal criteria, highlighted with cases of interest or annotated with events that may have impacted the data (Few, 2009: 55–82). Individual data points on charts can be clicked, revealing further case details in popup boxes. Few (2009: 55–82) also describes how charts can be adjusted by re-expressing data per capita, as percentages or per kilogram, for example. Charts can be re-visualised using different chart types and can have further variables and cases added. Axes can be rescaled to allow the data to be presented more effectively within the chart space. For example, professional soccer players' transfer fees or earnings are positively skewed with few players having above-median values. Therefore, charts showing such variables may need to be rescaled using logarithmic scales. Zooming and panning is also possible, allowing subranges of interest to be shown more closely. As charts are explored, some charts may be "bookmarked", allowing analysts to quickly return to them during analysis sessions.

COGNITION AND PERCEPTION

Successful visualisation requires an understanding of the messenger's and receiver's perspectives. Kirk's (2012: 16) model places the message centrally, identifying these two roles. The messenger communicates what they have discovered within data and ideas they are trying to convey. The receiver of the message may be a decision maker who not only needs to understand the message but be persuaded and inspired by it. The human brain processes information through perception and cognition. Knowledge of perception and cognition helps analysts improve the

42

impact and clarity of the information they provide to decision makers. Perception is the organisation and processing of sensory data that come from the external environment. Perception uses sensory stimuli to detect things without necessarily understanding them. Cognition, on the other hand, develops knowledge through thinking about the information we have sensed and considering ideas we have not necessarily experienced. Cognition is used to solve problems and initiate action. Perception and cognition are not completely separate due to information sharing, the need to "bind" sensory information to concepts that we understand, the role of attention in focussing on what we look at and listen to and the ability to understand complex objects composed of multiple perceived shapes (Tacca, 2011). Vision is the most powerful of our senses (Few, 2009: 6, 30–31); our ability to recognise texture, shape, size, colour, orientation, curvature, blur, spatial location and movement almost effortlessly benefits from knowledge and memory.

Just look around you right now or listen to your environment. You have just processed an enormous volume of information. Think about what it would take to write a computer program to process this information and learn from it. Consider how easily we can separate or combine shapes, deal with partially obscured objects, judge distance and shade, and so on. The visual features we consider primitive depend on the level of abstraction we use when dealing with information. You probably only needed to use a fraction of the information you just processed to identify where you are and the rough time of day. Similarly, the complexity of processing audio information is often taken for granted. Words can run into other words with no pause in between and yet we are able to recognise the separate words. Again, consider what a computer program must do when processing the sound of "Good morning, how are you?" just to separate this into five words that can be processed.

Despite the ability of the human brain to process complex information and recognise patterns through visual perception, we still often fail to recognise important concepts because of the way information is presented to us. Deception is also possible and information can be presented in deliberately misleading ways. Therefore, when we are providing information to decision makers, we should present it in ways that enhance the accuracy and speed of understanding. Providing information in such a fashion and tailored for the specific audience helps reduce time to insight (Sleeper, 2017).

With respect to sports performance analysis, two examples of enhanced presentation are voiceovers in feedback videos and dashboards. Feedback videos include the aspects of performance that coaches want to draw athletes' attention to. Match statistics may reveal a problematic area within a performance and this will be emphasised in the video sequences used. Sometimes, statistical information is included within the video to present these two types of information synergetically; however, it is poor practice to superimpose text points on video sequences. The players need to watch the video sequences rather than be distracted from the wealth of video information by having to read text, no matter how relevant it is. Therefore, such points are made in voiceovers during the video, allowing players to watch the video and listen to the points made in parallel. There are several theories as to how the brain processes information but given that players can discuss performance while actively watching feedback videos shows they are not distracted too much from observing video sequences while listening to audio information.

Dashboards are used to present a collection of key information in a manner that aids rapid understanding and decision making (O'Donoghue and Holmes, 2015: 68–84). Each piece of information within the dashboard needs to be presented in the right visual way to get the message across. Visual properties of charts allow information to be processed in the order of 200ms using short-term memory (Healey et al., 1996). The use of short-term memory can also be optimised when dashboards group similar information together.

Information should also be presented in ways that are familiar to us. For example, in biomechanics, animations allow viewers to evaluate techniques using their knowledge and ability to distinguish between the good and flawed ones. As technology has improved, these animations have progressed from two-dimensional stick figures to virtual skeletons or humans animated using data recorded from real athletes or patients.

VISUALISING TRENDS IN SPORTS PERFORMANCE

Trends are changing patterns over time that can be presented visually to identify improvements and fluctuations that occur (Farris, 2017). Data can be presented together with reference values to help viewers evaluate the data (Few, 2009: 96). Figure 3.1 shows how performance trends can

44

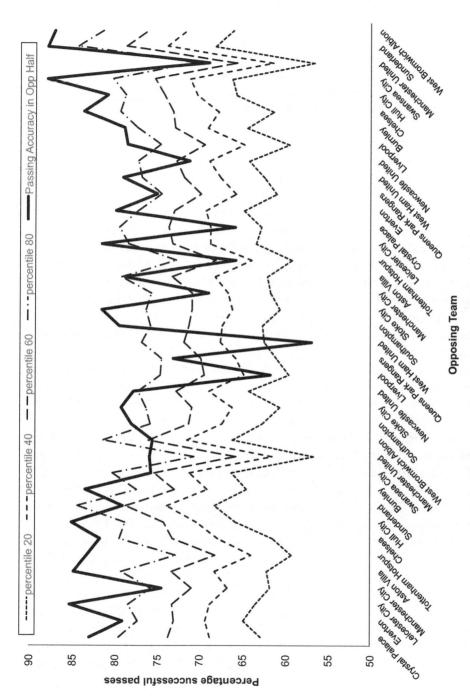

Figure 3.1 The percentage of passes made in the opposition half that successfully reach a teammate by Arsenal during the 2014–2015 English FA Premier League season (Nisotaki, 2016)

be evaluated using reference values; the particular example is the passing accuracy in the opposition half for the Arsenal soccer team during the 2014–2015 English FA Premier League season (Nisotaki, 2016). The thick black line represents Arsenal's passing accuracy in the opposition half. The other four lines are quintile norms for this variable that address opposition quality. The norms were calculated using all the performances against each opponent; for example, the norms for matches against Crystal Palace were calculated using the performances of Crystal Palace's opponents. This divides performances against Crystal Palace into five bandings: the highest 20% of values against Crystal Palace, the next highest 20%, the middle 20%, the second lowest 20% and the lowest 20%. Such norms could have been calculated using regression techniques to model passing performance in terms of relative team quality, which is represented by league points or position. However, soccer performance is made up of multiple attacking and defending abilities, meaning that we cannot simply expect passing performance to be correlated with success. Some teams may be relatively better at defending than passing whereas others may be much better at passing than their league position suggests because they have limitations in other areas of performance. Thus, the quintile norms shown in Figure 3.1 are evidenced by passing performances of teams' opponents. Consider the first match in which Arsenal played Crystal Palace. To assess Arsenal's performance in this match, we essentially ask "what are high, average and low passing performances for teams when they are playing against Crystal Palace?" This is because the specific competitive situation that Arsenal faced in this first match of the season was playing against Crystal Palace. Figure 3.1 shows that Arsenal's percentage of successful passes in the opposition half was in the highest 20% of English FA Premier League teams against this particular opponent. This approach allows performances to be considered relative to opposition quality rather than just in absolute terms. Consider matches against Manchester United and Sunderland. Manchester United is a strong opponent and teams' passing success when playing them is lower than when they play against other opponents. This is reflected by the quintile norms for passing success in the opposition half lowest in matches in which the opposition is Manchester United. Consider Arsenal's first match against Manchester United: Arsenal's passing accuracy in the opposition half is similar in this match to when they played Swansea City in the previous match. However, when we relate these two Arsenal performances to the norms for English FA Premier League teams against these two opponents, we

46

see that Arsenal's passing accuracy against Manchester United is comfortably in the top 20% of performances against this opponent but was just above the 60th percentile against Swansea City. This means that almost 40% of English FA Premier League performances against Swansea City involved a higher passing accuracy in the opposition half than Arsenal's value in this match. Sunderland, on the other hand, is a weaker opposition than Manchester United and teams tend to enjoy higher passing accuracy in the opposition half against Sunderland than they do against other opponents. As we can see, Arsenal's second performance against Sunderland involved a higher passing accuracy than their first match against them in both absolute and relative terms.

You should have noticed that the quintile norms displayed in Figure 3.1 are not parallel. This is because some opponents are more consistent than others at defending. This is reflected by opponents having narrower ranges of passing accuracy in the team's half than is the case for other teams in the league. Consider the first two matches that Arsenal played in the 2014–2015 season against Crystal Palace and Everton. We can see that the range of values for passing accuracy in the opposition half is much higher in matches against Crystal Palace than Everton; that is, Crystal Palace's defending could be said to be much more erratic than that of Everton. The most consistent team for controlling opposition passing was Newcastle United; the difference between the 20th and 80th percentile for passing accuracy of Newcastle United's opponents was 4.78%. Chelsea was the most erratic team for controlling opposition passing; the difference between the 20th and 80th percentile for passing accuracy of Chelsea's opponents was 7.64%. Thus, when we are playing against a given opponent, the quintile norms not only tell us how high or low our passing accuracy should be but also the range of passing accuracies we can expect against the given opponent.

Having discussed the reference values, which are presented as quintile norms, we can now consider Arsenal's performances in absolute and relative terms. Visualising trends seeks to highlight rates of change as well as fluctuations in variables of interest (Kirk, 2012: 68–69). For the first 17 games of the season, with four exceptions, Arsenal's passing accuracy in the opponents' half was in the highest 20% of performances seen against these opponents. However, Arsenal then had their worst passing performances of the season in two of the next three games (against Liverpool and particularly against West Ham United). Passing performances continued to be erratic from Arsenal's second match against Southampton to their second match against Newcastle United. The passing accuracy in these matches tended to alternate between the top 20% when considering opposition quality and the middle 20% or below. This period of erratic passing form ended once they played Liverpool for the second time. Passing performances were in the top 20% against the given opposition for the remaining eight matches of the season. This included a match against Manchester United in which the lower passing accuracy in the opponent's half is explained by the quality of the opposition.

DECISION MAKING IN DECATHLON PREPARATION

The decathlon

This section uses the decathlon in track and field athletics as an example of how data can be visualised to aid the decisions of coaches and athletes. The decathlon is made up of 10 disciplines, which are listed in Table 3.1. Athletes need to prepare optimally to maximise the points they achieve from the overall decathlon event. The questions that decathletes may have include:

- Which discipline(s) can be improved, adding the most points to the total?
- What level of improvement is feasible in each discipline in a given time scale and does the improvement level depend on the athlete's current ability in the discipline?
- Does improvement in one discipline risk a score reduction in other disciplines?
- Are there disciplines with common fitness and technical requirements that would all benefit from the same relevant training?
- Are some disciplines "weighted" more than others with performance variability impacting points awarded more than in other events?
- What are the types of athletes who compete in the decathlon and are certain types advantaged by the disciplines included and the scoring system?

All these questions are important but, ultimately, it is the first question that is of most interest. The other questions are related to this first question; consequently, data scientists need to understand the decathlon and how it is scored to help identify priorities for individual competitors.

48

Table 3.1 The scoring coefficients used for the decathlon (IAAF, 2001: 24)

Discipline	A	B	C
100m (s)	25.4347	18	1.81
Long jump (cm)	0.14354	220	1.4
Shot put (m)	51.39	1.5	1.05
High jump (cm)	0.8465	75	1.42
400m (s)	1.53775	82	1.81
110m hurdles (s)	5.74352	28.5	1.92
Discus throw (m)	12.91	4	1.1
Pole vault (cm)	0.2797	100	1.35
Javelin throw (m)	10.14	7	1.08
1500m (s)	0.03768	480	1.85

Ultimately, these priorities will be chosen by decision makers; therefore, the concern of this chapter is how data can be visualised to best inform the decision-making process.

The decathlon is scored using equation (3.1) for timed running disciplines, in which lower times are better, and equation (3.2) for throw and jump events, in which higher distances are better. In these equations, X is the athlete's distance or time measured in the units shown in Table 3.1 and the scoring coefficients A, B and C depend on the discipline being scored. The total points awarded for the decathlon is the sum of the points awarded for the 10 individual disciplines.

$$\text{Points} = A\,(B-X)^C \qquad\qquad (3.1)$$
$$\text{Points} = A\,(X-B)^C \qquad\qquad (3.2)$$

Data collection and checking

To understand the decathlon and start answering the questions posed earlier, we need to study it and for that we need data. This chapter is based on an analysis of 211 completed decathlon performances of 100 different decathletes during World and Olympic Championships between 2007 and 2017. These data were collected from publicly available results (https://en.wikipedia.org/wiki/Category:Decathlon_at_the_World_Championships_in_Athletics, accessed 26/7/17; https://en.wikipedia.org/wiki/Category:Decathlon_at_the_Olympics, accessed 26/7/17); the time or distance performed by each athlete in each discipline was recorded together with the points awarded for the discipline. The total points awarded for the decathlon were also recorded for each athlete. There were some initial pre-processing tasks that were necessary; for example, 1500m times in minutes and seconds had to be transformed into total seconds and some distances reported in metres (the three jumps) had to be converted into centimetres. Any incomplete performances in which athletes failed to complete all 10 events were excluded.

The data went through a thorough checking process that involved three stages. First, the equations used to compute points awarded were applied to the performances in each discipline to ensure that the points calculated and recorded were the same. When there was a discrepancy in the points recorded and those calculated from the performance, the error could have been in the recording of the performance or the corresponding points. Erroneous data were rechecked against the initial source and corrected if possible. In two cases, this did not resolve the problem and therefore a second source was consulted (www.iaaf.org/results, accessed 13/8/17), revealing that the initial source was inaccurate for these two cases and the data were corrected. This process also allowed verification that the same points-awarding system was applied during all decathlons from 2007 to 2017. The equipment and rules applying to decathlons had been studied prior to data collection and there were no obvious rule changes regarding points awarded. However, performing such a check on the data only takes 15 minutes in a spreadsheet package and is worth doing for extra reassurance.

Second, the total points each athlete achieved for the decathlon was summed from the points awarded for the 10 disciplines and compared with the total reported points to highlight any errors. An error at this stage could be in the recorded total points for the decathlon or in the performance (time or distance and corresponding points) for an individual event. When any mismatches in the totals occurred, the initial sources were rechecked and the data corrected. This revealed no additional errors to those already identified in the first stage of checking.

A third check was to examine the minimum and maximum points awarded for each discipline across all 211 performances. This highlighted one 110m hurdles performance in which an athlete was awarded 8 points, possibly due to falling at a hurdle before completing the race. It was decided to exclude this performance. Once this had been done, the minimum points awarded for any discipline was 381 for a 5 min 33.7s

50

performance in the 1500m and the maximum was 1,068 for an 8.03m long jump. The total scores for the decathlon ranged from 7,021 to 9,045 points.

There is one issue with excluding incomplete performances – it also reduces the volume of individual event data used to study athlete progression over successive seasons. One aim of analysing the decathlon is to identify areas in which points can be improved. Imagine the case in which an athlete, in 2015, completes all the events successfully but has three no jumps in the long jump. When we exclude this performance, we may also lose two year-to-year progression pairs (2014 to 2015 and 2015 to 2016) for the nine disciplines the athlete completed. There are advantages and disadvantages to including incomplete performances. The main advantage is that it increases the volume of individual discipline data used to analyse season-to-season progression. The main disadvantage is that some discipline performances may not be as competitive or may be experimental if the athlete has already failed to compete in one discipline in a decathlon. Such data might not be considered valid for individual disciplines within a competitive decathlon performance.

Range of points in different disciplines

Consider the question posed earlier: "Are some disciplines 'weighted' more than others with performance variability impacting points awarded more than in other events?" Figure 3.2 shows the spread of points awarded for the 10 disciplines within the 211 performances included in the analysis. This is a box and whiskers plot that represents the inter-quartile range as a box with the whiskers showing the range of the remaining values as long as they are within 1.5 inter-quartile ranges. Any outlier performances outside this range are shown as circles. This representation immediately shows the viewer which disciplines decathletes gain the most points for and, more importantly, which disciplines have the largest variance in points awarded. Comparisons, like this of decathlon disciplines, should consider the ranges, distributions and rankings of values across the situations or groups being compared (Kirk, 2012: 67–68). The pole vault and javelin have the largest inter-quartile ranges, which means that a performance's ranking gains or loses more points in these two disciplines than in others. Basically, the points

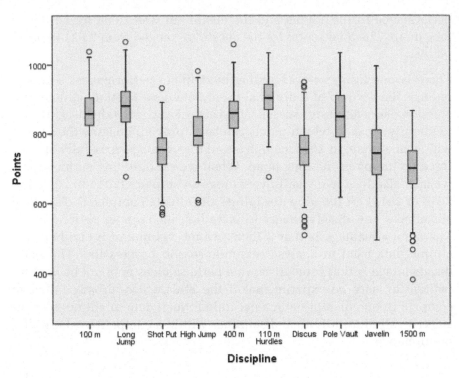

Figure 3.2 Distribution of points for the 10 disciplines (n=211)

difference between a quarter of the way down from the best performance and a quarter of the way up from the worst performance is greater in these two events than in any other.

We may also be interested in trends in points achieved by medallists and athletes in other places. These can be used to set targets for decathletes aiming for future decathlon competitions. Perhaps an athlete who achieved a silver or bronze medal is aiming for gold. Perhaps an athlete placed between 5th and 10th place in a previous championship is aiming for a medal. Perhaps an athlete placed between 15th and 20th is aiming to be in the top 10 places. Perhaps an athlete preparing for their first decathlon within an Olympic or World Championship has a personal best points score in a continental or domestic competition and sets a target placing based on a feasible improvement. Figure 3.3 shows the points required to achieve different placings in World and Olympic decathlons between 2007 and 2017.

52

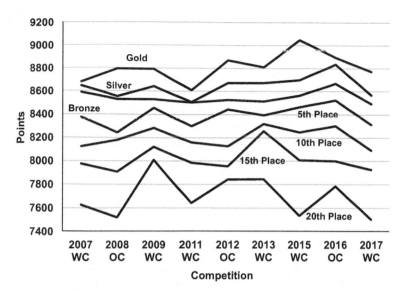

Figure 3.3 Points awarded in World (WC) and Olympic (OC) Decathlon Championships between 2007 and 2017

Relationships between different disciplines

Let us now consider the earlier questions of whether "improvement in one discipline risks a score reduction in other disciplines" and "Are there disciplines with common fitness and technical requirements that would all benefit from the same relevant training?" Visualising relationships between variables allows connections, associations and exceptions to be identified (Kirk, 2012: 69–70). However, in the decathlon, there are 45 pairs of events that could be correlated. A simple correlation matrix for the points awarded in the 10 disciplines would show pairwise relationships between the disciplines. However, there may be sets of three or more variables that are related. A principal components analysis can be used to identify such relationships between variables. This could be applied to the full set of 211 performances or to the best performances of the 100 individual athletes whose data are used. This chapter used the latter approach to avoid a situation in which the relationships were too specific to particularly successful athletes who had competed in several World and Olympic Championships. The initial exploratory principal components analysis extracted three components with eigenvalues of over 1.0 that together represented 64.3% of the variance in the data. However, the final two events (the javelin and the 1500m) were not loaded onto any of the three extracted components ($|r| < +0.500$). Therefore, a further principal components analysis was attempted to extract two additional components to hopefully encompass these two events resulting in all the extracted components having eigenvalues of 1.0 or over after they had been rotated; a component with an eigenvalue of less than 1.0 is not worth an original variable. This principal components analysis extracted five components that together represented 80.5% of the variance in the data. Rotation led to a reduction of the primary principal component's eigenvalue but elevated the fourth and fifth components' eigenvalues to greater than 1.0. Loading plots can be used to show relationships between disciplines within a multidimensional space (Miller, 2016: 13, 72). The loading plots in Figures 3.4(a) to 3.4(c) show how the points awarded for the individual disciplines load onto these principal components. The primary principal component is shown in Figures 3.4(a) and 3.4(b), revealing that it is highly correlated with points earned for the 100m ($r = +0.879$), long jump ($r = +0.755$) and 400m ($r = +0.844$) with a further positive correlation with the 110m hurdles ($r = +0.485$); thus, these four disciplines seem to be related through the common attributes of speed and power. PC2 (the second principal component) has heavy loadings from points earned for the shot put ($r = +0.828$) and the discus ($r = +0.908$) with a further positive correlation with the javelin ($r = +0.364$). Thus, the three throwing events are related. PC2 also has a negative correlation with points earned for the 1500m ($r = -0.484$), suggesting that making improvements in the shot put and discus could reduce performance in the 1500m. PC3, shown in Figure 3.4(b), has heavy loadings from points earned in the pole vault ($r = +0.860$) and the 110m hurdles ($r = 0.641$). These two disciplines may have similarities such as take-off ability. Figure 3.4(c) shows the loadings of disciplines onto PC4 and PC5. PC4 is highly correlated with points earned from the high jump ($r = +0.909$) and has a positive correlation with points earned from the long jump ($r = +0.455$), which can be interpreted as representing a jumping dimension within the data. Finally, PC5 has heavy loadings from points earned from the javelin ($r = +0.821$) and the 1500m ($r = +0.609$). This might possibly be explained by the javelin run-up benefitting from an efficient running technique in contrast to the preparation phases for the other two throwing events within the decathlon. Principal components analysis involves some subjective processes in deciding the number of principal components to extract, the solution to use and how principal

54

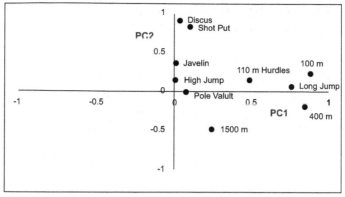

(a) Loading plot for principal components PC1 and PC2.

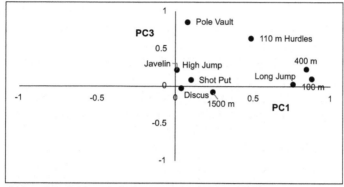

(b) Loading plot for principal components PC1 and PC3.

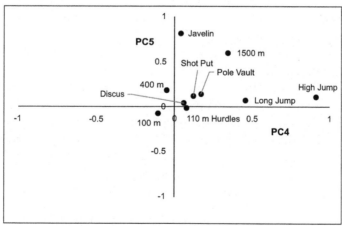

(c) Loading plot for principal components PC4 and PC5.

Figure 3.4 Loading plots for the five principal components extracted from decathlon data

components should be interpreted. There is a choice of factor rotation techniques that could be used, which, combined with alternative numbers of principal components to extract, lead to several solutions. Choosing one solution requires the analyst to consider the nature of the variables loading onto principal components within different solutions and which solution is most logical and consistent with relevant theory. This requires experience, knowledge and expertise.

Types of decathletes

We now turn to the question of whether there are different types of decathletes. This was explored by applying a hierarchical cluster analysis to the best performance for each of the 100 decathletes in the dataset. The data were first dimensionalised so that disciplines were represented by the percentage of the total score they contributed rather than the raw points earned. This was done to avoid a situation in which the level of a decathlete's success impacted the analysis; this is about the type of decathlete and how they earn their points rather than how many points they score. There are a range of solutions that could be produced using hierarchical cluster analysis; therefore, there is an element of analyst judgement just as there is with principal components analysis. A dendogram is a tree diagram showing the decomposition of the set of athletes into clusters; the clusters are continually split until there are 100 individual decathletes at the bottommost nodes of the dendogram. The vertical lines of a dendogram represent how far apart different clusters are; thus, we would ideally like to have short vertical lines within clusters, so that members are similar, but large vertical lines between different clusters. Once seven clusters had been determined (containing 76, 9, 7, 3, 2, 2 and 1 decathletes), the next five divisions of the data only identified small groups of one to three athletes rather than splitting the cluster of 76 into more substantial clusters of 10 or more members. Therefore, it was decided to select the seven-cluster solution. The cluster of one athlete was unavoidable because the first division of the data created this cluster along with one containing the remaining 99 decathletes.

Figure 3.5 shows the percentage of total points derived from the 10 disciplines for the mean member of the three main clusters. This shows that the modal cluster of 76 decathletes (C1) has a higher javelin score than the other two clusters but is not the highest performing of the three

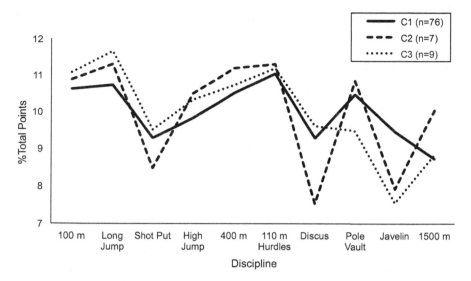

Figure 3.5 Percentage of decathlon points derived from the 10 disciplines by the three main clusters of decathletes

clusters in any other discipline. C1's next most successful disciplines relative to the other clusters are the shot put and the discus. The five disciplines in which they achieve a lower percentage of their total points than the other two clusters are not drastically below those two clusters. Cluster C2 is the most inconsistently performing cluster between disciplines with relatively good performances in the high jump, 400m, 110m hurdles, pole vault and 1500m but much fewer points for the shot put and discus than the other two clusters. Cluster C3 performs relatively well in the 100m, long jump, shot put and discus, but not so well in the javelin and pole vault. The line graph used in Figure 3.5 is just one way of visualising the performances of different clusters of athletes in various events.

The other four clusters represent small groups of one to three decathletes but may be important particularly if a decathlete we are working with is one of these types. Adding four further lines to Figure 3.5 might obscure patterns. An alternative would be to use a compound column chart. This would avoid multiple lines crossing each other but has the limitation of making differences between clusters more difficult to recognise due to the full 0–100% scale used. Our solution is to use a line graph like Figure 3.5 but not show all seven clusters at once. Instead, we might show the three main clusters in mid-colours like blues and greens using brighter colours like red or yellow to highlight an additional cluster of interest, only showing one additional cluster at a time. Interactive visualisation allows such a line graph to be interactively filtered so that only selected clusters of interest are shown at any time.

Feasible improvements in different disciplines

We now turn to the second of our initial questions: "What level of improvement is feasible in each discipline in a given time scale and does the improvement level depend on the athlete's current ability in the discipline?" It is one thing being able to identify a discipline in which a decathlete is not performing as well as they are in other disciplines. The next step is to set reasonable targets for improvement in that discipline. To do this, we need some knowledge of what level of improvement is possible over given periods of time. Within the dataset used in this chapter, there are 65 decathlon performances by an athlete who had other performances during the previous year. This allows paired analyses to look at the range of improvements possible in various disciplines within the decathlon. Figure 3.6 is a box and whiskers plot that reveals that some athletes improve the points awarded in a discipline, whereas others may see a decrease in the points awarded compared to a year earlier. The stars (asterisks) in this chart are "extreme values" that are more than three inter-quartile ranges outside the one for changes in points scored between successive calendar years. The discus, pole vault and javelin have the largest ranges of change in points, whereas the 400m and the shot put have the smallest.

The improvements shown in the median areas of Figure 3.6 may not be possible for all athletes. An athlete who is already earning points at the upper end for a given discipline will have less scope for improvement than other athletes whose points for the discipline may be in the lowest quartile. Table 3.2 summarises the data for those athletes who improved their points score in disciplines over successive calendar years. The pole vault was the discipline in which most athletes improved (n=47) whereas the shot put had the fewest athletes improve (n=27). In every discipline, the improvement in points was negatively correlated with the number of points the athlete had for the discipline a year earlier. This confirms that it is harder to improve the better you are. The regression models for

58

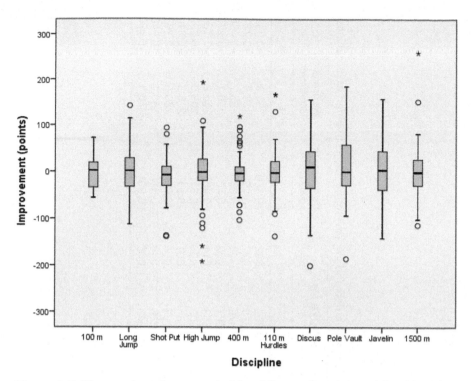

Figure 3.6 Changes in points awarded for different disciplines of the decathlon between successive calendar years (n=65)

predicted improvement based on the previous year's points in an event are significant for eight of the 10 disciplines. The main implication is that the range of improvement reduces as previous points earned from a discipline increases. Although the shot put has one of the lowest variabilities in performance change, performance in the shot put is related to performance in the discus, meaning there may be training that would benefit both disciplines.

The standard deviation for improvements applies when an athlete previously had the mean number of points for any of the improvers analysed. For example, we will consider the javelin, in which the largest improvements in points were made. An improving athlete who scored 742.6 points in this discipline a year ago would be expected to improve by 58.4 points (= 169.1–0.149 x 742.6). The standard deviation in improvement of ±42.1 points applies to athletes who previously earned 742.6 points

Table 3.2 Correlation and regression coefficients between points awarded and improvements made in different disciplines

Discipline (number of improving athletes)	Previous points	Improvement in points	ANOVA test		Correlation coefficient	Regression coefficients	
	mean±SD	mean±SD	F	p	R	a	b
100m (n=39)	874.2±70.1	20.2±17.1	0.852	.362	−0.150	52.3	−0.037
Long Jump (n=34)	878.4±66.5	45.2±37.4	5.814	.022	−0.392	238.9	−0.221
Shot Put (n=27)	739.0±57.7	26.1±25.0	0.878	.358	−0.358	85.2	−0.080
High Jump (n=42)	794.5±66.7	36.1±39.9	10.881	.002	−0.462	256.1	−0.277
400m (n=28)	850.1±59.2	30.4±34.2	6.869	.014	−0.457	254.9	−0.264
110m Hurdles (n=30)	889.0±73.9	41.9±42.9	9.903	.004	−0.511	305.9	−0.297
Discus (n=37)	717.6±70.1	48.7±42.9	12.66	.001	−0.515	275.3	−0.316
Pole Vault (n=47)	846.1±73.4	43.3±56.1	6.268	.016	−0.350	269.5	−0.267
Javelin (n=33)	742.6±97.7	58.4±42.1	4.218	.049	−0.346	169.1	−0.149
1500m (n=31)	679.9±81.3	40.6±50.6	52.045	.000	−0.801	380.1	−0.499

in this discipline. There is a greater range of improvement for athletes who scored fewer than 742.6 points for the javelin a year ago and a lower range for athletes who scored greater than 742.6 points. The 12 athletes with fewer than 700 points for the javelin a year earlier had a standard deviation in improvement scores of ±45.3 points, whereas those over 700 points (n=21) had a standard deviation of ±32.8 points.

Target setting

The analysis of the decathlon is used for a purely academic case study based on the performances of Thomas Van der Plaetsen (Belgium), the 2016 European Champion who finished eighth in the 2016 Olympic Decathlon with a personal best performance of 8,332 points. The question is what would this athlete need to do to win a medal at the next World or Olympic Championships? The highest score needed to achieve a bronze medal in a World or Olympic Championships shown in Figure 3.3 is 8,666 points. Given the retirement of double Olympic and double World Champion Ashton Eaton, we could set a target of 8,700 points, expecting this to give a good chance of winning a medal.

The athlete's performances in decathlon events were gathered from publicly available information (https://en.wikipedia.org/wiki/Thomas_Van_der_Plaetsen, accessed 15/8/17), revealing that two of his best decathlon performances for individual disciplines occurred during his best decathlon. Table 3.3 shows that there are eight other disciplines in which he had better performances in previous years. If he was to equal all 10 personal bests within a decathlon event, he would achieve a total of 8,651 points, which is short of the target. So which events should he focus on to give himself the best chance of achieving the target points total of 8,700? Table 3.3 shows the ranking of his best performances within the dataset of 211 performances used in this chapter. He is already one of best performers at the pole vault, high jump and long jump, so there is limited scope for improvement in these disciplines. His worst discipline is the 100m, which is surprising given the strong relationship between 100m time and long jump distance. However, Figure 3.2 shows that the 100m is one of the three disciplines with the lowest variability in points change. The discus, on the other hand, is one of the three disciplines with the largest variability in points change.

Table 3.3 Decathlon performances by Thomas Van der Plaetsen

Discipline	Personal best decathlon		Personal bests within a decathlon			
	Performance	Points	Performance	Points	Year	Rank
100m (s)	11.24	808	11.09	841	2013	133
Long Jump (m)	7.66	975	780	1010	2013	7
Shot Put (m)	12.84	657	14.12	736	2014	125
High Jump (m)	216	953	217	963	2011	2
400m (s)	49.63	832	48.64	878	2011	79
110m Hurdles (s)	15.01	848	14.59	900	2015	114
Discus (m)	43.58	738	44.32	753	2016	107
Pole Vault (m)	540	1035	540	1035	2016	1
Javelin (m)	62.09	769	65.31	818	2013	49
1500m (min:s)	4:34.21	717	4:34.21	717	2016	85
Total Points		8332		8651		

The process of determining where the athlete can best improve his points total uses the information in Table 3.3 as well as the analysis of potential improvements shown in Table 3.2. There are three stages to the process that are applied to each discipline. First, the athlete's current best performance within a decathlon is used as a starting point with which to add a points improvement value. Second, the 25th, 50th and 75th percentile in points improvement in the 10 disciplines are determined from the athletes ($27 <= n <= 47$) who improved in the given events. For example, the 25th, 50th and 75th percentiles for discus points improvements for the 37 improving athletes in the discipline were 14, 37 and 65 points, respectively. These percentiles are for the average improver; the values are higher for athletes with below-mean performance in the given discipline and lower for athletes with an above-mean performance. Therefore, a third stage is needed to determine a multiplying factor to apply to the percentiles in points improvement. This is only done for the eight disciplines in which level of performance has a significant influence on the amount of improvement. The regression equations shown in Table 3.2 are applied to the athlete's best performances within a decathlon to determine a predicted improvement for an athlete performing at the given level within the different disciplines. The factor by which the percentiles are multiplied is the predicted improvement for the athlete expressed as a fraction of the predicted improvement for the mean-improving athlete in the discipline. For example, the athlete has a predicted improvement of 37.4 points (= 275.3−0.316 x 753) for the discus

62

given his current best in a decathlon of 753. Now the mean-improving athlete is predicted to improve by 48.7 points according to Table 3.2. Therefore, the athlete's scope for improvement needs to be scaled down by 0.77 (= 37.4 / 48.7). Thus, the 25th, 50th and 75th percentiles in points improvement for the discus are scaled down from 14, 37 and 65 points to 10.8, 28.5 and 50.0 points, respectively.

Figure 3.7 shows the result of applying this process to each discipline for the athlete under consideration. The athlete's current best performances within a decathlon are shown as the thick solid black line. The thinner solid black line is the 50th percentile in points improvement for the discipline adjusted for the athlete's performance level. The dashed lines below and above the thin solid line are the 25th and 75th percentile in points improvement, respectively. The events with the biggest scope for improvement are the javelin (50th percentile in points improvement = 36), the discus (50th percentile in points improvement = 29), the 110m hurdles (50th percentile in points

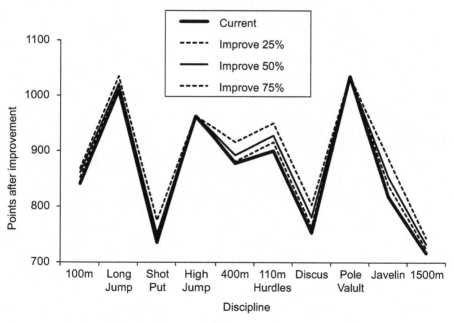

Figure 3.7 Predicted performance improvements for Thomas Van der Plaetsen

improvement = 28) and the 100m (50th percentile in points improvement = 20). If the athlete can improve in these four disciplines to a greater extent than the bottom quarter of improvers and maintain best scores within the decathlon for the other six events, he will achieve a total of 8,709 points, exceeding the target of 8,700 points. If the athlete made improvements in these four events equivalent to the 50th percentile, he would achieve a total of 8,763 points. The actual performances needed to achieve the required points can be determined by changing the subject of equations (3.1) and (3.2) so that performance, X, is the subject of the equation rather than points. Equations (3.3) and (3.4) determine the performance required in running and jumping/throwing events, respectively. Applying these to the points in the four disciplines in which a target improvement equivalent to the 25th percentile in improvements is set gives target performances of 11.04s for the 100m, 14.46s for the 110m hurdles, 44.84m for the discus and 66.66m for the javelin.

$$X = B - e^{(\ln \text{ Points } - \ln A)/C} \tag{3.3}$$
$$X = B + e^{(\ln \text{ Points } - \ln A)/C} \tag{3.4}$$

Keep in mind that the principal components analysis discussed earlier in this chapter showed that discus performance is negatively associated with 1500m performance. The athlete and his support team need to ensure that any developments made to improve discus performance do not result in points reduction in the 1500m. To summarise, the athlete needs to improve in the 100m, 110m hurdles, discus and javelin as described, avoid losing points in the 1500m, and equal his personal bests in the other five events to exceed the target of 8,700 points estimated as good enough to win a medal. World Championship and Olympic medals do not grow on trees!

SUMMARY

This chapter described the role of visualisation in evaluating trends in performance and decision making about priorities for training. Passing performance in English FA Premier League soccer was used as an example of trend monitoring. The absolute performance of the team was plotted against quintile norms for performances against the given opposition. This allows performance to be considered relative to the quality of the opposition in the given match. The decathlon in track and field athletics is a good example in which profiling can be applied because the event is made up of 10 different disciplines. In setting targets, we need to understand the type of decathlete we are dealing with, how good they are at the different disciplines and their scopes for improvement. The better an athlete is at a discipline, the more difficult it is to improve. Evidence can be derived from previous performances as to the spread of improvements possible in the different disciplines given the athlete's current ability. The variances of points scored in different disciplines means that improvement in some disciplines will yield more additional points than equivalent improvements in others. This can allow athletes and their support teams to identify the areas for improvement that are most feasible and will lead to the biggest gain in overall points for the decathlon. There is a clear role for visualisation in presenting such information to athletes, coaches and high-performance managers to help them make effective decisions.

REFERENCES

Farris, M. (2017) 'The Aspire Group's ticket marketing, sales and service philosophy', In C.K. Harrison and S. Bukstein (eds.), *Sports business analytics: Using data to increase revenue and improve operational efficiency* (pp. 69–88), London: Routledge.

Few, S. (2009) *Now you see it: Simple visualisation techniques for quantitative analysis*, Oakland, CA: Analytics Press.

Healey, C.G., Booth, K.S. and Enns, J.T. (1996) 'High-speed visual estimation using preattentive processing', *ACM Transactions on Computer-Human Interaction*, 3(2): 107–135.

IAAF (2001) 'IAAF scoring tables for combined events', https://web.archive.org/web/20071203030644/www.iaaf.org/newsfiles/32097.pdf, accessed 26th July 2017.

Kirk, A. (2012) *Data visualisation: A successful design process*, Birmingham, UK: Packt Publishing.

Miller, T.W. (2016) *Sports analytics and data science: Winning the game with methods and models*, Old Tappan, NJ: Pearson Education Inc.

Nisotaki, M. (2016) 'Trend analysis: Addressing opposition quality using regression analysis', M.Sc. Dissertation, Cardiff, UK: Cardiff Metropolitan University.

O'Donoghue, P.G. and Holmes, L.A. (2015) *Data analysis in sport*, London, UK: Routledge.

Sleeper, R. (2017) 'Data visualisation and data-driven storytelling', In C.K. Harrison and S. Bukstein (eds.), *Sports business analytics: Using data to increase revenue and improve operational efficiency* (pp. 201–218), London: Routledge.

Tacca, M.C. (2011) 'Commonalities between perception and cognition', *Frontiers in Psychology*, 2: 358.

Yau, N. (2011) *Visualise this: The flowing data guide to design, statistics and visualisation*, New York, NY: Wiley.

CHAPTER 4

SIMULATION AND MODELLING

INTRODUCTION

Simulation studies are a safe way of predicting aspects of sports performance of interest to decision makers. Real matches with real risks do not take place and yet reasonably valid information about sports can be generated. However, the simulation results are only as good as the underlying models of matches and tournaments used within simulators. These models typically represent matches by key variables and, therefore, cannot represent the full complexity of sports performance. There are many intangible factors such as coachability and leadership that are difficult to measure numerically (Alamar, 2013: 47). Nonetheless, the variability in sports performance attributed to factors not included in the model can be simulated using random numbers. Models of sports performance are produced by analysing previous cases in which key variables of interest and outcomes are known. Once the model is produced, future performances can be simulated, providing outcome predictions. We also need to be aware of the limitations of simulations and the assumptions they make. Consider the Fast4 format of tennis in which the first player to score 4 points wins the game even if the game has gone to deuce. We could use our knowledge of the probability of serving players winning points on different surfaces in women's and men's singles tennis to simulate traditional and Fast4 games to determine the difference in the probability of winning these two types of games. However, this assumes that tennis points will be played the same way under both systems. This does not invalidate such a simulation study but we do need to be aware of the limitations. The most important thing to understand about simulation studies is that they do not actually predict match outcomes! They simulate matches and tournaments many times to gain an understanding of the different outcomes possible and the probability with which they could occur. This chapter uses the outcomes of international rugby union matches as an example to evaluate the probability of different teams winning the 2019 Rugby World Cup. This information can be used for target setting and evaluation of team performance.

TOURNAMENT PREDICTION

Major sports tournaments occur in cycles; for example, a World Cup in rugby union or soccer occurs once every four years. The period between World Cups is referred to as a cycle. Sports governing bodies often set targets for squads such as reaching the quarter-finals or semi-finals of tournaments. To set reasonable targets, knowledge of the chances of reaching various stages of tournaments should be used. There is a role for simulation to determine squads' chances of reaching different tournament stages. Simulations studies have highlighted factors influencing success such as tournament structure (O'Donoghue, 2005), team quality (O'Donoghue and Williams, 2004), home advantage and travel (O'Donoghue, 2014) as well as recovery days between matches (O'Donoghue et al., 2016). Predictive modelling using simulation can also be used by betting agencies to help set odds for teams reaching various tournament stages. This allows them to take bets on teams' performances in the months and even years leading up to the tournament. This chapter discusses modelling assumptions, how they can be tested, and how models address any modelling assumption violations. The 2019 Rugby World Cup is used as an example because the tournament structure and draw were already made by the time of writing (summer 2017) even though not all the teams qualified yet. Therefore, we have more uncertainty in predicting the tournament than if all 20 teams contesting the tournament were known. Analytic principles are used to enhance the underlying model of rugby union performance.

MODELLING ASSUMPTIONS

The main message from this example is that models should not be straightjacketed by the assumptions of modelling techniques. Indeed, the ways in which data used to create models violate the assumptions of

68

modelling techniques are actually opportunities to enhance models with features that are relevant to the type of data used. A regression model is used to predict the points difference between two teams contesting a rugby match using the difference between their World ranking points. Regression models in sports are not able to predict exact values for individual cases. For example, in sports psychology, they are used to show general relationships between variables (Woodman et al., 2010). The data used to create models do not fit them exactly and the differences between actual and predicted values are referred to as residuals. The distribution of residual values about the predicted value can be used to estimate the probabilities of different match outcomes. They can also be used within simulation packages to estimate various outcome probabilities for tournaments composed of multiple matches (O'Donoghue and Williams, 2004; O'Donoghue et al., 2016). The assumptions of regression analysis that are relevant to this exercise are:

- There must be at least 20 cases per independent variable used in the model (Ntoumanis, 2001: 120–121).
- The residual values should be normally distributed (Vincent, 1999: 111).
- The residual values should be homoscedastistic (Anderson et al., 1994: 521); this means the distribution of residual values should be the same for all subranges of predicted values.
- The residual values should be independent (O'Donoghue, 2012: 151); this means there must be no order effects or temporal trends within residual values.

The overall approach to predictive modelling using a simple linear regression is made up of two stages. First, real data are used to assess the relationship between an independent and dependent variable and to form a regression model. The second stage is the prediction phase in which we go in the reverse direction using the model to determine predicted values for dependent variables for new cases in which we have values for the independent variables. In this section, we describe how regression models can be enhanced applying the analytics principles covered in Chapter 1. In particular, this section addresses limitations in data quality. Data used to model rugby performance may violate the assumptions of modelling techniques. The very nature of international rugby may be changing with an increasing number of upsets and surprise results in recent years. An analytics approach should deal with

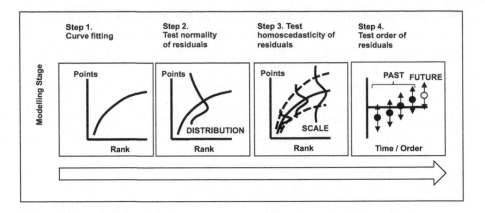

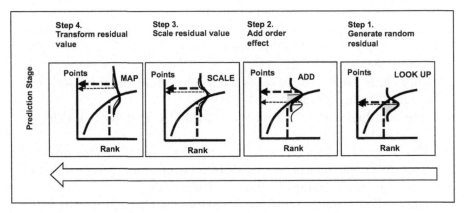

Figure 4.1 The overall approach to predictive modelling

these matters to improve the quality of the predictive model. In addressing such issues, both the modelling and prediction stages include additional steps as shown in Figure 4.1.

MODELLING STAGE

The first step of the modelling stage is to apply curve fitting to determine the type of relationship that exists between independent variables and the dependent variable. During this step, we consider the independent variables in isolation and then together. The relationship between an independent and dependent variable may be linear, logarithmic, inverse, quadratic or cubic. The decision about candidate models to use in each case depends on the statistical significance of the models as well as knowledge of the application domain. For example, one might reasonably expect the points difference in a sporting contest to increase as the gap in rankings between the two competitors increases. In such a situation, if a quadratic model turns out to be the most statistically significant, we would override the choice of model suggested by statistical analysis. Quadratic models will either be in a U shape or an inverted U shape, neither of which reflect our conceptual understanding of the relation between the two variables. There are other situations in which a quadratic model could be acceptable. During the initial curve fitting stage, we can reduce the number of independent variables used in the model because there may be some that are totally unrelated to the dependent variable.

Once the relationships between the independent variables and dependent variable are understood, we can produce a single model of the dependent variable including the full set of independent variables using multivariate regression analysis. If the statistics package used only provides multivariate regression using linear relationships, we can simply apply the necessary functions to the independent variables to account for their relationships with the dependent variable. For example, imagine if we have four independent variables x_1, x_2, x_3 and x_4 whose relationships with our dependent variable are linear, inverse, logarithmic and quadratic, respectively. In this situation, we would enter x_1, $1/x_2$, $\log x_3$, x_4 and x_4^2 into the multivariate regression analysis. We set significance levels for the inclusion and exclusion of independent variables, which allows the statistics package to show any significant models. A model could include one or more independent variables. We may have a situation in which one variable (x_1) is a significant predictor of the dependent variable and another independent variable (x_2) is not quite a significant predictor but the model including both x_1 and x_2 is more significant than the model that excludes x_2. In this case, we might choose the model that included both x_1 and x_2 because it is the most significant predictive model for our dependent variable and x_2 was only found to be not significant when it was considered in isolation.

The second, third and fourth steps of the modelling stage consider the residual values. These are the differences between actual values and values predicted by the model for the cases used to produce the model. The distribution of residual values is important because when we eventually make predictions, we need to add random variability about the predicted result that is evidenced by the variability that actually occurs. The normal distribution is important because we can determine the probability of a randomly generated value being less than some value of interest from it. This also means that we can go in the reverse direction, using a random probability between 0 and 1 to determine the value of the dependent variable equivalent to it. The second step of the modelling stage determines the distribution of the residual values. When we have selected the model to be applied at the end of the first step, we save the residual values so their distribution can be studied. Initially, the residuals are tested to see if they are normally distributed. This can be done with a Shapiro Wilk test if there are fewer than 50 cases used in the modelling stage or a Kolmogorov-Smirnov test if there are 50 or more cases. If the residuals are not normally distributed, we need to determine their distribution type so we have a way of mapping the residual values onto a normally distributed version of the residuals. The transformed normal distribution can then be used with random probabilities during the prediction stage. Skewness and kurtosis can be inspected using the variable explore facilities of statistics packages. However, what we really need is a way of mapping the distribution of residual values onto a normal distribution. This can be done using curve fitting with the ordered residual values and a synthesised set of normally distributed values with the same mean (0) and standard deviation as our residual values. The normally distributed version can be synthesised using the NORMINV function in Microsoft Excel (Microsoft Inc., Redmond, WA). For example, if we had 100 previous cases with a mean of 0 and a standard of 6 for the residual values, we would use NORMINV (p, 0, 6) with 100 values of p from 0.005 to 0.995 in steps of 0.01. The curve fitting exercise will yield a transformation function that maps residual values onto corresponding values of this normally distributed version of the residuals. There are some points to consider with curve fitting models used for this purpose. First, if the best transformation function turns out to be linear, we might as well not use it. A linear transformation will simply scale the non-normal distribution, it will not normalise it. A quadratic transformation function is problematic because, eventually, we wish to go in the other direction when making predictions. The problem here is that the solution to a quadratic equation gives two results because the square root term of the solution gives two answers (e.g. the square root of 4 could be 2 or -2). There is a similar problem with cubic transformation functions. A quadratic or cubic transformation function in which the x^2 term is negligible could be used because the inverse equation would produce a single value. Reciprocal, logarithmic and exponential transformation functions imply inverse functions that go in the other direction.

72

The third step of the modelling stage is to test if the transformed residual values are homoscedastic. If there is no relationship between the transformed residual values and the predicted value for the dependent variable, the transformed residual values are indeed homoscedastic. If, on the other hand, the spread of transformed residual values depends on the predicted value for the dependent variable, we need to understand how the spread of residual values increases or decreases as predicted values increase. When we eventually make predictions, we need to scale any randomly generated residual value to reflect the fact that the spread of residual values is not uniform. To understand if there is a "shotgun" effect in the transformed residuals, we need to correlate the absolute transformed residual values with the predicted values. If there is a positive correlation of greater than 0.250 (Pearson's r), there is a "shotgun" effect that increases the spread of transformed residuals as predicted values of the dependent variable increase. A simple linear regression analysis will produce a function for the mean transformed residual value for any predicted value of the dependent variable. This can then be used to scale the transformed residual values so we have a homoscedastic version that can be used during the prediction stage.

The fourth and final step of the modelling stage is to determine if the residual values (after transformation and scaling) are independent or whether there is some trend or order effect in them. The model thus far has normally distributed residual values that are independent of predicted values when the historical cases used to produce the model are considered as a whole. However, there may be a trend for the model to underestimate the dependent variable of interest for cases that occurred during one period of time and overestimate them for cases occurring during other periods. If this is happens, we should analyse this trend in the predicted values and extrapolate how much the model will over- or underestimate the dependent variable in the future. This information can then be used to modify predictions based on the model to account for the known order effect on the residual values.

PREDICTION STAGE

The modelling stage uses a series of four ordered steps to produce a model for our dependent variable in terms of our independent variables. The last three steps adjust residual values to produce transformed residual values that satisfy the assumptions of regression analysis, allowing us to make predictions using random numbers mapped onto the normal probability distribution. Therefore, during the prediction phase, we need to go in the reverse order to move from our adjusted residuals to the actual distribution of residuals when generating a predicted result.

The first step of the prediction stage is to determine a predicted value using the regression equation. This is the value on the line of best fit for the given value(s) of the independent variables. We then generate a random number between 0 and 1 to determine the adjusted residual value that will be added to the predicted value to account for variability about the line of best fit.

The second step applies any temporal modifier to the predicted value that may have been justified by extrapolating trends in the adjusted residual values. This modifier is added to the predicted value separately from the residual value that still has a couple steps to be applied to transform it back into the actual distribution of the residual values.

The third step of the prediction stage involves scaling the residual value in the reverse direction to that used in the model stage. For example, if we discovered a "shotgun" effect in the transformed residual values during the modelling phase such that transformed residual values needed to be divided by 1.2 for the given predicted value, for the residuals to be homoscedastic, the residual value generated during the prediction stage would need to be multiplied by 1.2. This means that, although the residual values used by the model satisfy the assumption of homoscedasticity, we are able to represent the differing variability of the dependent variable evidenced in various subranges.

Having generated a normally distributed residual value that has been appropriately scaled for the given predicted value, the fourth and final stage is to transform the residual value so it comes from the actual distribution of residual values observed for the dependent variable rather than from the normal distribution required for modelling purposes. This involves using the inverse of the mapping function used in the second step of the modelling stage. For example, if a logarithmic transformation had been applied to the residuals to produce a normally distributed version, we would use an exponential function to map our normally distributed residual value to one from the actual distribution. Once the four steps of the prediction stage have been applied, the final predicted

74

value is calculated by summing the expected value, residual value and temporal modifier.

THE RUGBY WORLD CUP

Having introduced the approach to predictive modelling, we can apply it to the Rugby World Cup. All 191 matches from Rugby World Cup tournaments played between 2003 and 2015 were used to create a model of international rugby union matches. These World Cup rankings were not used prior to 2003 and tournaments played up to 1991 only awarded 4 points for a try rather than 5. Therefore, matches from Rugby World Cup tournaments prior to 2003 were not used to create the model.

The dependent variable of interest is the points difference (PD) between the higher and lower ranked teams contesting a match. If this value is positive, the match went to form, if it is negative, the match was an upset and if it is zero, the match was a draw. Three independent variables were considered during the construction of the predictive model. These variables represented the general concepts of team quality, home advantage and recovery from previous matches. The relative quality of the two teams contesting the match is represented by the difference in the world ranking points of the higher and lower ranked teams within the match, RD. Home advantage is represented by the difference between how far two teams travelled to the tournament, DD. Each team's distance travelled is crudely estimated using the giant circle distance between their capital city and the tournament host nation's capital. The third independent variable is how many more recovery days the higher rank team had since their previous match than the lower ranked team, RecD.

The relationship between each independent variable and the dependent variable is initially considered for each independent variable in isolation. The main variable associated with match outcome according to research evidence is relative quality of the teams or individuals contesting the match (O'Donoghue, 2014; O'Donoghue and Williams, 2004; O'Donoghue et al., 2016). Therefore, the relationship between RD and PD is considered first. Curve fitting found that linear ($p < 0.001$), logarithmic ($p < 0.001$), inverse ($p = 0.015$), quadratic ($p < 0.001$) and cubic ($p < 0.001$) models were all significant predictors of PD when RD was used as an independent variable. The most significant of these was the linear model, which also avoided PD decreasing for values of RD over 30, as was the case with the quadratic model.

Curve fitting found that the best model of PD in terms of DD was the quadratic model. However, none of the models using DD as an independent variable were significant ($p \geq 0.435$). Furthermore, none of the models of PD using RecD as an independent variable were significant, but the linear model based on RecD was close to significant ($p = 0.059$). Having explored the relationships between the independent variables and PD in isolation, it was decided to exclude DD from the model. RD was included because it is a highly significant predictor of PD and RecD was included because it was close enough to being significant in isolation that a model using both RD and RecD might be a more significant predictor of PD than a model based solely on RD. The fact that linear models were the most significant when RD and RecD were used in isolation meant that these independent variables could be entered into the multivariate regression analysis without being transformed in any way. RD and RecD were entered into the analysis using the "Stepwise" method with p values of 0.05 and 0.20 used for entry and removal of independent variables, respectively. The statistics package excluded RecD ($p = 0.491$) and produced the model for PD shown in equation (4.3).

$$PD = -4.127 + 2.592 \text{ RD} \qquad (4.3)$$

Having decided on this linear model of PD, we can now move to the second step of the modelling phase and explore the residual values. These values were saved and found to have a mean±SD of 0.0±18.229; that is, considerable variability about the expected result! A Kolmogorov-Smirnov test concluded that the distribution of the residual values was sufficiently normal ($p = 0.200$). Therefore, a mapping function was not needed to transform the residuals into normally distributed ones. There were three outliers and one extreme value identified while exploring the residuals. The extreme value was Australia's 142–0 win over Namibia in 2003. Given the World Cup rankings of the teams at the time, the first outlier was Ireland's 20–43 loss to Argentina in 2015, which was not just an upset but a particularly large margin of victory for Argentina; the second outlier was Wales' 66–0 win over Fiji in 2011, which was also a much larger win than one might expect; and the final outlier was New Zealand's 58–14 win over Namibia in 2015 because New Zealand was expected to win by a much greater margin. It was decided not to remove these outliers and extreme value because they were legitimate real rugby results and not due to measurement error. Excluding these values would artificially reduce the variability in international rugby results.

The third step of the modelling stage revealed a "shotgun" effect in the residuals; the absolute residual values had a positive correlation of +0.270 with both RD and the predicted value for PD (denoted as PD'). This mild heteroscedasticity in the data meant the standard deviation of the residual values was lower for lower PD' values and higher for higher PD' values. A regression equation for absolute residual values (AbsRes) in terms of predicted points difference, PD', is shown in equation (4.4).

$$AbsRes = 9.968 + 0.163*PD' \qquad (4.4)$$

AbsRes represents the mean of the absolute values that would occur for matches with an expected point difference of PD'. What we need to generate random variability about the expected result is the standard deviation of the residual values that would occur for matches with an expected point difference of PD'. Now the mean of absolute residuals for the standard normal distribution is 0.7977 and the standard deviation of the standard normal distribution is 1. Therefore, AbsRes needs to be multiplied by 1 / 0.7977 (= 1.2536) to determine the standard deviation to apply for the given predicted point difference PD'. When we multiply equation (4.4) by 1.2536, we get equation (4.5). This standard deviation for the residuals is used instead of a uniform standard deviation of 18.229.

$$SDres = 12.496 + 0.204 \; PD' \qquad (4.5)$$

An analysis of variances tests compared the residual values between the four Rugby World Cup tournaments that made up the dataset used to create the model. There was almost a significant difference between the four tournaments (p = 0.058) with a pattern of residual values decreasing as shown here.

- Rugby World Cup 2003: residual values 5.6±20.6
- Rugby World Cup 2007: residual values 0.0±19.1
- Rugby World Cup 2011: residual values -1.0±16.6
- Rugby World Cup 2015: residual values -4.5±16.5

This meant that, on average, higher ranked teams were winning matches by smaller margins and the chance of upsets was increasing. Although the ANOVA test itself was not significant, the post hoc comparison between the 2003 and 2015 tournaments was significant ($p = 0.043$). Considering this trend, it was decided to apply a modifier of -6.5 points to the predictions made for the 2019 tournament.

Table 4.1 shows the teams drawn in each pool and the sources of the remaining qualifiers. Consider the Pool A match between Ireland and Japan. At the time of writing, Ireland was ranked 4th in the World Cup with 85.39 points whereas Japan was ranked 11th with 73.79 points (www.worldrugby.org/rankings/mru?lang=en, accessed 30/8/17). Thus, the difference in the two teams' ranking points is 11.6. Applying equation (4.3) gives an expected margin of victory for Ireland of 25.9 points (= -4.127 + 2.592 x 11.6). However, teams may do better or worse than expected and there is a range of possible points differences. The standard deviation of the residual values for a match of this expected points difference is given by applying equation (4.5). This gives a standard deviation of 17.780 (= 12.496 + 0.204 x 25.9). Anticipating that the chance of upsets is going to increase, we apply a modifier of -6.5 to the expected value, giving an expected 19.4 point winning margin for Ireland. Therefore, the points difference is normally distributed with a mean of 19.4 points and a standard deviation of 17.780. Points differences between -0.5 and +0.5 round to 0, which is a drawn match. The probability of this is 0.0123. The probability of Japan winning (points difference less than -0.5) is 0.1315 and the probability of Ireland winning (points difference greater than 0.5) is 0.8561.

Table 4.1 Chances of teams winning pools of the Rugby World Cup 2019 (Japan)

Pos	Pool A		Pool B		Pool C		Pool D	
	Team	%	Team	%	Team	%	Team	%
1st	Scotland	63.1	N Zealand	87.8	England	85.8	Australia	50.8
2nd	Ireland	34.6	S Africa	12.0	Argentina	9.4	Wales	36.8
3rd	Japan	1.0	Italy	0.1	France	4.6	Oceania 1	8.3
4th	Europe 1	0.7	Repechage 1	0.0	Oceania 2	0.2	Georgia	4.1
5th	P Off Wnr	0.7	Africa 1	0.0	America 1	0.0	America 2	0.0

SIMULATION

A simulator was implemented in Matlab to run the 2019 Rugby World Cup 100,000 times. This means that the pool match between Ireland and Japan described previously is simulated 100,000 times as are the other 39 pool matches. Random numbers are used with the normal distribution of points differences for each match to simulate variation about the expected result. Therefore, Ireland should win 85.61% of the matches against Japan, Japan should win 13.15% and 1.23% of the matches between these two teams should be drawn. If we assume that the highest ranked teams from the World Cup regions identified in Table 4.1 at the time of writing will qualify for the 2019 World Cup, the remaining participants in the tournament will be:

- Europe 1: Romania
- Africa 1: Namibia
- Oceania 1: Fiji
- Oceania 2: Samoa
- America 1: USA
- America 2: Uruguay
- Play Off Winner: Tonga
- Repechage Winner: Spain or Russia or Canada

The ranking points for these teams were used within the simulator with the percentage of tournaments in which each team topped their pool shown in Table 4.1. Two notable predictions of the simulator are that Scotland (currently ranked 6th in the World Cup) is more likely to win Pool A than 4th-ranked Ireland and Argentina (currently ranked 10th in the World Cup) is more likely to qualify from Pool C than France, which is ranked 8th. This largely happened because of the -6.5 point modifier, making the matches between teams ranked close together the most likely to be upsets.

Figure 4.2 shows the teams expected to reach various stages of the knockout tournament and their chances of doing so. New Zealand's chance of winning the tournament appears to be greater than their chance of making the final! Note that the 48.7% chance shown for New Zealand reaching the final in Figure 4.2 is via the lower half of the knockout tournament. There is an additional 10.2% chance that New Zealand will come second in Pool B and make the final via the top half of the knockout structure. However, although New Zealand is the most likely team

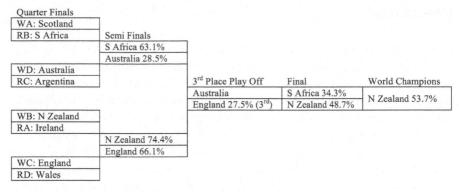

Quarter Finals				
WA: Scotland				
RB: S Africa	Semi Finals			
	S Africa 63.1%			
	Australia 28.5%			
WD: Australia				
RC: Argentina		3rd Place Play Off	Final	World Champions
		Australia	S Africa 34.3%	N Zealand 53.7%
		England 27.5% (3rd)	N Zealand 48.7%	
WB: N Zealand				
RA: Ireland				
	N Zealand 74.4%			
	England 66.1%			
WC: England				
RD: Wales				

Figure 4.2 Knockout stage of the Rugby World Cup 2019 (Japan)

to win the tournament, there is a 46.3% chance that someone other than New Zealand could win. When the simulator was run 100,000 times, 12 of the 20 teams won the tournament at least once and all but three teams were deemed to have a chance of making the semi-finals. So is the prediction correct? The prediction is not actually a single prediction – it is not predicting how far each team will get in the tournament. Instead, this predictive model is generating probabilities recognising that the outcome of the Rugby World Cup is not certain.

The simulation results can be used for target setting; for example, South Africa could set a target of reaching the final, given the 34.3% chance of this happening according to the model, but also acknowledge that reaching the semi-final would be acceptable. A team might also consider whether their chances in the tournament might be enhanced by coming second in the pool rather than first. The simulator predicts that England has an 85.8% chance of winning Pool C and an additional 11.3% chance of coming second, giving an 97.1% overall chance of qualifying. However, winning Pool C places England in the bottom half of the knockout tournament along with the World Cup's strongest team, New Zealand. England is ranked 2nd in the World Cup and might have a better chance of reaching the final if it came second in Pool C. This could be determined by adjusting the simulator after the pool stage to give England a 97.1% chance of qualifying from the pool and placing them in the upper half of the knockout tournament in any tournament runs in which they qualified. A final word of caution is that the Rugby World Cup draw is made a long time before the tournament actually happens. The draw for the 2015 Rugby World Cup placed Australia,

England and Wales in the same pool because Wales was ranked 9th in the World Cup at the time of the draw. By the 2015 Rugby World Cup, these three teams were all ranked in the top five teams. Hence, team strength can change dramatically over a two-year period, indicating the simulation runs may have to be repeated periodically as we approach tournaments.

SUMMARY

The outcomes of individual sports performances and tournaments are not certain, which is why betting agencies accept wagers on such events. The probabilities of different outcomes of sports matches can be modelled using previous data. This chapter used a continuous outcome variable for matches (points difference), which was modelled in terms of relative quality of the teams contesting matches. Analysis of residual values from previous case data allows a probability distribution for the points difference variable to be produced. This can then be used within a simulation package in which random numbers are applied to probability distributions to generate a range of expected results. The random variation applied is evidenced by previous case data and may require models to map actual distributions onto a normal distribution to predict outcomes. This mapping process overcomes the issue of data failing to satisfy the assumption of normality required by regression analysis. When the variation of expected results depends on the relative quality of the teams involved, this can be built into the model. Similarly, when the assumption of independence does not hold, it may be an opportunity to enhance the predictive model. For example, the strength in depth in international rugby is increasing and this trend can be extrapolated to future tournaments.

REFERENCES

Alamar, B.C. (2013) *Sports analytics: A guide for coaches, managers and other decision makers*, New York, NY: Columbia University Press.

Anderson, D.R., Sweeney, D.J. and Williams, T.A. (1994) *Introduction to statistics: Concepts and applications*, 3rd edn., Minneapolis/St. Paul, MI: West Publishing Company.

Ntoumanis, N. (2001) *A step by step guide to SPSS for sport and exercise studies*, London: Routledge.

O'Donoghue, P.G. (2005) 'The role of simulation in sports tournament design for game sport', *International Journal of Computer Science in Sport*, 4(2): 14–27.

O'Donoghue, P.G. (2012) *Statistics for sport and exercise studies: An introduction*, London: Routledge.

O'Donoghue, P.G. (2014) 'Factors influencing the accuracy of predictions of the 2014 FIFA World Cup', *International Journal of Computer Science in Sport*, 13(2): 32–49.

O'Donoghue, P.G., Ball, D., Eustace, J., McFarlan, B. and Nisotaki, M. (2016) 'Predictive models of the 2015 Rugby World Cup: Accuracy and application', *International Journal of Computer Science in Sport*, 15(1): 37–58.

O'Donoghue, P.G. and Williams, J. (2004) 'An evaluation of human and computer-based predictions of the 2003 Rugby Union World Cup', *International Journal of Computer Science in Sport*, 3(1): 5–22.

Vincent, W.J. (1999) *Statistics in kinesiology*, 3rd edn., Champaign, IL: Human Kinetics.

Woodman, T., Zourbanos, N., Hardy, L., Beattie, S. and McQuillan, A. (2010) 'Do performance strategies moderate the relationship between personality and training behaviors? An exploratory study', *Journal of Applied Sport Psychology*, 22(2): 183–197.

82

CHAPTER 5

GEOSPATIAL DATA ANALYSIS

INTRODUCTION

Geospatial analyses have been used effectively on data from diverse domains, including meteorological and crime data, and within more recent times, applied in a broad sense to sports data. This chapter begins by discussing the various data formats likely to be encountered and the types of software that can be gainfully employed. We then discuss descriptive procedures and some common tools and techniques for geospatial analysis, including "hotspot" analysis.

Geospatial data as a long list of coordinates reveals little about the underlying phenomena but when these are visualised on a map, with the ability for analysts to interact with these visual displays, this opens up the data for interpretation. This visual presentation of geospatial data is particularly useful to decision making in areas such as exercise and health, sports recruitment and sports marketing.

Significant progress has been made in the analysis of trajectories with the emerging research trends of semantic trajectories and computational movement analysis. Trajectories can be derived from a diverse set of sources – for instance, GPS/RFID or analysis of video – and studies include soccer and basketball. We present some latest findings in this area, concluding with the related fields of mining spatio-temporal data.

THE EVOLUTION OF GEOSPATIAL ANALYSIS

Geographical information systems (GIS)

Just over a decade ago, professional (and often times prohibitively expensive) geographical information systems (GIS) were required for working with and visualizing geospatial data. Open-source tools were hard to use and working with geospatial data across the Internet was not yet realised. It was only when Google Maps and Google Earth were released (in 2005) that geospatial data came within reach of anyone with an Internet connection or mobile device with a map-driven application tool. ESRI's flag-ship commercial GIS offering is ArcGis (www.arcgis.com, accessed 27/11/17), which offers an extremely powerful platform for geospatial data but is rivalled by the open-source system QGIS (www.qgis.org, accessed 27/11/17), which includes an interface to the arguably more difficult-to-use (for beginners) system GRASS (https://grass.osgeo.org, accessed 27/11/17). The more sophisticated spatial analysis or routines provided in GRASS can be accessed through the SEXTANTE plugin for QGIS (https://plugins.qgis.org/plugins/sextante/, accessed 27/11/17).

Global Positioning System (GPS)

The Global Positioning System (GPS) has also significantly influenced the development of geospatial analytics. Satellite navigation for cars and portable devices with GPS chipsets have each played their part. The desire to record one's location is becoming increasingly common, and most forms of social media have the option of geotagging.

The open-source software movement has also had a major influence and it is now possible to build geospatial applications from freely available toolkits and libraries, such as PROJ.4, PostGIS, OGR and Mapnik (links in the software section at the end of the chapter).

Alongside this software and hardware development, various standards and data formats (e.g. GML, KML, GeoRSS, WKT) have been proposed and critiqued, such as the Open Geospatial Consortium (www.opengeospatial.org, accessed 27/11/17) formats and protocols for sharing and storing geospatial data.

84

CORE GEOSPATIAL CONCEPTS

The term *geospatial* refers to information located on the earth's surface using coordinates, often in the form of latitude and longitude values. Because of the volume of data often involved, spatial extensions to standard relational databases have needed to be developed. Similarly, because of the natural presentation of geospatial data on a map, many GISs have developed their own file formats, often adhering to different standards and, therefore, not all geospatial data points are compatible.

These different standards and data formats are because of the complicated shape of the earth, which is not actually a perfect sphere, and therefore representing points, lines and areas on the surface of the earth is quite a complex process.

Location

The coordinate system of latitude and longitude is a common way to measure position. A metaphor to explain this system is to imagine the earth as a sphere whereby we can connect any point on the surface with the centre. We then measure this line against two references. The equator is a centre line around the earth and the latitude is the angle the point makes against this reference line going north-south. In a similar fashion, we can measure east-west against another reference line, the Greenwich meridian (in the UK), and this is the longitude of the point. Arbitrarily, points north of the equator are positive and those below are negative, and points west of Greenwich are negative and those east are positive.

Distance

Considering the aforementioned lines from the centre to the surface, we can measure the distance between two points not only by the distance on the surface of the earth but also by the angle between the two lines from the centre. The distance measure on the surface is referred to as the linear distance, or the actual travelling distance.

Projections and coordinate systems

It is important to know that there are multiple types of coordinate systems, either projected or unprojected. An example of an unprojected system is the longitude and latitude previously described because in this system, the actual values refer to a specific point on the earth. The downside of such a system (using angles of lines to the centre of the earth) is that computations are complex, such as calculating the distance between points.

Projected coordinates are the numerous ways in which the three-dimensional shape of the world is "projected" onto a two-dimensional representation. The coordinates refer to a point in a two-dimensional space, which represents the surface of the world. This is also known as a Cartesian system. To define such a projection, normally a point of origin and measurement units are specified. This system permits much faster calculations of distance and other computations compared with complex angular calculations if the data were unprojected. There are literally hundreds of different projections and none of them are perfect; this is not because of the "imperfect" shape of the earth but because you cannot represent a three-dimensional surface correctly in two dimensions. In practice then, some projections represent certain areas of the earth's surface accurately while adding major distortions elsewhere and, therefore, these projections are useful only for those specified areas. It is therefore vital that the projection is known when working with geospatial data; without knowing the projection, it is not possible to plot data or perform accurate calculations. Fortunately, this is a well-studied area and tools exist to transform one projection onto another.

An example of a projected system is the Universal Transverse Mercator (UTM) system, which uses 60 zones to cover the entire world. A different projection is used within each zone to reduce errors, each defined with their own point of origin. Relative to these origins, all points are calculated – northing and easting values – always positive increments from the origin or reference point.

Datums

A related concept important to understand is that of a *datum*. Geographic, or unprojected, coordinates (latitude and longitude) systems

86

are based on a spherical or ellipsoidal representation of the world. If it is ellipsoidal, there are two axes defined, the longer and shorter axes. If it is spherical, all that is required is the radius of the sphere. This is the datum, the shape that is used to approximate the earth, which is actually a squashed form of ellipsoid and therefore difficult to model. The datum is this chosen model.

All coordinates are referenced to a datum. The projections mentioned previously are the series of transformations that convert the location of points on a curved surface, the datum, to locations on the flat plane. The datum is therefore an integral part of the projection, as projected coordinated systems are based on geographic coordinates, which are in turn referenced to a datum. It is possible and even common for datasets to be in the same projection but be referenced to different datums and therefore have different coordinate values.

The various coordinate systems refer to one or other datums, without which the projection will not make sense. The projections are the calculations used to relate the points on the particular three-dimensional space to locations in two-dimensional space. Therefore, the datum is a crucial part of the projection. Data can actually use the same projection but associate with distinct datums.

There are three main reference datums that might be encountered when working with geospatial data:

- NAD 27: North American Datum of 1927. As all datums, it has a model for the three-dimensional shape of the earth, using a spheroid called the Clarke Spheroid of 1866. The point of origin used is the Meades Ranch in Kansas. This datum is used for North America.
- NAD 83: North American Datum of 1983. Here, the model of the earth is more complex than the previous spheroid and is called the 1980 Geodetic Reference System, or GRS 80. This datum is used for Mexico, Central America and North America (US and Canada).
- WGS 84: World Geodetic System of 1984. This is the most common datum in use today. A different model again is used, the Earth Gravitational Model of 1996, or EGM 96. The points of reference are based on a reference meridian from the International Earth Rotation and Reference Systems Service (IERS). When referring to locations in the US, this datum is essentially the same as NAD 83. It is

the system used by the satellites of the Global Positioning System (GPS) and, therefore, any data that is sourced from a GPS device will use this.

Many geospatial data will reference datums other than the popular WGS 84 and you should not assume that a particular datum was used. For instance, the same coordinate could be 100 metres away if referencing a different datum. You will no doubt encounter data referencing different datums and, on many occasions, it will be necessary to convert between them.

Features and geometries

Features exist in the real world at a particular location, such as a specific landmark, house or shopping centre. Many times, a feature will not be easy to characterise by a set of coordinates; for instance, a natural feature with indistinct boundaries, such as an estuary. Geometries, on the other hand, are precise geospatial constructs representing simple points to complex vectors.

USING GEOSPATIAL DATA

The initial stages involve preparing and pre-processing the spatial data, such as checking the datums and converting between projections. Next is the interesting part – actually using the data. There are many things that can be done with geospatial data, including determining the proximity between points (such as player positions), calculating how far a player has run based on their GPS-acquired tracklog, creating buffer zones around a point and determining the intersection between two shapes.

An important part of working with geospatial data is visualisation. Visualisation of data provides invaluable insight, not only for inspection but also for transformation and determining the kinds of computation to apply to the data.

The concept of mash-ups has emerged in recent years, popularized by the use of the Google Maps application programming interface (API), which has had an enormous effect on geospatial analyses, placing

88

within reach of a new generation of analysts sophisticated computations that were only dreamed of a few years before. The ability to combine several datasets through a common geospatial index is termed a *mash-up*. Often, these are web applications available to anyone with access to the Internet. An example of a mash-up might be the integration of sports fans' home locations with placement of sports grounds or playing fields. There are clearly alternatives to Google Maps but this platform has definitely been the inspiration of this type of analysis. MapServer, Mapnik and OpenLayers can also provide this functionality and overlay data on a map.

We already introduced the idea of map projections and it is interesting to note that those used by Google's products are deliberately simplified, which can lead to errors in both visualisation (mash-ups/overlaying data) and analysis.

The following sections look at GIS- and spatial-enabled databases that can remedy these limitations.

COMMON TOOLS FOR GEOSPATIAL DATA

GIS software packages

In addition to the actual data that represents the geospatial features, GIS data can contain:

- Metadata about the datum, projection and coordinate system; the measurement system and file-level details such as last access date/times.
- Attributes attached to the features, such as a player having "age", "fitness", "name" and so on.
- Information about how to display the data, such as colours of points and thickness of linestrings.

GIS data come in two main formats: raster and vector. Raster is generally used for image data, such as bitmaps. Examples would be aerial photographs, scanned paper maps (digital raster graphic, DRG) and elevation data (digital elevation model, DEM).

As the name suggests, vector data is mathematical, which can be used in analyses. This is the most common kind of data that a GIS would use.

Examples include the vector formats of points (player positions), lines (tracklogs of a player's movements within a game) and polygons (perhaps a "convex hull" defining the outline of a player's positions within a game).

The simplest vector is the point, described by its coordinates within its coordinate system. More complex is a linestring or path (for instance, a tracklog), represented as a linked set of segments of lines. These segments range from point to point, whereas the original source of the data, perhaps a player's curving run, is complex to represent otherwise and, therefore, the linestring is a simplification or representation of the actual event. Linestrings are used in layers in GIS for various contours of cities, countries, rivers and roads, for example. Polygons are similar to linestrings, being sequences of line segments; however, the distinction is that the polygon "line" actually joins itself – it is "closed" and encloses a space within its shape. Polygons are used for any kind of object, whether houses, bridges, city features and so on.

Some common vector format geospatial data that might be encountered include:

- Shapefile: an open specification, developed by ESRI, for storing and exchanging GIS data. The shapefile (ESRI Shapefile Technical Description, www.esri.com/library/whitepapers/pdfs/shapefile. pdf, accessed 27/11/17) is a common file type used in geospatial analysis. All commercial and open-source software will accept the shapefile in their GIS formats. It is comprised of a set of three files with different extensions but the same base name; for example, player1.shp, player1.shx and player1.dbf. SHP is the feature geometry, SHX is the shape index position and DBF is the attribute data.
- Simple Features: this is an OpenGIS standard for storing geographical data (points, lines, polygons) along with associated attributes.
- TIGER/Line: commonly encountered when working with US datasets. A text-based format used by the US Census Bureau to represent roads, buildings, rivers and coastlines. More recent data comes in the shapefile format.

In addition to these "major" data formats, there are also so-called micro-formats often used to represent smaller sections of geospatial data. Example usage could be for representations within a program or for

90

data transfer over networks. However, they can be used for persistence or storage of data. An example is Well-known Text.

Well-known Text (WKT) is a simple text-based description of a geospatial object, such as a point, line or polygon. Instead of text, the alternative Well-known Binary (WKB) uses binary data to represent individual features. The following shows a geometry defining the boundary of Headingley Rugby Stadium, UK, converted into a WKT string:

```
POLYGON ((53.816029–1.581314,
53.816093–1.583039,
53.816734–1.583040,
53.816684–1.581245))
```

As can be seen, the WKT string is a simple way of describing a geometry, with Headingley rugby stadium represented as a polygon comprised of four x,y coordinates. However, WKT text strings can be much more complex, comprising many thousands of points with complex polygons. However complex the geographical feature, it can still be represented as a WKT string.

The WKT strings can also be used to represent a spatial reference encompassing a projection, datum and/or coordinate system. For example, here is a WKT string using the D_GDA_1994 datum, GRS_1980 coordinate system and reference point (0,0), which is Greenwich, converted into a WKT string:

```
GEOGCS["GCS_GDA_1994",DATUM["D_GDA_1994",SPH
EROID["GRS_1980",6378137.0,298.257222101]],PRIMEM
["Greenwich",0.0],UNIT["Degree",0.0174532925199433],
AUTHORITY["EPSG",4283]]
```

Additional micro-formats include:

■ GeoJSON: a variant of the JSON data format for representing geographic data structures.

- Geography Markup Language (GML): an XML-based format for exchanging GIS data.
- GPS Exchange Format (GPX): an XML-based format for exchanging GIS data, particularly waypoints, tracks and routes, favoured by many sports applications.
- KMZ/KML (Keyhole Markup Language): another XML-based format. This GIS format is mainly used for Google Earth. KMZ (KML-Zipped) is a compressed version of the file. It replaced KML as the default Google Earth geospatial format. In 2008, KML/KMZ became an international standard of the Open Geospatial Consortium.

Here are some examples of the same data – two points – represented in some of these formats:

```
<kml xmlns:atom="www.w3.org/2005/
Atom" xmlns:gx="www.google.com/
kml/ext/2.2" xmlns="www.opengis.
net/kml/2.2">
 <Document>
  <name>example.kml</name>
  <Style id="pushpin">
   <IconStyle id="mystyle">
    <scale>1.0</scale>
    <Icon>
     <href>http://maps.google.com/mapfiles/
     kml/shapes/placemark_circle_highlight.
     png</href>
    </Icon>
   </IconStyle>
  </Style>
  <Folder>
   <Placemark>
    <name></name>
    <styleUrl>#pushpin</styleUrl>
    <Point>
     <coordinates> -6.228433907,
     53.33515936</coordinates>
    </Point>
   </Placemark>
```

```
Time, Smooth Vel., GPS
Time, GPS Latitude, GPS
Longitude,
1:19:48.32, 0.646, 14:30:00,
53.33515936, -6.228433907,
1:19:48.43, 0.661, 14:30:00,
53.33515926, -6.228433207,
```

geospatial data analysis

```
   <Placemark>
    <name></name>
    <styleUrl>#pushpin</styleUrl>
    <Point>
      <coordinates> -6.228433207,
      53.33515926</coordinates>
    </Point>
   </Placemark>
    </Folder>
  </Document>
</kml>
```

KML format

```
<?xml version="1.0"
encoding="UTF-8"?>
<gpx
version="1.1"
creator="RunningFreeBird – www.
runningfreebird.com/"
xmlns:xsi="www.w3.org/2001/
XMLSchema-instance"
xmlns="www.topografix.com/GPX/1/1"
xsi:schemaLocation="www.topografix.
com/GPX/1/1 www.topografix.com/
GPX/1/1/gpx.xsd"
xmlns:gpxtpx="www.garmin.com/
xmlschemas/ TrackPointExtension/v1">
<trk>
<name><![CDATA[Running 6/29/10
1:19 pm]]></name>
<time>2010–06–29T01:19:48Z</time>
<trkseg>
<trkpt lat="53.33515936" lon=
"-6.228433907"><ele>57.7</ele><time>
2010–06–29T01:19:48Z</time>
</trkpt>
<trkpt lat="53.33515926" lon=
"-6.228433207"><ele>57.7</ele><time>
2010–06–29T01:19:48Z</time></trkpt>
```

GML and WKT format

```
<gml:Point gml:id="rfb1"
srsName="http://www.
opengis.net/def/crs/
EPSG/0/27700">
   <gml:pos srsDimension=
"2">53.33515936
6.228433907</gml:pos>
 </gml:Point>
<gml:Point gml:id="rfb2"
srsName="http://www.
opengis.net/def/crs/
EPSG/0/27700">
   <gml:pos srsDimension=
"2">53.33515926
6.228433207</gml:pos>
 </gml:Point>
Or:
  <gml:LineString>
   <gml:coordinates>
53.33515936, 6.228433907
53.33515926, 6.228433207
</gml:coordinates>
   </gml:LineString>

WKT
POINT (53.33515936
```

</trkseg>	6.228433907)
</trk>	POINT (53.33515926
</gpx>	6.228433207)
	LINESTRING (53.33515936
	6.228433907, 53.33515926
	6.228433207)
GPX	GML

The OpenStreetMap (OSM, http://openstreetmap.org, accessed 27/11/17) GIS format is another XML-based file format, although the more efficient, smaller PBF format (Protocolbuffer Binary Format) is an alternative. OpenStreetMap is a crowdsourcing GIS project interfaced on a website where people can collaborate to create and edit geospatial data.

The geometries remain the same but with different naming conventions. Points are represented as nodes, lines are ways and polygons are areas. There are also relations, which are collections of other elements. Any element (node, way or relation) can have a number of tags associated with it, providing additional information about that element. It is possible to freely obtain geospatial data from OpenStreetMap by using the API – either to download the subset of data you are interested in or the entire OpenStreetMap database, called Planet.osm. Alternatively, it is

Figure 5.1 GPX tracklog data projected over OpenStreetMap layers

possible to download data nicely packaged into smaller chunks and convorted into other data formats.

Here is an example of what OpenStreetMap XML data look like:

```xml
<?xml version="1.0" encoding="UTF-8"?>
<osm version="0.6" generator="CGImap 0.3.3 (9787 thorn-01.
openstreetmap.org)"
copyright="OpenStreetMap and contributors" attribution="http://
www.openstreetmap.org/copyright" license="http://
opendatacommons.org/licenses/odbl/1-0/">
 <bounds minlat="51.5085000" minlon="-0.1563000"
maxlat="51.5138000" maxlon="-0.1465000"/>
 <node id="102053" visible="true" version="11"
changeset="13457341" timestamp="2012-10-11T17:44:21Z"
user="Metanautics fixes" uid="900987" lat="51.5130481"
lon="-0.1581734"/>
 <node id="108253" visible="true" version="3"
changeset="18178728" timestamp="2013-10-04T13:39:44Z"
user="mjmm17" uid="716353" lat="51.5121181"
lon="-0.1450357"/>
 <node id="3256088661" visible="true" version="1" changeset=
"27744491" timestamp="2014-12-28T01:06:39Z" user="Amaroussi"
uid="1016290" lat="51.5135354" lon="-0.1575604">
  <tag k="bus" v="yes"/>
  <tag k="local_ref" v="P"/>
  <tag k="name" v="Marble Arch Station"/>
  <tag k="public_transport" v="stop_position"/>
  <tag k="source" v="Survey of 2014-12-24"/>
 </node>
 <way id="26996713" visible="true" version="3"
changeset="21149754" timestamp="2014-03-17T06:51:23Z"
user="Amaroussi" uid="1016290">
  <nd ref="295907939"/>
  <nd ref="295907948"/>
  <tag k="highway" v="residential"/>
  <tag k="lit" v="yes"/>
  <tag k="name" v="Red Place"/>
 </way>
</osm>
```

Spatially enabled databases

We have seen that it is possible to represent points, linestrings and polygons using WKT format and, therefore, technically it is possible to insert these text values into a text field in a relational database for storage. However, there would be no simple way to query the data other than retrieving the text values one-by-one and recreating the spatial objects, upon which some calculations could then be carried out. Perhaps a raft of additional indexes could be created to alleviate this problem.

However, a much better solution would be to insert the spatial objects into a database that makes use of the spatial characteristics of the data (as opposed to a purely textual representation), otherwise known as a spatially enabled database. Features of such a database include:

- A specific geometry field that stores spatial data types.
- The ability to make spatial queries; for example: select all events (e.g. "tackles") within a certain bounded area (bounding box).
- The ability to perform the equivalent of regular database "joins" on spatial data, called "spatial joins".
- The ability to derive entirely new objects from built-in spatial operations and insert into the database; for example: set "possible_sales" to the intersection of the "double_income_no_kids" or "disposable_income" and "sports_fans" polygons.

In the same manner that regular databases (non-spatial) utilise indexes to optimise querying strategies, spatially enabled databases use spatial indexes. The purpose is the same, to optimise and therefore speed up complex calculations, meaning that such databases can handle very large amounts of data. Typically, the heavy lifting should be carried out by the database, where possible, before retrieving into an application because the database is optimised for these forms of computationally intensive procedures.

An example of a powerful open-source spatial database is PostgreSQL with the PostGIS spatial objects plugin. This database has support for different geometry types, spatial types, indexes and functions, allowing querying and managing information about locations and mapping. PostGIS has a reputation as a geospatial powerhouse and supports the following features:

geospatial data analysis

- Accepts data in a wide range of common formats, such as WKT and WKB, but also GML, KML, SVG and the geographical variant of JSON, GeoJSON.
- Fast bounding-box calculations based on spatial indexes; for instance, whether one area overlaps, touches, is equivalent to, is contained by or is to the left or right of another, and so on.
- Equivalent calculations on the actual spatial object and not just the bounding box ("lighter" databases just do the equivalent bounding-box calculations).
- A wide range of functions for calculating interesting values about a spatial object, such as distances between points, lengths of lines and the nearest point to an object.
- Recalling the importance of datums and coordinate reference systems, PostGIS can transform data between the different systems and even modify the data in many ways, such as scaling and rotating.

SpatialLite is also open source like Postgres/PostGIS but is more restrictive. It extends the serverless SQLite database engine through spatial capabilities and can hold all spatial and non-spatial files in one file. It supports the following features:

- Can handle all major forms of spatial data types, such as points, lines and polygons.
- Columns are designated to handle a specific spatial data type with particular spatial references using an identifying code. This enforces storage of data in the correct fields in the database.
- Accepts data in a range of common formats, such as WKT and WKB, and can translate between these geometries and others.
- Similar to PostGIS, various geometrical functions like distances between points or polygons create buffer zones and the equivalent quicker operations use the more coarse-grained bounding-box representations of the spatial objects.
- Similar to PostGIS, transforms data between coordinate reference systems, scaling and rotating, etc.
- Support for fast spatial relationship calculations using minimum bounding rectangles.
- Different forms of indexing to speed up calculations, such as R-Tree and bounding box indexes.

The well-known database MySQL (used by Facebook and Twitter) also has spatial extensions with many functions available. As an example, the following SQL statement creates a database table, with a field designed to hold polygon data types:

```
CREATE TABLE playerzones (
id INTEGER AUTO_INCREMENT PRIMARY KEY,
player CHAR(255),
convexhull POLYGON NOT NULL,
INDEX (player),
SPATIAL INDEX (convexhull))
```

The POLYGON keyword is part of the extended SQL language and the field "polydata" is designated as this type. The last line of this code creates a spatial index on this field, which now facilitates optimised queries of the following kind:

```
SELECT player FROM playerzones WHERE MBRContains(convexhull,
thisTacklePoint)
```

Imagine a set of convex hulls created from the tracklogs of a team's players during a given game or season of games. We are interested in the players that could potentially have tackled an opponent in a particular location on the pitch. The operation MBRContains() works by creating a minimum bounding rectangle (MBR), or bounding box, around the spatial object. It is a fast routine because it is simpler to work out if a point is within a rectangular-shaped box than the more convoluted original spatial object, although of course there is now the possibility of false positives being generated, as the bounding box is clearly larger in size than the original polygon. Nonetheless, this could be used to retrieve data quickly (false positives and all) and more accurate calculations could then be carried out by an application accessing this recordset.

Finally, from the commercial world, there are two important spatial data offerings: Oracle and Microsoft's SQL Server.

For a long time, Oracle was seen as the industry standard in relational database management systems. Unsurprisingly, there are spatial extensions available for this platform, termed Oracle Spatial. The features supported include all those previously mentioned for PostGIS and MySQL, such as spatial data types and indexes, spatial joins and queries, and transformations of data. Additionally, Oracle Spatial employs various exploratory or analytical techniques from the field of data mining, useful geocoding functions and can handle data in raster format.

Microsoft's SQL Server is another widely used relational database system. Again, this database supports the full range of expected geospatial operations and data types.

Like the previous databases, Microsoft implemented a standard specified by the Open Geospatial Consortium. This means that the naming convention employed matches the previously mentioned open-source databases but with a slight difference, stemming from the preferred implementation using object-oriented syntax. As an example, SQL Server uses some_geometry.STIntersects(some_point) rather than ST_Intersects(some_geometry, some_point).

Unlike the previous databases, a potentially significant limitation is that SQL Server does not support transformations based on coordinate systems.

ANALYSING POINT DATA

Having covered the issues related to the kinds of geospatial data formats likely to be encountered and the issues of projections and storage, and related software, we are now in a position to review the types of analytics that can be performed.

Centrographic statistics

The most basic descriptors for the spatial distribution of point data are *centrographic statistics*. Consider the analysis of a single row of data, determining the statistics of mean, standard deviation, skewness and kurtosis – these then have their equivalents for two-dimensional data (e.g. easting and northing). As expected, the simplest statistic is the *mean centre*, which is the mean of the two coordinates. The *standard distance deviation* and *standard deviational ellipse* are measures of the dispersion of points around the mean centre. The *centre of minimum distance* is defined as the point nearest to all other points, calculated by summing the distance to all other points, for all points, and returning the smallest value.

A different description of the data is provided by the *convex hull*, which is simply a boundary drawn around the distribution of points. This polygon contains within it all the points of the data. This feature clearly shows the geographical range of a dataset, and it is possible to compare one convex hull to another to determine differences in size and orientation, degrees of overlap and so on. Useful as it is, a convex hull is vulnerable to extreme values, with one outlier indicating the size of the hull is artificially inflated to include that point. Outliers have a much more significant effect on a convex hull than, for instance, the mean centre, the influence of which is diminished because all points are averaged.

Spatial autocorrelation for zonal data

Often, it makes sense to analyse data according to zones or specific spatial areas. Consider a playing field divided into defence, midfield and offence, for instance. Here, we could sum the individual data points within these areas and compare them against those values derived from other zones. In this case, all the data are assigned to a single position, often the *centroid*, and the number of data points in the area becomes an *attribute*.

When analysing spatial data, it is useful to consider the concept of complete spatial randomness, which means there are no clusters or patterns, no correlation or any form of spatial arrangement. Spatial autocorrelation, however, is a departure from randomness in which there is some pattern or arrangement of points that are related to each other in some way and violate the assumption of statistical independence. There are several ways to measure spatial autocorrelation at the area level or for individual-level data with count or interval attributes, such as Moran's "I" statistic, Geary's "C" statistic or the Getis-Ord "G" statistic (Geary, 1954; Getis and Ord, 1992; Moran, 1950).

Hotspots, heat maps and clusters

The use of maps to present point data is particularly useful to decision making in areas such as exercise and health, sports recruitment and

100

sports marketing. Furthermore, the ability to overlay an aggregated feature such as a hotspot, heat map or cluster is powerful.

Hotspots are artificial constructs that do not exist in reality but are areas
where there is a high degree of point data clustering. Precisely where the
hotspot begins is impossible to determine, as it is defined by a gradient
and not a hard and fast border. However, an imaginary line is drawn to
indicate this hypothetical border location, which then gives the possibility of determining, for instance, whether something is inside or outside
the hotspot.

There are many techniques to identify hotspots, some of which are
derived from the area of statistics known as *cluster analysis*, aimed at
grouping points together into coherent clusters. A number of cluster
analysis typologies have been developed, as cluster routines typically
fall into several general categories (Everitt et al., 2011):

- The easiest technique to understand is the *mode*, a count of points at
  different locations. The location with the largest count is a hotspot.
  The *fuzzy mode* is derived from this, including a buffer zone around
  each point to include points found in the immediate vicinity; for
  example, within a 5m or 10m search radius. The calculation is now
  the number of points that occur at each location within this defined
  radius.
- *Hierarchical* techniques create successively higher-order clusters,
  based upon point patterns grouped on the basis of some criteria
  (e.g. nearest neighbour). The second-order clusters are grouped into
  third-order clusters, and so on, and this hierarchy of clusters can be
  displayed with a dendogram (an inverted tree diagram). The *nearest
  neighbour* implementation defines a *threshold distance* that is used
  to compare against the distances for all pairs of points. Only points
  that are closer to one or more other points than the threshold distance are selected for clustering. Additionally, the minimum number
  of points can be specified that need to be included in a cluster.
- *Partitioning* techniques, frequently called the *K-means* technique,
  partition the points into a specified number of groups, defined prior
  to execution. Thus, all points are assigned to one, and only one,
  group. The routine tries to find the best positioning of the k centres
  and assigns each point to the nearest centre. The technique is useful
  when control over the grouping is desired through the definition of
  k (e.g. 11 for a soccer match).

- *Density* techniques identify clusters by finding dense concentrations of points. *Kernel density interpolation* (sometimes called *kernel density estimation*) generalizes point locations to the entire region by providing density estimates for all parts of a region (i.e. at any point). Surface or contour maps can be used to show the intensity at all locations. An example of this approach can be found in the spatio-temporal analysis of tennis matches (Mora and Knottenbelt, 2016) in which the court and its immediate surrounding area are divided into a grid of equally sized rectangles (100×100 rectangles for the players and 200×200 for the ball) and time spent by the player or ball in that area is shown by a colour representing the normalized frequency. For instance, the heat map of the player's positions across all the videos analysed shows that players spend most of their time in the centre behind the baseline, occasionally coming closer to the net.

Space-time analysis

There are several space-time measures and techniques, such as the Knox and Mantel indexes, spatiotemporal moving average (STMA) and correlated walk analysis (CWA).

The STMA is the moving mean centre of n observations where n is called the *span*, assuming a default value of 5. The span is centred on each observation so there is an equal number on both sides, except of course for the events towards the beginning and end.

CWA is a method with a statistical origin in Random Walk Theory used for analysing the spatial and temporal sequencing of incidents. This routine makes guesses about the time and location of the next event based on the spatial and temporal distribution effectively operating as the previously described STMA for prediction.

ANALYSING TRAJECTORIES

Recent advances in localization (GPS, RFID) have provided the opportunity to track individuals in space-time, producing streams of spatiotemporal (x,y,t) points, called trajectories.

The section covers: data cleaning and preparation; definition of moving objects and trajectories; computational movement analysis and semantic

102

trajectories; developing a taxonomy of movement patterns; representation and storage of data; and spatiotemporal information mining.

There is great demand for this technology in sports scene analysis. Major tennis tournaments are able to track the players and balls and provide 3D reconstructions of each point played. Similarly, football coaches routinely analyse match video archives to learn about an opponent's behaviours and strategies. Software can automatically provide basic statistical information about the match and performance of the players, such as how far a player ran, the top/average speed of players, the number of passes and goal shots, the ball speed of free kicks, density plots of players, most favoured positions and measurements of how offside a player went. However, recent advances in tracking technologies are producing data at previously unseen spatial and temporal granularities. This spatiotemporal data has necessitated the development of new techniques for modelling and analysis because the traditional, static spatial analysis toolbox lacks methods for this data concerned with dynamic processes (Gudmundsson and Horton, 2017).

New research into trajectory management has developed efficient storage and indexing techniques, as well as methods for knowledge discovery. Many works have focused on the geometric aspect of raw mobility data. Now, however, there is a demand to understand the semantic behaviour of moving objects, utilising data patterns that are interpreted or explained through information derived from the underlying application domain.

Various groups converge on this area according to Melorose et al. (2015):

- GIS researchers with experiences in modelling uncertainty, sensitivity and scale, such as segmenting the trajectories of players on a "pitch" into semantically meaningful segments or interpolating a player intensity surface on a pitch.
- Database researchers and developers of various types of moving object databases aimed at data management and querying issues around moving objects. For instance, each player on a pitch might represent a leaf in a dynamic tree optimised for fast queries.
- Computational geometers using new measures for the representation and discovery of movement patterns; for instance, using a convex hull representation of player positions to datamine "flocking" effects.

Whether it is the use of exploratory analysis approaches, techniques for indexing, or development of new datamining algorithms, all these approaches progress the ability to infer high-level knowledge from low-level tracking data.

Consider the following high-level rule from McQueen et al. (2014) based upon low-level features derived from positional data (player-tracking data collected by the STATS SportVu system):

Automatically Recognizing On-Ball Screen
IF [
there is a player who is dribbling the ball (i.e. the ball-handler)
AND there is an offensive player within 10 feet of the ball-handler (i.e. the screener)
AND the screener is not in or near the paint (see in-set figure for definition of "near")
AND the screener is no more than 2 ft. further from the basket than the ball-handler is
AND there is a defensive player <= 12 ft. from the ball-handler (i.e. the on-ball defender)
AND the basketball is not in the paint] for >=13 consecutive frames
AND the ball-handler is the same for every frame THEN
identify as action

Data cleansing and preparation

The most common way to model moving entities is as point objects moving through time, producing a sequence of time-stamped observations.

Much effort still needs to be spent in data preparation because GPS measurements from mobile devices suffer from sampling errors and the recorded position of a moving object is not always correct; therefore, the recorded data may be unreliable, imprecise, incorrect and contain noise. This is because noise can be introduced into GPS signals from several sources, such as effects from the ionosphere, and because satellite clocks can produce noise of plus or minus 15m. To remove erroneous data, various methods for detecting "outliers" can be used, presupposing that a "smoothed" approximation of a curve to the raw data is the actual route or path taken. This stage is a simple form of data cleansing upon which

104

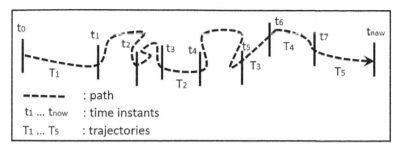

Figure 5.2 A spatiotemporal path and its trajectories

the more complicated semantic tagging and representation of the route is based. After the initial processing stages, efforts are put towards combining the cleaned mobility tracks from the GPS devices with contextual data from the environment, which are now referred to as semantic trajectories (see Figure 5.2).

A moving object creates a spatiotemporal path comprised of many trajectories defined by a semantic segmentation of the path. Each trajectory is defined by a time interval having a beginning and end $[t_{begin}, t_{end}]$ and can meet, but not overlap with, other trajectories on the path of this moving object. Trajectories may in turn be divided into smaller semantic segments with a new sequence of subintervals in which the object position may move (defined as moves) or stay still (defined as stops). Therefore, a trajectory is seen as a sequence of moves punctuated by stops.

The problem then is how to partition a trajectory into a number of meaningful segments (subtrajectories). It is possible to identify uniformity within movement characteristics, such as the object's speed or heading, to define a segment. Therefore, determining these meaningful movement characteristics and relevant segments is clearly dependent on the context. Within different domains, the same trajectory could represent quite different activities. Analysis of these features requires expert knowledge and context information. What actually is the activity the object is performing during the time it is tracked? How are the many "stops" and "starts" of the trajectory, changes in velocity and so on to be interpreted? Automatic extraction of events from a trajectory is a hard task.

Complex moving objects and trajectories

Movement data ranges from comparatively simplistic tracklog modelling to extremely complex types involving three-dimensional shapes
moving through space, such as massive weather events with hurri-
canes or cyclones, which produce complex movement data. Figure
5.3 depicts movement types discussed by Gudmundsson and Horton
(2017):

Semantic trajectories modelling and analysis

There are two classes of trajectories – those involving the dynamics of
single-object trajectories and *sequence behaviours* and those involving

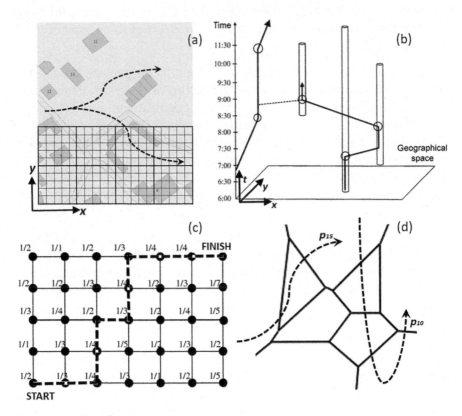

Figure 5.3 Four basic movement spaces

several moving objects that focus partly on the interactions between the objects, or indeed coordination, an example being *flocking behaviour* (Parent et al., 2013).

According to Melorose et al. (2015), Laube and colleagues initiated study into the new field of flocking behaviour, in which a flock is defined as a group of moving entities that move in spatial proximity for a defined time interval. This group of objects has a defined bounding box or disc. The approach has been criticized for its simplicity, including ignoring membership issues (entities leaving and entering the group), but nonetheless their work initiated the first considerations of how to handle these dynamic groups of multiple objects.

Laube (2014: 87) later came to define the new field of computational movement analysis as "the interdisciplinary research field studying the development and application of computational techniques for capturing, processing, managing, structuring, and ultimately analysing data describing movement phenomena, both in geographic and abstract spaces, aiming for a better understanding of the processes governing that movement". Traditionally, research on mobility data management has centred on moving object databases and statistical analysis. These works primarily focus on:

- Data models: definitions and extensions of trajectory-related data-types such as moving points/regions.
- Data management or trajectory database management systems: efficient storage of mobility data with ad hoc indexing and querying techniques.
- Data mining: design of trajectory mining and learning algorithms (e.g. clustering, classification, outlier detection, finding convoys, sequential pattern mining).

Progress has been made in segmenting trajectory data, defining similarity in movement patterns, detecting clusters and so on. Work also progresses in the area of semantic annotation of structures and patterns. Melorose et al. (2015) and Yan et al. (2013) propose a model for semantic annotation that progressively transforms the raw mobility data into semantic trajectories enriched with segmentations and annotations.

Of course, it is not just individual players or groups (flocks) of players that need to be tracked, there is also the ball in many sports. Much work has been conducted through IBM SecondSight analytics in basketball (rebounding and so on). In soccer, Gyarmati and Anguera (2015) provide an approach to the automatic extraction of passing strategies by looking for repeating patterns of pass events during soccer games. The locations on the field where passes happened are input to the system. For each pass, information is gathered regarding the position on the field (x and y locations) both for the passer and receiver of the ball. The ball possession of each team is considered individually, resulting in a set of two-dimensional sequences for each team for each game. A dynamic programming algorithm is then used to compare pass sequences present in the datasets.

Gyarmati and Stanojevic (2016) continue this approach in their QPass system. Instead of just being concerned with quantitative analysis of soccer players' passing ability focused on descriptive statistics, their "merit-based evaluation of soccer passes" consider a players' real contribution to the strategy of their team in relation to passing and ball possession; for instance, whether the player is able to help the build-up of an attack or can maintain ball possession, or whether there is a change in the field values owed to a pass. They derived an album of pass trajectories for different gaming styles from seasons data; major events like passes and shots are annotated. The events are accompanied by the identity of the players and location information. Among other insights, losing ball possession and *not* having the ball at a particular part of the field could in fact lead to better chances to win a game.

Representation and storage

We have stated some methods used for processing moving object data and the difficulties related to designating movement segments with formal semantic descriptions (e.g. semantic trajectories, episodes like stops and moves) and diverse movement patterns (e.g. moving clusters). A further issue is how to store this data in a movement data warehouse (MDW). Current support for such data is limited to storing and querying raw movement (i.e. the spatiotemporal position of an object). However, it is not just the raw data but its various descriptions and measures that need to be stored in a database or data warehouse, which must facilitate powerful information analyses and reasonable performance.

We have seen that the various spatially enabled databases have additional representations of the original polygon data as minimum bounding boxes and these are examples of a trajectory segmentation approach, which leads to simplification of the original objects into smaller, less complex primitives better suited for storage and retrieval purposes. Retrieval, querying and investigating are efficient processes because index structures can be created over these minimum bounding boxes used to store the trajectories. Usually, the objective is to find segmentation for all the trajectories to minimise cost; that is, the total number of segments is bounded by some number k. Suggestions for cost functions range from minimising the volume of the bounding boxes to complex combinations of many different attributes.

Various authors explore how conceptual modelling could provide applications with direct trajectory support (i.e. movement data structured into countable semantic units) as a first class concept (Spaccapietra et al., 2008).

Examples of database work for moving object data include the set of data types defined by Guting (Güting and Schneider, 2005; Güting et al., 2000), covering spatial, temporal and moving types. The approach includes both a formal theory for moving objects (points and regions) and a full implementation. Guting's work includes both an abstract and discrete view of spatiotemporal paths. The former describes a path as curves defined by infinite sets and the latter view adopts a finite representation that approximates the trajectory as a polyline. The discrete model presented is a possible implementation of the abstract model.

A semantic model for an MDW is proposed by Fileto et al. (2014), introducing definitions for movement segments, patterns and their classes and categories. These constructs are semantically enriched with references to concepts and/or instances of these concepts arranged in distinct hierarchies.

Knowledge discovery and spatiotemporal information mining

The dynamic world is comprised of spatial regions at varying degrees of scale. Typically, small-scale spaces are comprised of clearly defined objects with a high degree of longevity. Large-scale spaces, however, are comprised of spatial objects with vague boundaries and are likely to undergo transformations and interact with each other in complex ways.

The field of geographic or spatiotemporal data mining has been established for over a decade (Miller and Han, 2009; Roddick and Lees, 2006). Example technology includes spatial and spatiotemporal rules mining.

The kinds of spatiotemporal information queries that would make sense over the aforementioned regions and contained objects (also events and processes) are diverse and hard to quantify. Although, traditionally, information queries seldom go beyond simple retrievals of data records, automatic query support for spatiotemporal information mining must extend what is recorded in the database to what can be inferred from it. Yuan et al. (2002) present a typology of queries that includes attribute queries, three types of spatial queries, three types of temporal queries and four types of spatiotemporal queries.

Knowledge discovery methods can be advantageously developed for the analysis of large sports datasets. Classifiers and predictive models can be developed to potentially detect specific events within sports; for example, predicting whether a certain play or strategy will result in a scoring opportunity. To this end, the toolbox of artificial intelligence, or AI, methods can be applied, including decision trees, association rules, support vector machines, neural networks and Bayesian methods.

Various authors utilise differing techniques to this problem of discovering patterns within moving object data (e.g. Cao et al., 2009). Djordjevic et al. (2011) developed a tool that given a sequence of events with time stamps detects if there is a periodic pattern. In addition, because an object is not expected to visit exactly the same location at every time instant of each period, the patterns are not rigid but differ slightly from one occurrence to the next.

Machine learning technology applied to positional data

Increasingly, there is a demand for knowledge-rich technologies that can represent and analyse player- and ball-tracking data. In parallel, there are so-called deep learning approaches that do not rely so much on explicitly coded domain knowledge but upon large datasets (with encoding of classes). Shah and Romijnders (2016) apply deep learning recurrent neural networks in the form of sequence modelling to predict in relation to basketball trajectories whether a three-point shot is successful. Alternative approaches may use complex physics models;

110

however, this approach is purely data driven and takes advantage of the powerful deep learning paradigm. In fact, the authors demonstrate their approach outperforms a static feature-rich machine learning model in predicting whether a three-point shot is successful. This suggests deep learning models may offer an improvement to traditional feature-based machine learning methods for tracking data.

SOFTWARE

We have mentioned open-source and commercial GIS and spatial databases that contain a huge array of powerful functions (e.g. QGIS and Postgres/PostGIS). There are many freely available machine learning libraries for most platforms that integrate with most programming languages. The following are a few of the most useful:

- PROJ.4, OGR and Mapnik
- Python libraries:
  - [XYZ]
  - Geodjango framework as ORM: http://geodjango.org/
  - Python Spatial Analysis Library: https://pypi.python.org/pypi/PySAL
- Kevin Toohey's R package SimilarityMeasures determines distance between two polygonal curves. Robust and fast similarity search for moving object trajectories.
- SaTScan is free software that analyses data using spatial, temporal or space-time scan statistics. It is designed for the following interrelated purposes: detect spatial or space-time clusters and see if they are statistically significant; test whether a point pattern is randomly distributed over space, time or space and time.
- CRIMESTAT: originally designed for crime analytics, it provides a comprehensive set of routines for point data (www.nij.gov/topics/technology/maps/pages/crimestat.aspx).

REFERENCES

Cao, H., Mamoulis, N. and Cheung, D.W. (2009) 'Periodic pattern discovery from trajectories of moving objects', *Geographic Data Mining and Knowledge Discovery*, 20. https://doi.org/doi:10.1201/9781420073980.ch15

Djordjevic, B., Gudmundsson, J., Pham, A. and Wolle, T. (2011) 'Detecting regular visit patterns', *Algorithmica*, 60(4): 829–852. https://doi.org/10.1007/s00453-009-9376-2

Everitt, B.S., Landau, S., Leese, M. and Stahl, D. (2011) 'Cluster analysis', *Quality and Quantity*, 14. https://doi.org/10.1007/BF00154794

Fileto, R., Raffaetà, A., May, C., Roncato, A. and Klein, D. (2014) 'A semantic model for movement data warehouses', *Proceedings of the 17th International Workshop on Data Warehousing and OLAP* (pp. 47–56), Shanghai, China, November 2014.

Geary, R.C. (1954) 'The contiguity ratio and statistical mapping', *The Incorporated Statistician*, 5: 115–145.

Getis, A. and Ord, J.K. (1992) 'The analysis of spatial association', *Geographical Analysis*, 24(3): 189–206. https://doi.org/10.1111/j.1538-4632.1992.tb00261.x

Gudmundsson, J. and Horton, M. (2017) 'Spatiotemporal analysis of team sports – A survey', *ACM Computing Surveys*, 50(2): 1–34. https://doi.org/10.1145/3054132

Güting, R.H., Böhlen, M.H., Erwig, M., Jensen, C.S., Lorentzos, N.A., Schneider, M. and Vazirgiannis, M. (2000) 'A foundation for representing and querying moving objects', *ACM Transactions on Database Systems*, 25(1): 1–42. https://doi.org/10.1145/352958.352963

Güting, R.H. and Schneider, M. (2005) 'Preface', In R.H. Güting and M. Schneider (eds.), *Moving objects databases* (pp. xvii–xxi). San Francisco: Morgan Kaufmann. https://doi.org/10.1016/B978-012088799-6/50001-3

Gyarmati, L. and Anguera, X. (2015) 'Automatic extraction of the passing strategies of soccer teams', *2015 ACM KDD Workshop on Large-Scale Sports Analytics*, 0–3. http://arxiv.org/abs/1508.02171

Gyarmati, L. and Stanojevic, R. (2016) 'QPass: A merit-based evaluation of soccer passes', *2016 ACM KDD Workshop on Large-Scale Sports Analytics*, 0–3. https://arxiv.org/abs/1608.03532

Laube, P. (2014) *Computational movement analysis*, New York, NY: Springer.

McQueen, A., Wiens, J. and Guttag, J. (2014). 'Automatically recognizing on-ball screens', *2014 MIT Sloan Sports Analytics Conference, Boston, MA, USA*, 28 February–01 March 2014 .

Melorose, J., Perroy, R. and Careas, S. (2015) 'The SIGSPATIAL special', *Statewide Agricultural Land Use Baseline 2015*, 1(1). https://doi.org/10.1017/CBO9781107415324.004

Miller, H.J. and Han, J. (2009) 'Geographic data mining and knowledge discovery: An overview', In H.J. Miller and J. Han (eds.), *Geographic data mining and knowledge discovery* (pp. 3–32), London: Taylor and Francis.

Mora, S.V. and Knottenbelt, W.J. (2016) 'Spatiotemporal analysis of tennis matches', 2–5. https://doi.org/10.475/123

Moran, P.A.P. (1950) 'Notes on continuous stochastic phenomena', *Biometrika*, 37(1/2): 17. https://doi.org/10.2307/2332142

Parent, C., Pelekis, N., Theodoridis, Y., Yan, Z., Spaccapietra, S., Renso, C., . . . Macedo, J. (2013) 'Semantic trajectories modeling and analysis', *ACM Computing Surveys*, 45(4): 1–32. https://doi.org/10.1145/2501654.2501656

Roddick, J.F. and Lees, B.G. (2006) 'Spatiotemporal data mining paradigms and methodologies', *Geographic Data Mining and Knowledge Discovery*, 27–44. https://doi.org/doi:10.1201/9781420073980.ch2

Shah, R.C. and Romijnders, R. (2016) 'Applying deep learning to basketball trajectories', *KDD '16*, 4. https://doi.org/10.475/123

Spaccapietra, S., Parent, C., Damiani, M.L., de Macedo, J.A., Porto, F. and Vangenot, C. (2008) 'A conceptual view on trajectories', *Data and Knowledge Engineering*, 65(1): 126–146. https://doi.org/10.1016/j.datak.2007.10.008

Yan, Z., Chakraborty, D., Parent, C., Spaccapietra, S. and Aberer, K. (2013) 'Semantic trajectories: Mobility data computation and annotation', *ACM Transactions on Intelligent Systems and Technology*, 4(3): 1–38. Article No. 49. https://doi.org/10.1145/2483669.2483682

Yuan, M., McIntosh, J., Shaw, K., Ladner, R. and Abdelguerfi, M. (2002) 'A typology of spatialtemporal information queries', *Mining Spatiotemporal Information Systems*, 1–20.

CHAPTER 6

SPATIOTEMPORAL ANALYSIS

INTRODUCTION

Chapter 5 covered geospatial analysis. The use of more localised spatiotemporal data is commonplace in sports, particularly in sports performance analysis. There is a distinction between spatial and temporal aspects, although the temporal aspects often involve changes in spatial data over time. Vast volumes of GPS data and other player- and ball-tracking data can be generated quickly and used to analyse tactical movement as well as work rate within sports. This chapter discusses a range of approaches from algorithmic methods to neural networks for identifying tactical patterns within these data. Such algorithms and neural networks have limitations and identify many false positive events as well as fail to identify actual events within player and object movement data. Therefore, there is a clear role for human verification during data analysis as well as decision making. This chapter discusses visual presentation of data including pitch diagrams of player movement and event locations to assist with such tasks. The use of graphical techniques such as Voronoi diagrams and centroid location maps to highlight patterns in spatiotemporal data are discussed with reference to player movement in team games. The integrated use of video and quantitative data also helps to overcome the limitations of solely relying on quantitative analysis of movement data.

ALGORITHMIC METHODS

Tactical movement patterns in team games are understood by sports practitioners. Coaching literature in many team games shows diagrams of player movement within playing areas when describing tactics (Bangsbo and Peitersen, 2002, 2004). Spatiotemporal aspects of team games include space creation (Bangsbo and Peitersen, 2004), space restriction (Bangsbo and Peitersen, 2002), depth and width (Daniel, 2003), concentration of players (Worthington, 1980) and balance of defence (Olsen, 1981). Many of these tactical formations and movements were described in the coaching literature several decades before automatic ball and player technology was developed. The development of accurate ball- and player-tracking technologies (Carling et al., 2008) has motivated the development of algorithms to specifically identify tactical behaviours described by practitioners (Lames and Siegle, 2011; Lemmink and Frencken, 2011; O'Donoghue, 2011). One early spatiotemporal analysis of such data was Gréhaigne et al.'s (1997) process for identifying sectors of the playing surface covered by players. The distance a player could travel within the next second was positively related to their current movement speed whereas their scope for changing direction was negatively associated. Gréhaigne et al.'s (1997) principles were the foundation for a later system that identified defensive patterns vulnerable to penetration by opposition through passes (Knudsen and Andersen, 2015). The development of systems to recognise tactical aspects from geospatial data was described by O'Donoghue and Holmes (2015: 116–121). There are five steps to this process: requirement analysis, system specification, system design, evolutionary implementation and validation. Requirements analysis selects an important and relevant tactical aspect of play. This is operationalised using geometry and trigonometry during system specification. System design involves identifying the data structures and algorithms necessary for the system to recognise the tactical aspect of interest. These are then implemented and tested on a function-by-function basis using an evolutionary prototyping approach. The fifth step is verification and validation. Verification tests that the system satisfies its specification; in other words, it does what the developer intended. This involves testing specific geometric properties using test case scenarios. Validation involves checking that the system actually recognises the same tactical events as human expert observers would. This evaluation process involves experts observing match videos and noting the times of the tactical events of interest. This list of events is then compared to those identified by the system so that any false positive and false negative cases can be considered. These steps are not performed in a sequence because some steps need to be repeated when working on exploratory algorithms for aspects of sports that are difficult to quantify. For example, O'Donoghue et al. (2017: 102–104) described how different subsets of criteria specified for identifying given tactics are evaluated during the validation stage, potentially leading to a revision of the system specification.

DATA REDUCTION

Centroids

There is a large volume of spatiotemporal data that can be recorded during team games. A player-tracking system recording 22 players for 90 minutes at 10 Hz will record 1,188,000 coordinates. Therefore, analysts try to reduce the volume of data they need to analyse to the most critical data associated with success. One way of doing this is to analyse key frames with respect to ball possessions. For example, in analysing challenge events in soccer, O'Donoghue and Holmes (2015: 123–124) only considered three instants during each possession: the start of the dribble, the end of the dribble that coincided with the ball being passed and the pass being received by a teammate. An alternative way of reducing the data is to use summary variables within each frame rather than the coordinates for every player and the ball. Passos (2017: 82–104) discussed centroids, inter-player distances, inter-player angles, length and depth of areas covered by groups of players and how these data can be used to analyse team member interactions. Team centroid is a collective variable that simplifies team data by reducing it to the mean location of team members. The disadvantage of doing this is that information about the depth and width of the team formation is lost. Furthermore, important behaviours by key individuals will be concealed when solely using team centroids.

Length and width

Length and width can apply to an entire team or unit of a team such as the defence, midfield or forwards. These variables are the minimum length and width of a rectangle that can be placed around the players of interest in parallel with the side lines of the playing surface. Length and width can be used with or instead of centroids. Passos (2017: 95–97) also described length per width ratio, which can further reduce the volume of data analysed.

116

Area

The area of the rectangle placed around the players of interest can be used as a variable that can be calculated simply. Figure 6.1 shows an alternative form of "surface area" described by Frencken et al. (2011) and Lopes et al. (2013), which fits the smallest convex hull around the set of players of interest; in this case, the 10 outfield players. The length of the perimeter of this area can also be used as a summary measure of a team's formation.

Voronoi diagrams can also be used in spatial analysis. They divide the playing area into subareas; one for each player of interest such that the player is closer to any point in that area than any other player. Fonseca et al. (2013) described how separate Voronoi diagrams for the two teams contesting a match can be superimposed on each other to allow overlapped and free areas to be determined for subsets of players.

Distances

Various distances can be used instead of coordinates. For example, determining distances of players to the centre of the goal they are attacking can halve the amount of data analysed. Similarly, distances from the centre circle or the team's centroid can be computed for each player.

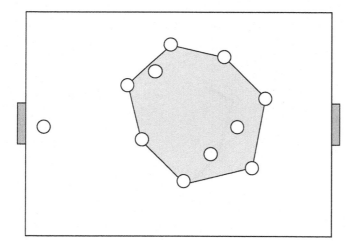

Figure 6.1 Area of the smallest convex hull containing the outfield players of a team

Distances can also be computed between pairs of players on the same team, opposing players or players and the ball. The term *dyad* is used to represent a pair of players of interest. For example, attacker-defender dyads can be analysed using the distances between the two players within each dyad.

Angles

Passos (2017: 85–91) describes how inter-player angles can indicate the use of evasive movements by the attacking player within a dyad as well as how players keep the ball carrier and opposing goal (or basket) in view during critical moments of possessions. When defining the angles used, we need to specify their reference lines or directions.

Isochrones

An isochrone connects points plotted at some point in time. Figure 6.2 uses an isochrone to represent the location of the back four of a football team at an instant during the match. The total length of the isochrone could be used to characterise the concentration or spread of the defence at some point. Alternatively, key angles within the isochrone could be used to reduce the volume of data analysed. The maximum distance

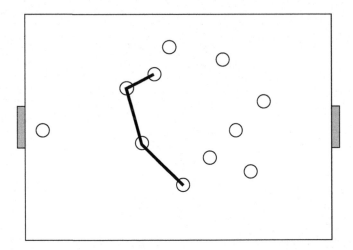

Figure 6.2 An isochrone for the back four of a soccer team

118

between a pair of players within the isochrone could indicate vulnerability in the defence, although we need to be careful about the central defenders crossing over, which could lead to a misinterpretation of gaps in the defence by such an analysis.

PROCESSING THE DATA

Artificial neural networks

As has already been mentioned, movement in sports, especially in team games, is dynamic and complex. For this reason, artificial neural networks have been used in the analysis of sports techniques (Lamb and Bartlett, 2013) and broader playing patterns in team games (Memmert and Perl, 2009; Perl et al., 2013). Artificial neural networks can be trained to recognise complex patterns, classifying these patterns using supervised or unsupervised learning algorithms. This section describes the use of artificial neural networks to recognise tactical patterns associated with successful possessions. A simple example is used in which 416 possessions from a single English FA Premier League match are analysed. There were 26 players who participated in the match. However, the data were pre-processed so only the 22 players on the pitch were represented for any instant in the game. This meant that when a player was substituted, a single pair of columns (X and Y) represented the player and the substitute once he entered the field. The player coordinates were recorded using a commercial automatic player-tracking system (Prozone3: Prozone Sports Ltd, Leeds, UK). The artificial neural networks only use the location of players and the ball at the instant the possession commences. Knowing the player in possession of the ball at the start of each possession also allowed the ball's location at the start of each possession to be determined. Possession outcomes are classified as successful if there is a scoring opportunity or the attacking team enters the attacking third (n = 122); otherwise, they are classed as unsuccessful (n = 294). The times at which possessions commenced as well as the outcomes of possessions were determined using a manual video analysis process. All data were transformed so that the team in possession is playing from left (negative X values) to right (positive X values). The remainder of this chapter discusses ways the data can be processed using supervised and unsupervised learning algorithms. These alternatives were implemented in Matlab R2017a (Mathworks, Natick, MA).

Linear filter for classification

Linear filter networks can be used to predict some numerical value for cases of interest or for classification purposes. When predicting a numerical value, a pure linear transfer function is used by an output neuron. When linear filter networks are used for classification purposes, there is typically a neuron in the output layer for each outcome class of interest. These neurons use hard limiting or logsig transfer functions to force values between 0 and 1; values of 1 or close to 1 predict the class represented by the given neuron.

Backpropagation algorithm

In this section, we compare two feedforward networks: one that uses team centroids and the ball's location at the start of possessions (ADB-network) and the other that uses team centroids without the ball's location (AD-network); A, D and B denote the use of the location of the attacking team's centroid, defending team's centroid and ball, respectively. The distance from each team centroid and the ball to the centre of the goal being attacked was entered into the neural networks. The middle layer neurons and output neuron used the tansig and logsig transfer functions, respectively. The weights were initialised to random values so if any train-test cycles used the same training cases, they would not necessarily predict the same possession outcomes. A range of middle layer sizes were studied for each neural network type with the neural networks trained using the backpropagation algorithm.

The system used to study the two networks employed an overall control system to iterate the training and testing of the neural network 200 times for each middle layer size from 1 to 8 neurons. The system was run twice as shown in Figure 6.3 – once for the AD-network and once for the ADB-network. Therefore, there were two input neurons used the first time the system was run (the distance of the attacking and defending teams' centroids to goal) and three input neurons the second time (the distance of the ball to goal was also used). The networks were attempting to distinguish between two types of possession: successful and unsuccessful. Therefore, only one output neuron was needed, which was intended to output 1 if a successful possession was predicted and 0 if the possession was predicted to be unsuccessful.

120

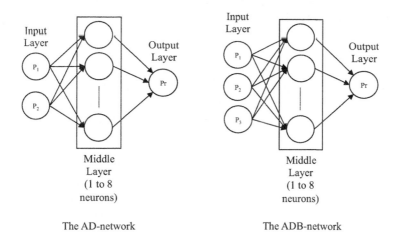

Input Layer

P₁

P₂

Output Layer

Pr

Middle Layer
(1 to 8 neurons)

The AD-network

Input Layer

P₁

P₂

P₃

Output Layer

Pr

Middle Layer
(1 to 8 neurons)

The ADB-network

Figure 6.3 Feedforward networks where P1, P2 and P3 are the distances of the attacking team's centroid to goal, the defending team's centroid to goal and the ball to goal

The possessions were randomly sorted so that the neural network was trained using a different dataset during each of the 3,200 train-test runs. On each occasion, 208 possessions were used to train the network and the other 208 possessions were used to test the predictive accuracy of the network. The system recorded accuracy, sensitivity and specificity statistics for each train-test cycle, allowing mean values for each combination of network type and middle layer size to be determined. Accuracy is the percentage of all possessions for which the neural network predicted the correct outcome. Sensitivity is the percentage of successful possessions for which the neural network correctly predicted a successful outcome. Specificity is the percentage of unsuccessful possessions for which the neural network correctly predicted an unsuccessful outcome.

During each train-test cycle, the input vector was set up using the distances for the 208 training cases. The target outcome was copied from the original data for the 208 training cases. Exploratory analysis revealed that the trained networks rarely produce clear-cut outcome values around 0 and 1. This meant that a post-processing action was needed to predict the outcomes from the neural network outputs. The 208 cases used to train the network were reapplied to the trained network to determine the outputs they would produce. These output values were sorted into ascending order. The proportion of actual successful possessions that occurred within these 208 cases was known, allowing a threshold value for predicting success to be determined. The number of cases varied between each train-test cycle due to the random sorting of cases. However, the post-processing of outputs meant that the correct proportion of training cases would be predicted to be successful in each train-test cycle even if there were some false positive and false negative predictions.

As mentioned, the network was trained with 208 randomly selected possessions during each train-test cycle. Within each cycle, the remaining 208 cases were used to test the accuracy of the trained network. This was done by setting up the input vector using the distance variables for those cases and applying the "sim" command in Matlab to predict the outcome for each test possession. Where the output exceeded the threshold value determined during training, the possession was predicted to be successful; otherwise, the outcome was predicted to be unsuccessful. As each possession was tested, accuracy, sensitivity and specificity statistics were determined.

The accuracy levels were very similar between the two neural network models with the ADB-network becoming more accurate when the middle layer had six or more neurons in it. The highest accuracy levels were achieved by the ADB-network when the middle layer contained seven and eight neurons. The variability in accuracy decreased for both types of network as the middle layer increased in size. Figure 6.4 shows that

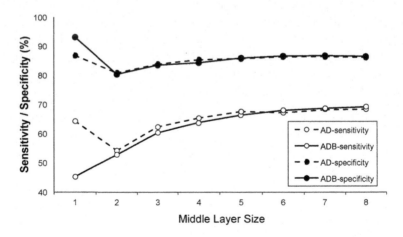

Figure 6.4 Specificity and sensitivity of alternative feedforward networks

specificity was higher than sensitivity for both types of network, irrespective of the size of the middle layer. The highest sensitivity value (69.23%) was achieved by the ADB-network when its middle layer contained eight neurons. The highest sensitivity values for each type of network were achieved when there was a single neuron in the middle layer. However, this was at the expense of also having a relatively low specificity value. When higher sensitivity scores were achieved with middle layers of six or more neurons, the ADB-network had higher sensitivity and specificity scores than the AD-network.

The mean values for accuracy, sensitivity and specificity are useful for broad comparisons between the two network types. However, we are also interested in finer differences between the two network types, such as the possessions correctly recognised by one neural network but not the other. A supplementary system was developed to apply the two neural networks, each implemented with a middle layer of eight neurons, on 200 occasions using a single set of 208 training possessions with the remaining possessions used to test accuracy. The weights were randomised at the start of each train-test cycle so different trained networks could be produced even though the same training data was used. During the testing stage, the number of correctly predicted outcomes was counted for each network type for each possession. Whenever the count exceeded 100 (50% of the iterations), the network was deemed to have predicted the outcome correctly. An isochrone was plotted for each possession starting at the attacking team's centroid with the ball location in the middle and the defending team's centroid at the other end. Each test possession was plotted on a pitch diagram distinguishing between correctly and incorrectly predicted outcomes.

The Venn diagram in Figure 6.5 shows there were 58 possessions that were actually successful. Thirty-seven of these (sensitivity = 63.8%) were correctly predicted by the AD-network and 41 (sensitivity = 70.7%) were correctly predicted by the ADB-network. Of particular interest is the false negative case predicted by the ADB-network and the five false negative cases predicted by the AD-network that were correctly predicted by the other network. These can be illustrated on pitch diagrams using isochrones to connect the team centroids and the ball.

This exercise found that the predictive accuracy of two network types increased as the size of the middle layer increased, although the rate of increase declined above middle layers of five neurons. The similarity in

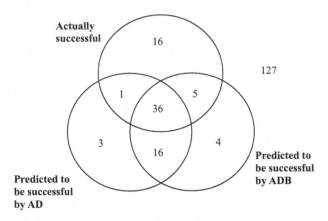

Figure 6.5 Accuracy of predictions by the AD- and ADB-networks

accuracy levels between the two networks may be explained by attacking and defending players positioning themselves strategically in relation to the current ball position (Gréhaigne and Godbout, 2013). Therefore, the ball location details utilised by the ADB-network provided only limited additional information beyond player locations in predicting possession outcomes.

It is important to consider the contribution of false positive and false negative predictions in selecting the best neural network structure to use rather than just looking at the overall accuracy level. If the ADB-network was analysed using middle layer sizes from 1 to 4, the highest accuracy level would be with one middle neuron (accuracy 79.0%. sensitivity 45.3%, specificity 93.0%). However, we might choose to use the ADB-network with four middle layer neurons because of the relative seriousness of false negative predictions in relation to false positives (accuracy 78.4%, sensitivity 63.9%, specificity 84.3%). There is no set rule or equation for this and the decision depends on the application area. In the future, predictive models might use something like the Desired Relative Seriousness measure used in statistical power analysis (Murphy et al., 2009).

A disappointing aspect of both neural network performances was the tendency to predict possession outcomes largely on the basis of the X coordinate of the attacking team. All the possessions predicted to be successful were located in the other team's half of the pitch despite the clear overlap of locations of possessions of different outcomes. An

124

explanation for the apparent mechanical classification of possessions is the quantitative nature of the pre-processed data used. Neural networks were designed to be used with more complex pattern-like data (Lamb and Bartlett, 2013; Perl et al., 2013). It should also be considered that a one-frame snapshot of a possession is very limited information and possession outcomes also depend on behaviours beyond this instant in time. A further explanation for the lack of accuracy in recognising successful possessions that started in the team's own half is due to the nature of sports performance. The neural network may recognise situations in which teams have a greater opportunity of success than other situations but, in reality, there are occasions in which teams achieve successful outcomes that were not likely and others in which they fail to achieve successful outcomes despite being in a favourable situation.

Perceptrons using heat maps

Perceptron networks are used to recognise graphical patterns such as character recognition (Hirwani and Gonnade, 2014). The locations of players on a playing surface is a different problem than character recognition because much less of the area analysed is taken up with the player locations than in the case of character pixels and the players appear as a series of dots with no connecting lines. A more fundamental problem is that although there are multiple ways of presenting characters, there is much greater variation in the patterns of players that can be observed on a playing surface during a game. Considering that the modal pitch size in the English FA Premier League is 105 x 68m, if we were to use 1m x 1m cells to represent the playing surface, we would have 7,140 cells with no more than 22 of these containing a player's centre of gravity. Indeed, a single 1m x 1m cell could contain more than player but the main issue is the overwhelming majority of the cells are empty. This is unsuitable for analysis by perceptron networks. However, there are ways in which data can be pre-processed to allow perceptron networks to be applied.

The first way in which data can be pre-processed is to use a smaller number of larger cells to represent the playing area. For example, we could divide a soccer pitch into 140 cells of 7.5m x 6.8m. This would increase the likelihood of more than one player located in a single cell but would reduce the number of empty cells considerably. An exploratory exercise applying this approach to the data used in the backpropagation example revealed some promise in predicting possession outcomes. The perceptron used 140 input nodes to represent the playing area. This essentially rearranges a two-dimensional structure of 140 cells into a single input vector of 140 elements. Each input neuron had a value of 1 if there were one or more outfield players of the attacking team in the cell; otherwise, the value was 0. There was a single output neuron that yielded a value of 1 if a possession was predicted to be successful; otherwise, the output value was 0. The perceptron network was trained using 208 of the possessions in the match and tested using the remaining 208 possessions. The overall accuracy level was 68.3% with 29 of the 56 successful possessions correctly predicted (sensitivity = 51.8%) and 113 of the 152 unsuccessful predictions successfully predicted (specificity = 71.2%). These results need to be viewed in context. The perceptron only looked at the broad locations of outfield players of the attacking team at the instant the possession started. Players of the defending team could also be included by adding another 140 input nodes but this would not be recommended unless we have a much larger number of training possessions. In this example, the 140 cells that the playing area is divided into is comparable with the number of training possessions used.

A further way of pre-processing player location data for use in a perceptron would be to use data from more than one instant in time. For example, if we restricted the study to possessions of 3s or longer and looked at the locations of players from the start of the possession to 2.0s into the possession, we would have 21 locations per player if the data were recorded at 10 Hz. Other tactical analyses could apply this approach using much broader time periods rather than individual possessions. Heat maps have been used in soccer (Strudwick, 2016: 555) to show the areas covered by players. This would allow the pitch to be represented by a larger number of cells (say, 7,140 cells of 1m x 1m) and most cells to contain non-zero values. Each input value would be between 0 and 1, representing the proportion of match time the cell was occupied by players. Data from multiple matches could then be entered into the neural network to determine if there is an association between player movements and broad match outcomes.

Perceptrons using Boolean facts

As previously mentioned, perceptrons are typically used in pattern recognition applications, such as character recognition, and input neurons have values of 0 or 1, although values in between can be used to represent "noise" in the data. This raises the possibility of using 1 and 0 to represent the truth of Boolean propositions. Although many artificial intelligence methods use fuzzy logic and recognise uncertainty, logic programming has been used in artificial intelligence through programming languages such as PROLOG (Clocksin and Mellish, 1984). Here, we describe an exploratory exercise to represent elements of tactical formations in soccer as a series of Boolean facts that can be entered into a perceptron network. The purpose of the network, as before, is to predict the outcome of possessions based on the locations of players at the beginning of possessions. Consider the formation of players shown in Figure 6.6; we do not use the same numbering system as many teams and assume a 4–4–2 formation with players 10 and 11 representing the two forwards. Also, during data recording, X represents where players are located lengthwise (from one end of the pitch to the other) whereas Y represents location with respect to the sides of the pitch (widthwise).

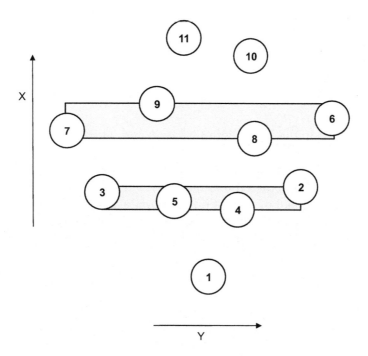

Figure 6.6 A soccer team formation playing up the page (the grey boxes represent areas covered by the four defenders and the four midfielders)

There are many statements we can make about this formation that will be true or false, represented by 1 or 0, respectively, when entering such information into a perceptron network. This is a list of 19 Boolean propositions that were determined during pre-processing of the 416 possessions from the English FA Premier League match we are using as a case study. These facts relate to the 19 outfield players of the team in possession of the ball as well as the ball's location:

1 Player 2 is ahead of player 6 (player 2 has a greater X value).
2 Player 3 is ahead of player 7 (player 3 has a greater X value).
3 Player 2 is to the right of both players 4 and 5 (player 2 has a greater Y value).
4 Player 3 is to the left of both players 4 and 5 (player 3 has a lower Y value).
5 Player 2 is behind the ball (player 2 has a lower X value than the location of the ball).
6 Player 4 is behind the ball (player 4 has a lower X value than the location of the ball).
7 Player 5 is behind the ball (player 5 has a lower X value than the location of the ball).
8 Player 3 is behind the ball (player 3 has a lower X value than the location of the ball).
9 Player 6 is to the right of both players 8 and 9 (player 6 has a greater Y value).
10 Player 7 is to the left of both players 8 and 9 (player 7 has a lower Y value).
11 Player 4 is ahead of at least one of the players 8 and 9 (player 4 has a greater X value than the minimum X value for players 8 and 9).
12 Player 5 is ahead of at least one of the players 8 and 9 (player 5 has a greater X value than the minimum X value for players 8 and 9).
13 The rectangle formed by the defenders overlaps with the rectangle formed by the midfielders in the X direction (the maximum X value for players 2, 3, 4 and 5 is greater than the minimum X value for players 6, 7, 8 and 9).
14 The width of the defenders is within the width of the midfielders (the minimum Y value for players 2, 3, 4 and 5 is greater than the minimum Y value for players 6, 7, 8 and 9 and the maximum Y value for players 2, 3, 4 and 5 is less than the maximum Y value for players 6, 7, 8 and 9).

128

15 The width of the midfielders is within the width of the defenders (the minimum Y value for players 6, 7, 8 and 9 is greater than the minimum Y value for players 2, 3, 4 and 5 and the maximum Y value for players 6, 7, 8 and 9 is less than the maximum Y value for players 2, 3, 4 and 5).

16 Player 10 is the furthest player forward (player 10 has a greater X value than all other players' X values).

17 Player 11 is the furthest player forward (player 11 has a greater X value than all other players' X values).

18 Player 10 is inside the four wider players (player 10 has a greater Y value than players 2 and 6 and a lower Y value than players 3 and 7).

19 Player 11 is inside the four wider players (player 11 has a greater Y value than players 2 and 6 and a lower Y value than players 3 and 7).

There are many more Boolean propositions that can be suggested involving the ball, the team with the ball and the team without the ball, as well as expressions combining two or all three. Indeed, these expressions relate to a single instant in the match. When team formation data come from more than one instant in time, we can have facts about how formations change over time. The Boolean propositions do not need to be mutually exclusive and in the current example, it is not possible for all the propositions to be true. For example, proposition 14 may be true, proposition 15 may be true, neither 14 nor 15 could be true but it is not possible for both 14 and 15 to be true.

These 19 Boolean propositions were applied to the 416 possessions from our case study match. There were 208 possessions used to train the perceptron network to recognise whether possessions were successful with the remaining 208 possessions used to test the accuracy of the trained network. As with the previously described perceptron, a single output neuron was used to represent whether a possession was predicted to be successful. The perceptron correctly predicted less than half of the 65 successful possessions (29 out of 65 giving a sensitivity score of 44.6%) with 114 of the 143 of the unsuccessful possessions correctly predicted (specificity 79.7%) and an overall accuracy of 68.8% (the outcomes of 143 of the 208 possessions were successfully predicted).

Self-organising maps

The neural network models mentioned up to now use supervised learning techniques whereby they are provided with training cases including the variable they are attempting to predict. Self-organising maps involve unsupervised learning in which the network trains to identify clusters of related cases. The classes of patterns identified can then be used in further analyses. Self-organising maps not only create and use a classification scheme but also represent topological relationships between the different classes. Self-organising maps have been used to analyse temporal patterns in action sequences within volleyball (Jäger et al., 2007) as well as patterns of play in handball (Pfeiffer and Perl, 2006) and soccer (Grunz et al., 2012).

Self-organising maps have a layer of input neurons and a competitive layer. The input layer has neurons that can take any numerical value. The competitive layer has a neuron for each class. Therefore, the analyst, although not knowing what the classes are going to be, needs to specify the number of classes that can be determined. There is a set of weights within the competitive layer corresponding to each cluster type. Each set of weights contains the same number of values as in the input layer. The values of these weights are intended to be values of the input variables for central members of the given cluster. Initially, the weights are randomised but as training cases are considered, the weights change to represent the classes discovered. As each training case is considered, the neurons of the competitive layer are compared to it. The neuron that the case is closest to "wins" and its weights are adjusted to reflect the updated set of cases associated with it. It is possible, when setting a number of classes, that some may end up "dead neurons" if they never win. This means that we may end up with fewer classes than requested.

A simple exercise is used here to explain how self-organising maps can be used with spatiotemporal data. The 416 possessions from the English FA Premier League match are used to train the self-organising map. There is no predetermined set of tactical classes to train the network to recognise so the data do not need to be split into training and test cases. In this example, only the back four of the defending team are considered. The four variables used are the X and Y coordinates of the back four's centroid, the depth and width of the back four. We initialise the self-organising feature map with four input neurons and a competitive layer of 16 neurons formed into a 4 x 4 feature map. Once the network is trained, we can access the four weights for each of the 16 clusters to determine their typical coordinates, depth and width.

Table 6.1 shows the weights for the 16 clusters as well as the number of possessions belonging to each cluster and the outcomes of these

130

Table 6.1 Clusters identified by training a self-organising feature map

Possession cluster	Frequency	Weights				Outcome	
		X	Y	Width	Depth	Unsuccessful	Successful
1	51	39.8	0.7	14.3	4.1	9	42
2	22	33.0	-9.7	24.7	5.1	4	18
3	23	21.3	-14.6	27.9	6.8	19	4
4	30	10.0	-11.8	24.9	5.5	26	4
5	20	28.1	6.1	25.9	5.4	8	12
6	22	18.4	-4.5	35.2	9.0	12	10
7	13	6.7	-10.1	34.2	10.7	10	3
8	18	2.2	-5.8	26.4	12.2	17	1
9	45	15.3	9.8	28.6	6.0	36	9
10	17	13.3	2.9	38.9	11.3	11	6
11	25	1.8	-7.4	43.7	20.0	18	7
12	14	-10.1	-6.9	33.3	21.2	14	0
13	23	5.8	11.1	32.8	9.0	22	1
14	29	3.9	4.7	46.7	16.6	25	4
15	28	-11.3	-0.8	42.0	27.2	28	0
16	36	-25.6	-2.2	21.8	34.5	35	1
Total	416					294	122

possessions. The cluster variable can now be crosstabulated with other variables such as team and possession outcomes. Differences between the two teams would suggest that they adopt different tactics or give the ball away in different areas of the field. In our example, there was no significant association between team and cluster (p = 0.146). The more interesting question is whether some clusters are more successful than others. A chi square test of independence revealed a significant association between possession type and outcome (p < 0.001) with clusters 1 and 2 having 82.4% and 81.8% success rates, respectively, which is in contrast to the other 14 possession types in which the success rate was always below 50%. The main variable distinguishing the first two clusters from the remaining clusters was the X coordinate; these possessions commenced nearer to the opposition goal than any other possessions.

SUMMARY

There is a vast amount of spatiotemporal data that can be gathered during sports performances using player-tracking technology. These data can be analysed using algorithmic techniques or artificial intelligence. Algorithmic approaches are challenging in that they require analysts to specify aspects of play in a mathematical form that covers all cases of the given tactic identified. This is not really possible and so analysts need to have strategies to identify and deal with false positive and false negative predictions by algorithms. Artificial neural networks can undergo supervised learning to distinguish possessions of differing outcomes. As before, there will be false positive and false negative predictions made. A further issue is that although weights within trained artificial neural networks can be inspected, the mechanisms by which they predict the success of possessions are not as transparent as the way in which analyst-written algorithms distinguish between different tactics. Unsupervised learning is an alternative approach that can lead to the identification of possession types not considered by the analyst but that may be associated with success.

REFERENCES

Bangsbo, J. and Peitersen, B. (2002) *Defensive soccer tactics: How to stop players and teams from scoring*, Champaign, IL: Human Kinetics.

Bangsbo, J. and Peitersen, B. (2004) *Offensive soccer tactics: How to control possession and score more goals*, Champaign, IL: Human Kinetics.

Carling, C., Bloomfield, J., Nelson, L. and Reilly, T. (2008) 'The role of motion analysis in elite soccer: Contemporary performance measurement techniques and work rate data', *Sports Medicine*, 38: 839–862.

Clocksin, W.F. and Mellish, C.S. (1984) *Programming in prolog*, 2nd edn., Berlin, Germany: Springer-Verlag.

Daniel, J. (2003) *The complete guide to soccer systems and tactics*, Spring City, PA: Reedswain Publishing.

Fonseca, S., Milho, J., Travassos, B., Araújo, D. and Lopes, A. (2013) 'Measuring spatial interaction behaviour in team sports using superimposed Voronoi diagrams', *International Journal of Performance Analysis in Sport*, 13(1): 179–189.

Frencken, W., Lemminck, K., Delleman, N. and Visscher, C. (2011) 'Oscillations of centroid position and surface area of soccer teams in small-sided games', *European Journal of Sports Sciences*, 11: 215–223.

Gréhaigne, J.F., Bouthier, D. and David, B. (1997) 'Dynamic-system analysis of opponent relationships in collective actions in soccer', *Journal of Sports Sciences*, 15: 137–149.

Gréhaigne, J.-F. and Godbout, P. (2013) 'Collective variables for analysing performance in team sports', in T. McGarry, P.G. O'Donoghue and J. Sampaio (eds.), *Routledge handbook of sports performance analysis* (pp. 101–14), London: Routledge.

Grunz, A., Memmert, D. and Perl, J. (2012) 'Tactical pattern recognition in soccer games by means of special self-organizing maps', *Human Movement Science*, 31(2): 334–343.

Hirwani, A. and Gonnade, S. (2014) 'Character recognition using multilayer perceptron', *International Journal of Computer Science and Information Technologies*, 5(1): 558–661.

Jäger, J.M., Perl, J. and Schöllhorn, W.I. (2007) 'Analysis of players' configurations by means of artificial neural networks', *International Journal of Performance Analysis of Sport*, 3(7): 90–103.

Knudsen, N.S. and Andersen, T.B. (2015) 'Methodology to detect gaps in a soccer defence', *International Journal of Computer Science in Sport*, 14(2): 18–24.

Lamb, P. and Bartlett, R. (2013) 'Neural networks for analysing sports techniques', In T. McGarry, P.G. O'Donoghue and J. Sampaio (eds.), *Routledge handbook of sports performance analysis* (pp. 225–236), London: Routledge.

Lames, M. and Siegle, M. (2011) 'Positional data in game sports – Validation and practical impact', *8th International Symposium of Computer Science in Sport*, Shanghai, China.

Lemmink, K.A.P.M. and Frencken, W. (2011) 'Tactical match analysis in soccer: New perspectives?', *World Congress of Science and Football VII, Book of Abstracts* (p. 22), Nagoya, Japan.

Lopes, A., Fonseca, S., Leser, R. Baca, A. and Paulo, A. (2013) 'Using spatial metrics to characterize behaviour in small-sided games', In D. Peters and P.G. O'Donoghue (eds.), *Performance analysis in sport IX* (pp. 258–266), London: Routledge.

Memmert, D. and Perl, J. (2009) 'Game creativity analysis by means of neural networks', *Journal of Sports Sciences*, 27: 139–149.

Murphy, K.R., Myors, B. And Wolach, A. (2009) *Statistical power analysis: A simple and general model for traditional and modern hypothesis tests*, 3rd edn., New York, NY: Routledge.

O'Donoghue, P.G. (2011), 'Automatic recognition of balance and in soccer defences using player displacement data', *8th International Symposium of Computer Science in Sport*, Shanghai, China.

O'Donoghue, P.G. and Holmes, L. (2015) *Data analysis in sport*, London: Routledge.

O'Donoghue, P.G., Holmes, L. and Robinson, G. (2017) *Doing a research project in sport performance analysis*, London: Routledge.

Olsen, E. (1981) *Fotball taktikk*, Oslo, Norway: Norwegian School of Sport Sciences.

Passos, P. (2017) 'Team member interaction analysis', In P. Passos, D. Araújo and A. Volossovitch (eds.), *Performance analysis in team sports* (pp. 74–109), London: Routledge.

Perl, J., Tilp, M., Baca, A. and Memmert, D. (2013) 'Neural networks for analysing sports games', In T. McGarry, P.G. O'Donoghue and J. Sampaio (eds.), *Routledge handbook of sports performance analysis* (pp. 237–247), London: Routledge.

Pfeiffer, M. and Perl, J. (2006) 'Analysis of tactical structures in team handball by means of artificial neural networks', *International Journal of Computer Science in Sport*, 5(1): 4–14.

Strudwick, A. (2016) *Soccer science*, Champaign, IL: Human Kinetics.

Worthington, E. (1980) *Teaching soccer skills*, London: Henry Kimpton Publishers Ltd.

CHAPTER 7

MACHINE LEARNING AND SPORTS

INTRODUCTION

This chapter provides a rationale for applying artificial intelligence (AI), especially to pattern recognition tasks in which statistical techniques are difficult to apply. The chapter introduces the wider area of machine learning using the example of injury data analysis. Supervised and unsupervised learning are differentiated, as are the various decision-making tasks. AI approaches including association rules, relation learning, graph-based approaches and semantic webs are covered. The chapter then describes various types of neural networks and deep learning, identifying general purpose toolkits that can be used. Critically important within the section on artificial neural networks are data dimension reduction tasks done in preparation for neural network analysis. These include factor and principle components analyses.

ChyronHego, Prozone and other such companies have developed hardware and software enabling data gathering on a large scale about ball sports. Mounted around the sports venue in question, whether a basketball court or football ground, is optical tracking hardware sufficiently sophisticated to track the velocities of balls and players encountered in these sports. This provides a great opportunity for sports analysts to gain critical insights into their team's performance, which could translate to a competitive edge over rivals. There is therefore a need for automated techniques to code events (Jonsson et al., 2006) and analyze data collected about sports matches. This chapter includes techniques from statistics and its close cousin, machine learning.

134

Pre-processing of image/video data into human activities (Cho et al., 2017; Raman and Maybank, 2015; Yi et al., 2017; Ziaeefard and Bergevin, 2015), or even determining intermediate steps such as derivation of meaningful *optical flow fields* (Eweiwi et al., 2014; Gómez-Conde and Olivieri, 2015; Mehmood et al., 2009), is difficult. Extracted from videos, an optical flow field is the estimation of motion derived from sequences of ordered images. Other data likely to be encountered are those from various sensors (accelerometer, GPS, etc), which likewise present their own specific issues for pre-processing (Liu et al., 2015).

There is a significant gap between low-level sensor data and the desired extrapolated high-level concepts features. Present analytical systems operating on the raw video feed usually employ various levels of scale from which these concepts and features are extracted, resulting in a significant overhead of computing resources (Sigari et al., 2016). Any representation that offers reduction of computation or is capable of delivering a higher-level understanding is of great benefit. For instance, Tzelepis et al. (2016) note the significant effort put into representation of what constitutes an "event" and how to reason with the generated concepts, and they review the approaches this concept receives in the text, visual and audio fields.

STATISTICAL TECHNIQUES

Clustering technologies

Statistics, and its close cousin artificial intelligence (AI), contain many similar technologies; for instance, clustering technologies can be found in both. Whereas cluster and factor analyses (Everitt et al., 2011) are found in statistics, neural networks and other approaches are found in AI. All these can be gainfully applied to sports data, including ways of extracting factors (dimensions), clusters and kernels from the data. Clustering can clearly provide valuable insights – we have seen in the chapter on geospatial techniques the notion of "hotspots" providing valuable visual information about a dataset. However, we noted that where the gradient begins that indicates the outline of a "hotspot" or "kernel" is subject to argument. Knauf (2014) and Knauf et al. (2016) use a kernel-based approach to clustering trajectories on team tactics in soccer, represented as a set of time/positions-tuples. They use their approach to represent, find and compare groups of related trajectories. The authors note specific challenges with pre-processing this data because they are noisy and often unstructured due to the continuous nature of the game and individual short-term aims of the players.

Dimensionality reduction

The more dimensions a dataset has, the more data required to create a good model, whether it is a decision tree or any other kind of classifier. This is the so-called curse of dimensionality, and so a common procedure is to use a technique to reduce the dimensionality while maintaining as much variance as possible. This is true for any area of data analytics and we find this also in feature-based action recognition.

Various approaches can be taken, such as principal components analysis (PCA) or factor analysis, or the reduction to just two dimensions in multidimensional scaling (MDS) (Coxon and Davies, 1982). MDS is an alternative to factor analysis and has the added benefit of projecting into two dimensions, enabling a visual inspection and determination of meaningful axes. Whatever approach is taken – factor analysis, PCA or MDS – it is important to note a limitation in the separation of the phases: reducing the dimensionality and subsequently clustering. By separating these stages, dimensionality reduction, the first stage, might not contain the features useful for the second stage of classification. Additionally, a technique like PCA does not consider the importance of class separability. This has led to certain approaches that attempt to combine the pre-processing and machine learning stages (Kong et al., 2011) into a single process with dimension reduction optimized for class separability.

Survival analysis for sports injuries

Survival analysis, or failure time analysis, was developed primarily in the health sciences (Kleinbaum and Klein, 2012) to model the time periods within which a population sample "succumbs" to an event, or indeed whether they "survive" to the end of the study period. Consider a set of rugby players, some of whom have suffered a concussion in their list of sports injuries. Survival analysis can tell us whether the concussion leads players to be more susceptible to future injuries compared to those who were not concussed. In fact, a high proportion of professional rugby union players sustain multiple injuries over consecutive seasons, and this particular statistical technology can be used to measure this (Moore et al., 2017). Of the common injuries, concussion has the highest match injury incidence (Gardner et al., 2014; Holtzhausen et al., 2006).

Data mining and machine learning

As previously detailed in other chapters, the field of data mining is concerned with finding patterns, associations, clusters and similarities in a set of data. There are many disparate data mining techniques, derived in the main from AI models but also from statistics and mathematics. Data mining is actually the last stage of the *knowledge discovery from databases* process, which is concerned in the earlier stages with data pre-processing, cleaning, transformation and so on. These demand significant efforts regardless of the dataset being mined.

The more data, the more significant the pre-processing stages; certainly with videos of sporting events, the volume of data is huge and this is a significant challenge (Hosseini and Eftekhari-Moghadam, 2013). Pre-processing invariably includes screening out of insignificant or redundant data; in the case of videos, this means removing frames. Only those sections of video that contain important events – for instance, rucks, mauls and tackles in rugby – might be included in a certain analysis to focus on the salient semantic parts and facilitate faster processing. Other analyses might demand a different extraction of features for detection of specific events. An interesting approach is to use the increase in sound (from the cheering of spectators) in a video sequence to indicate frames that contain significant events to be used in the following modelling process (Kolekar et al., 2009).

Previously, we looked at geospatial and spatiotemporal aspects of sports data, whereas this section includes modelling technologies from machine learning and artificial intelligence.

The modelling phase of a data mining system has the ability to generate patterns or rules, not all of which constitute discovery of useful knowledge; in fact, in all likelihood, most patterns are not interesting. Therefore, it is important to explicitly state what kinds of patterns are

137

indeed interesting. Han and Kamber (2011) define a pattern as *interesting* if:

- It can be easily understood by humans.
- It is valid (within acceptable parameters) when presented with unseen data.
- It is both useful and novel.

An interesting pattern represents knowledge; however, it takes a domain expert to review the pattern and decide whether it is actually new knowledge, useful to the task at hand, unlike the many uninteresting patterns (or rules, or networks, etc) that have also been generated.

In certain situations, generating all rules or patterns will result in a prohibitive number to review; therefore, a measure can be refined to reduce these numbers. There are many measures of interestingness; for instance, based on the concepts of support (how many datapoints are affected) and confidence (likelihood of truth), values for which the knowledge engineer sets acceptable thresholds. Additionally, new knowledge could be defined as something that might be unexpected, which causes a revision of concepts or offers strategic insights. Therefore, there may be a mixture of objective and subjective measures employed to generate what is hoped to be the most relevant and useful set of patterns. For instance, data mining of association rules makes use of interestingness measures and other constraints to maximise the relevance of the derived rules.

Fayyad et al. (1996) define the following categories of data mining:

- Classification: the output class is known (termed "supervised") and the task is to determine if a mapping from the input features to these classes exists. For instance, neural networks, decision trees and naïve Bayes approaches fall into this category.
- Clustering: in this case, there are no known output classes; instead, the focus is on determining whether certain data can be grouped or clustered together based on a form of similarity. Termed "unsupervised" because of the lack of output classes. Neural networks again fall into this category, such as self-organising maps (Kohonen networks), and the many forms of clustering known in statistics.
- Series analysis: this data is time stamped, providing a sequence of events or values over time. Han and Kamber (2011) detail important classes used to describe time-series data: movements over a long

138

time scale; variations of cyclical movements; variations of seasonal movements; and movements that have no pattern, or are seemingly random. Using this categorisation, it should be possible to make various time-forecasting predictions.

■ Association: association rules model links between two or more features; for instance, *"if player_speed >20 and player_skills > 15 then scoregoals"*. Each rule is associated with values of confidence and support (defined previously).

RULE-BASED APPROACH

Recall from the earlier chapter the high-level rule (McQueen et al., 2014) based upon low-level features derived from positional data:

Automatically Recognizing On-Ball Screen
IF [
there is a player who is dribbling the ball (i.e. the ball-handler)
AND there is an offensive player within 10 feet of the ball-handler (i.e. the screener)
AND the screener is not in or near the paint (see in-set figure for definition of "near")
AND the screener is no more than 2 ft. further from the basket than the ball-handler is
AND there is a defensive player <= 12 ft. from the ball-handler (i.e. the on-ball defender)
AND the basketball is not in the paint] for >=13 consecutive frames
AND the ball-handler is the same for every frame THEN
identify as action

Fuzzy rules also exist (Dubois and Prade, 1996), which are variants of the rule-based "if-then" construction because they include linguistic variables. They are inspired by the human mind's ability to manage uncertainty and there are no discrete values, just membership in the sets defined by the linguistics variables, e.g. slow, medium and fast – see Figure 7.1.

Lim et al. (2015) present a review of fuzzy set-oriented approaches to human motion analysis. Similarly, Hosseini and Eftekhari-Moghadam (2013) apply a fuzzy rule approach for detecting events and marking up

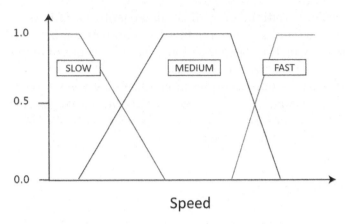

Figure 7.1 Fuzzy membership for player speed

of soccer video data. The inputs to their system are 11 visual features and several audio features. These are considered suitable and effective enough to cover most semantic events taking place in soccer games. Visual features include ASR "Detection of jersey block based on face block location", SBCP "Detection of straight bar in corner point using Hough transform" and PGA "Computation of Hue histogram". These are then used to derive fuzzy rules such as the following:

Rules from low-level visual features
(1) If ASR is High Then Event is Offside
(2) If ASR is Low And SBCP is High Then Event is Corner
(3) If ASR is Low And SBCP is Low And PGA is High Then Event is Goal-A
(4) If ASR is Low And SBCP is Low And PGA is Low And PGB is High Then Event is Goal-B

Motivated by the need for transparency over neural networks and support vector machines (SVMs), Song and Hagras (2016, 2017) also utilise fuzzy logic-based systems for video event activity detection within long video sequences of soccer games. An important feature is measuring similarities between two temporal sequences, which may vary in speed.

140

Association rules

We previously defined association rules, or link analysis, also known as *affinity analysis* or *association* with the features of support and confidence. Discovery of rules for video indexing, summarisation, classification and semantic event detection are documented in Vijayakumar and Nedunchezhian (2012).

Verhein and Chawla (2006) define association rules related to spatiotemporal data. These spatiotemporal association rules, or STARs, describe how entities move between regions over time. The technique divides the space into regions and the algorithm then searches for interesting ones, defined as a large number of entities leaving (sink), entering (source) or entering and leaving (thoroughfare). See Figure 7.2 for a definition of "interesting" patterns or rules.

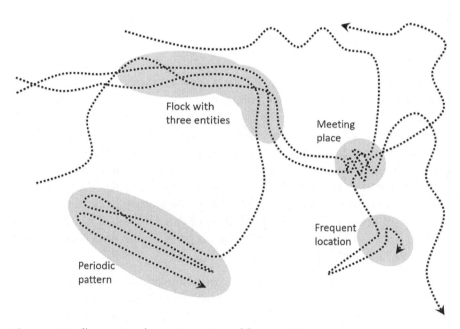

Figure 7.2 Illustrating the trajectories of four entities moving over 20 time steps

DECISION TREE CLASSIFICATION RULES

Decision trees are a classification technique that uses repeated decisions over specific attributes, and depending on the evaluation of the test, a branching occurs. Hence, little by little, a tree-like structure is built up. At the ends of the branching are leaf nodes, which are the actual classification of the data that meets all the decisions along the way. Having built the model, it is possible to prune it to make it more general but, in any case, the tree can be used by pushing data through the repeated test/decisions until finally reaching an end node, which then becomes the classification.

Catal et al. (2015) utilise a decision tree for accelerometer-based activity recognition as one of their classifiers. Their machine learning task is to recognise physical activities such as sitting, walking and jogging performed by humans from raw accelerometer data. In addition to the decision tree, they also use neural network and statistical techniques (e.g. logistic regression).

INDUCTIVE LOGIC PROGRAMMING

Inductive logic programming (ILP) is a well-known framework for representing and reasoning with relational data. A significant benefit is that complex domain knowledge can be encoded as constants, variables and predicates (facts or clauses, representing relations between variables) and various inferencing methods can be used to learn new knowledge. ILP can be presented with a series of negative and positive examples and can incorporate a model that classifies them accordingly. An example of using ILP for its representation of rich, relational forms is characterising scoring chances (Van Haaren et al., n.d.; Van Haaren et al., 2015). An example of a variable is Player p_i and that of a predicate, $Pass(p_i, p_j)$.

Again, a complete match is split into subsequences of interesting events. These are then split into a number of phases, such as starting with a throw-in or free kick and ending when a foul is made or when the ball goes out of play. A positive example is when the team manages to take a shot and all else is represented as a negative example. For instance, *shot(Phase)* indicates whether a shot was attempted in a phase (*Phase*). Predicates include *pass(Phase, Player1, Player2, Zone1,*

142

Zone2); for example, in a *Phase*, *Player1* in *Zone1* passed the ball to *Player2* in *Zone2*, cross(*Phase*, *Player1*, *Player2*, *Zone1*, *Zone2*) and *set_piece(Phase, Player1, Player2, Zone1, Zone2)* have similar meanings.

GRAPH-BASED APPROACHES

Graph-based approaches are based on entities and their relationships, or nodes and edges. The entities may be sports player locations, events or other features. The entities are associated by way of the relationships between them.

Moving away from event detection in sports video analysis, Zhu et al. (2009) focus on tactic analysis using a graph-based method. Based on the multi-object trajectories, a weighted graph is constructed (in which values are assigned to edges) via the analysis of interaction between the ball and the players. From the weighted graph, an aggregate trajectory is calculated.

Passing patterns have also been studied, such as analysing strategies by building occupancy maps based on ball movements (Lucey et al., 2013).

Team activity data can also be represented as a network (Kostakis et al., 2017) but this time, the network is temporal; in fact, it is a sequence of time-stamped edges that capture interactions between players. The nodes in the network represent states. The edges represent transitions between the nodes. There is a small set of node operations that facilitates transitions between these nodes. The problem is then to identify the various team gameplays and map them to the various segments.

Zhu et al. (2013) model multi-object interactions using a "string of feature graphs". These elements use a graph-based spectral technique and a dynamic programming scheme for working with the complete strings.

TEXT DATA AND NATURAL LANGUAGE PROCESSING

Natural language processing (NLP) is a field that cross-cuts computer science, artificial intelligence and computational linguistics, and is concerned with the interactions between computers and human, or so-called "natural", languages.

Different from the state-of-the-art sports video analysis methods that heavily rely on audio/visual features, approaches like Montoliu et al.'s (2015b) and Xu et al.'s (2008) incorporate web-casting or author-topic model text into sports video analysis.

The approach taken by Montoliu et al. (2015a) is based on pattern recognition and machine learning techniques. The strategy used is based on the Bag-of-Words (BoW) technique and characterizes short football video clips. These explain the team performance and train advanced classifiers in automatic recognition of team activities. They define specific football actions such as Ball Possession, Quick Attack and Set Piece.

NEURAL NETWORKS AND DEEP LEARNING

A neural network is modelled after the biological network of cells in the human brain. It consists of several layers of nodes, each node having the ability to take inputs and pass on an output signal. Each input has a factor that determines the amount of influence it will have on the output.

An example of supervised learning, recurrent neural networks are applied to basketball trajectories (Shah and Romijnders, 2016) to predict whether a three-point shot will be successful. The models are capable of learning the trajectory of a basketball without any physics knowledge.

In unsupervised learning, the system only receives input information without any direction on expected output. The system learns to classify patterns based on those it has been exposed to during unsupervised learning. There are many types of unsupervised networks, including self-organizing maps (SOMs, or Kohonen networks), Grossberg nets, instar, outstar, bi-directional associational maps and Hopfield networks. For example, in two studies, recurrent (Sun et al., 2016) and hierarchical (Ding et al., 2016) self-organizing maps are applied to human activity prediction.

Ijjina and Krishna Mohan (2016) apply *deep neural networks* to human action recognition. They developed a hybrid deep neural network model, referred to as a homogeneous convolutional neural network (CNN). The group of classifiers employed by the neural network is built by distinguishing the input features and varying initial weights.

REFERENCES

Catal, C., Tufekci, S., Pirmit, E. and Kocabag, G. (2015) 'On the use of ensemble of classifiers for accelerometer-based activity recognition', *Applied Soft Computing Journal*, 37: 1018–1022. https://doi.org/10.1016/j.asoc.2015.01.025

Cho, N.G., Park, S.H., Park, J.S., Park, U. and Lee, S.W. (2017) 'Compositional interaction descriptor for human interaction recognition', *Neurocomputing*, 267: 169–181. https://doi.org/10.1016/j.neucom.2017.06.009

Coxon, A.P.M. and Davies, P.M. (1982) *The user's guide to multidimensional scaling: With special reference to the MDS(X) library of computer programs*, London and Exeter, NH: Heinemann Educational Books. file://catalog.hathi trust.org/Record/000769244

Ding, W., Liu, K., Cheng, F. and Zhang, J. (2016) 'Learning hierarchical spatio-temporal pattern for human activity prediction', *Journal of Visual Communication and Image Representation*, 35: 103–111. https://doi.org/10.1016/j.jvcir.2015.12.006

Dubois, D. and Prade, H. (1996) 'What are fuzzy rules and how to use them', *Fuzzy Sets and Systems*, 84(2): 169–185. https://doi.org/10.1016/0165-0114(96)00066-8

Everitt, B.S., Landau, S., Leese, M. and Stahl, D. (2011) 'Cluster analysis', *Quality and Quantity*, 14. https://doi.org/10.1007/BF00154794

Eweiwi, A., Cheema, M.S. and Bauckhage, C. (2014) 'Learning spatial interest regions from videos to inform action recognition in still images', *CEUR Workshop Proceedings*, 1226: 137–147. https://doi.org/10.1016/j.patrec.2014.07.017

Fayyad, U., Piatetsky-Shapiro, G. and Smyth, P. (1996) 'From data mining to knowledge discovery in databases', *AI Magazine*, 17(3): 37. https://doi.org/10.1609/aimag.v17i3.1230

Gardner, A.J., Iverson, G.L., Williams, W.H., Baker, S. and Stanwell, P. (2014) 'A systematic review and meta-analysis of concussion in rugby union', *Sports Medicine (Auckland, N.Z.)*, 44(12): 1717–1731. https://doi.org/10.1007/s40279-014-0233-3

Gómez-Conde, I. and Olivieri, D.N. (2015) 'A KPCA spatio-temporal differential geometric trajectory cloud classifier for recognizing human actions in a CBVR system', *Expert Systems with Applications*, 42(13): 5472–5490. https://doi.org/10.1016/j.eswa.2015.03.010

Gudmundsson, J., Laube, P. and Wolle, T. (2008) 'Movement patterns in spatiotemporal data', In S. Shekhar and H. Xiong (eds.), *Encyclopedia of GIS* (pp. 726–732), Berlin: Springer. www.springerlink.com/content/h01539/#section=145928&page=1

Han, J. and Kamber, M. (2011) *Data mining: Concepts and techniques*, Vol. 12, Elsevier. https://doi.org/10.1007/978-3-642-19721-5

Holtzhausen, L.J., Schwellnus, M.P., Jakoet, I. and Pretorius, A.L. (2006) 'The incidence and nature of injuries in South African rugby players in the Rugby Super 12 competition', *South African Medical Journal = Suid-Afrikaanse Tydskrif Vir Geneeskunde*, 96(12): 1260–1265.

Hosseini, M.S. and Eftekhari-Moghadam, A.M. (2013) 'Fuzzy rule-based reasoning approach for event detection and annotation of broadcast soccer video',

Applied Soft Computing Journal, 13(2): 846–866. https://doi.org/10.1016/j. asoc.2012.10.007

Ijjina, E.P. and Krishna Mohan, C. (2016) 'Hybrid deep neural network model for human action recognition', *Applied Soft Computing Journal*, 46: 936–952. https://doi.org/10.1016/j.asoc.2015.08.025

Jonsson, G.K., Anguera, M.T., Blanco-Villaseñor, Á., Luis Losada, J., Hernández-Mendo, A., Ardá, T., . . . Castellano, J. (2006) 'Hidden patterns of play interaction in soccer using SOF-CODER', *Behavior Research Methods*, 38(3): 372–381. https://doi.org/10.3758/BF03192790

Kleinbaum, D.G. and Klein, M. (2012) *Survival analysis*, New York, NY: Springer.

Knauf, K. (2014) 'Spatio-temporal convolution kernels for clustering trajectories', *2014 KDD Workshop on Large-Scale Sports Analytics, New York, NY, USA*, 25 August 2014.

Knauf, K., Memmert, D. and Brefeld, U. (2016) 'Spatio-temporal convolution kernels', *Machine Learning*, 102(2): 247–273. https://doi.org/10.1007/s10994-015-5520-1

Kolekar, M.H., Sengupta, S. and Seetharaman, G. (2009) 'Semantic concept mining based on hierarchical event detection for soccer video indexing', *Journal of Multimedia*, 4(5): 298–312.

Kong, Y., Zhang, X., Hu, W. and Jia, Y. (2011) 'Adaptive learning codebook for action recognition', *Pattern Recognition Letters*, 32(8): 1178–1186. https://doi.org/10.1016/j.patrec.2011.03.006

Kostakis, O., Tatti, N. and Gionis, A. (2017) 'Discovering recurring activity in temporal networks', *Data Mining and Knowledge Discovery*, 31. New York, NY: Springer. https://doi.org/10.1007/s10618-017-0515-0

Lim, C.H., Vats, E. and Chan, C.S. (2015) 'Fuzzy human motion analysis: A review', *Pattern Recognition*, 48(5): 1773–1796. https://doi.org/10.1016/j.patcog.2014.11.016

Liu, L., Peng, Y., Liu, M. and Huang, Z. (2015) 'Sensor-based human activity recognition system with a multilayered model using time series shapelets', *Knowledge-Based Systems*, 90: 138–152. https://doi.org/10.1016/j.knosys.2015.09.024

Lucey, P., Oliver, D., Carr, P., Roth, J. and Matthews, I. (2013) 'Assessing team strategy using spatiotemporal data', *KDD*, 1366. https://doi.org/10.1145/2487575.2488191

McQueen, A., Wiens, J. and Guttag, J. (2014). 'Automatically recognizing on-ball screens', *2014 MIT Sloan Sports Analytics Conference, Boston, MA, USA*, 28 February–01 March 2014 .

Mehmood, K., Mrak, M., Calic, J. and Kondoz, A. (2009) 'Object tracking in surveillance videos using compressed domain features from scalable bitstreams', *Signal Processing: Image Communication*, 24(10): 814–824. https://doi.org/10.1016/j.image.2009.06.006

Montoliu, R., Martin-Félez, R., Torres-Sospedra, J. and Martinez-Usé, A. (2015a) 'Team activity recognition in Association Football using a Bag-of-Words-based method', *Human Movement Science*, 41: 165–178. https://doi.org/10.1016/j.humov.2015.03.007

146

Montoliu, R., Martín-Félez, R., Torres-Sospedra, J. and Rodríguez-Pérez, S. (2015b) 'ATM-based analysis and recognition of handball team activities', *Neurocomputing*, 150(Part A): 189–199. https://doi.org/10.1016/j.neucom.2014.09.053

Moore, I.S., Mount, S., Mathema, P. and Ranson, C. (2017) 'Application of the subsequent injury categorisation model for longitudinal injury surveillance in elite rugby and cricket: Intersport comparisons and inter-rater reliability of coding', *British Journal of Sports Medicine*, Published Online First: 01 March 2017. https://doi.org/10.1136/bjsports-2016-097040

Raman, N. and Maybank, S.J. (2015) 'Action classification using a discriminative multilevel HDP-HMM', *Neurocomputing*, 154: 149–161. https://doi.org/10.1016/j.neucom.2014.12.009

Shah, R.C. and Romijnders, R. (2016) 'Applying deep learning to basketball trajectories', *KDD '16*, 4. https://doi.org/10.475/123

Sigari, M.-H., Soltanian-Zadeh, H. and Pourreza, H.-R. (2016) 'A framework for dynamic restructuring of semantic video analysis systems based on learning attention control', *Image and Vision Computing*, 53: 20–34. https://doi.org/10.1016/j.imavis.2015.07.004

Song, W. and Hagras, H. (2016) 'A big-bang big-crunch type-2 fuzzy logic based system for soccer video scene classification', *FUZZ-IEEE'16*, 2059–2066.

Song, W. and Hagras, H. (2017) 'A type-2 fuzzy logic system for event detection in soccer videos', *IEEE International Conference on Fuzzy Systems, Naples, Italy*, 9–12 July 2017. https://doi.org/10.1109/FUZZ-IEEE.2017.8015426

Sun, Q., Liu, H., Liu, M. and Zhang, T. (2016) 'Human activity prediction by mapping grouplets to recurrent Self-Organizing Map', *Neurocomputing*, 177: 427–440. https://doi.org/10.1016/j.neucom.2015.11.061

Tzelepis, C., Ma, Z., Mezaris, V., Ionescu, B., Kompatsiaris, I., Boato, G., . . . Yan, S. (2016) 'Event-based media processing and analysis: A survey of the literature', *Image and Vision Computing*, 53: 3–19. https://doi.org/10.1016/j.imavis.2016.05.005

Van Haaren, J., Dzyuba, V., Hannosset, S. and Davis, J. (2015) 'Automatically discovering offensive patterns in soccer match data', *Lecture Notes in Computer Science (Including Subseries Lecture Notes in Artificial Intelligence and Lecture Notes in Bioinformatics)*, 9385: 286–297. https://doi.org/10.1007/978-3-319-24465-5_25

Van Haaren, J., Hannosset, S. and Davis, J. (n.d.) 'Strategy discovery in professional soccer match data', *KDD-16 Workshop on Large-Scale Sports Analytics, San Francisco, California, USA*, 14 August 2016.

Verhein, F. and Chawla, S. (2006) 'Mining spatio-temporal association rules, sources, sinks, stationary regions and thoroughfares in object mobility databases', *Lecture Notes in Computer Science (Including Subseries Lecture Notes in Artificial Intelligence and Lecture Notes in Bioinformatics)*, 3882(574): 187–201. https://doi.org/10.1007/11733836_15

Vijayakumar, V. and Nedunchezhian, R. (2012) 'Mining video association rules based on weighted temporal concepts', *International Journal of Computer Science Issues*, 9(4): 297–303. www.engineeringvillage.com/share/document.url?mid=cpx_17fa65e13b8c077a32M4d322061377553&database=cpx

Xu, C., Wang, J., Lu, H. and Zhang, Y. (2008) 'A novel framework for semantic annotation and personalized retrieval of sports video'. *IEEE Transactions on Multimedia*, 10(3): 421–436. https://doi.org/10.1109/TMM.2008.917346

Yi, Y., Cheng, Y. and Xu, C. (2017) 'Mining human movement evolution for complex action recognition', *Expert Systems with Applications*, 78: 259–272. https://doi.org/10.1016/j.eswa.2017.02.020

Zhu, G., Xu, C., Huang, Q., Rui, Y., Jiang, S., Gao, W. and Yao, H. (2009) 'Event tactic analysis based on broadcast sports video', *IEEE Transactions on Multimedia*, 11(1): 49–67. https://doi.org/10.1109/TMM.2008.2008918

Zhu, Y., Nayak, N., Gaur, U., Song, B. and Roy-Chowdhury, A. (2013) 'Modeling multi-object interactions using "string of feature graphs"', *Computer Vision and Image Understanding*, 117(10): 1313–1328. https://doi.org/10.1016/j.cviu.2012.08.009

Ziaeefard, M. and Bergevin, R. (2015) 'Semantic human activity recognition: A literature review', *Pattern Recognition*, 48(8): 2329–2345. https://doi.org/10.1016/j.patcog.2015.03.006

CHAPTER 8

GENOMICS IN SPORTS

INTRODUCTION

This chapter provides a gentle introduction to genetics and discusses the processes of analysing genomics data to identify markers and pathways and their potential value in sports. Identification of genomics markers linked to biological processes crucial for sports performance, such as those related to metabolism and muscle development, are particularly useful to decision making in sports science. The chapter also provides a hands-on activity to analyse sample genomic data for two individuals.

BRIEF INTRODUCTION TO GENOMICS

All of us carry genetic information that influences our physical and behavioural characteristics. For example, genes may decide eye colour, muscle strength or the way we respond to treatment. This genetic information is stored at about 3 billion positions that each contains two characters. However, unlike English language, which consists of 26 characters, nature encodes all genetic information with just four characters: A, C, T and G. These four letters A C T G, called *nucleotides* Adenine (A) Cytosine (C) Guanine (G) and Thymine (T), are basically organic molecules consisting of the elements carbon, nitrogen, hydrogen and oxygen. The 3 billion positions are arranged as a set of 23 *chromosomes*. Every human has two pairs of 23 chromosomes (a total of 46 chromosomes). A particular location in the genome can be identified by

Table 8.1 Genome and bases inherited from parents

Position in genome	1 2 3 4 5 6 7 . . 3 billionth position (approx)
Base inherited from mother	T A G A C A T . . .
Base inherited from father	G A T A C A T . . .

two numbers: first, the chromosome number and, second, the position within the chromosome. The regions in the genome that code for proteins are known as *genes*.

At each of the 3 billion positions on the human genome, one will find a set of two characters out of A, C, T and G. These characters are called *bases*. There are only two characters at every position because one is inherited from the mother and another from the father. This set of two characters is called a *genotype*. Table 8.1 shows a genome example of an individual with bases inherited from parents. This genome can also be represented as "(T/G), (A/A), (G/T), (A/A), (C/C), (A/A), (T/T) . . . 3 billionth position".

For this individual, the genotype at position 1 is "T/G"; "T" must have been inherited from the mother and "G" must have been inherited from the father. Similarly, the genotype at position 2 is "A/A", "A" having been inherited from both the mother and father.

On average, the genome of one individual is 99.5% similar to that of another, which means all humans carry almost identical genetic information. However, at about 0.5% of the locations in the genome, individuals carry different genotypes. Such differences are called *single nucleotide polymorphisms* (SNPs) and, because of these, no two humans are completely identical.

The following is an example of the genomes of two individuals. These genomes differ at positions 1 and 6. At the first position in the genome, the first individual has genotype T/T (T from the mother and T from the father) and the second individual has genotype T/G (T from the mother and G from the father). At the sixth position, the first individual has genotype C/C (C from the mother and C from the father) and the second individual has genotype C/T (C from the mother and T from the father). So if the genome of individual 1 is treated as a reference genome, the genome of individual 2 will have SNPs at locations 1 and 6.

150

Individual 1 **(T/T)**, (A/G), (G/A), (A/T), (C/T), **(C/C)**, (T/A) . . . 3 billionth position

Individual 2 **(T/G)**, (A/G), (G/A), (A/T), (C/T), **(C/T)**, (T/A) . . . 3 billionth position

Phenotype is another commonly used term in genomics, meaning a physical characteristic. For example, some commonly found phenotypes in elite sports persons are greater body and appendicular lean mass, strong muscles that can powerfully contract at high speeds and an efficient cardiovascular system. There is a strong relationship between phenotypes and genotypes. Differences in genotypes may lead to differences in phenotypes. Note that all genomic positions in this book are based upon the Homo sapien (human) genome build 38, also known as GRCh38 (available from www.ncbi.nlm.nih.gov/assembly/GCF_000001405.37, accessed 28/11/17).

USE OF GENOMICS IN SPORTS

Nature versus nurture has been a long running debate and nurture undoubtedly plays an important part towards success in sports (Baker and Farrow, 2015). However, this chapter is focused on nature and how it may be used in sports. As discussed in the previous section, differences in genotypes can lead to changes in phenotypes. It is important to identify genotypes or genome markers associated with phenotypes that are significant in sports. Such genome markers can then be used in sports for talent identification, developing personalised training and nutritional programmes and personalised treatment for injuries. A major international initiative to find and validate genomic markers of athletic performance is led by the Athlome Project Consortium (Pitsiladis et al., 2016).

A number of genomic locations or genes have been linked to phenotypes important for sports. Guilherme et al. (2014) and Guth and Roth (2013) provide an excellent summary of developments on using genetics for sports. For example, it has been shown that the ACTN3 gene affects muscle performance, the FTO gene affects body and appendicular lean mass and the ACE and PPARGC1A genes affect cardiovascular performance. A study by Del et al. (2017) found that individuals with "T" at location 66,560,624 on chromosome 11 are more likely to have muscle injury during a competitive sport. A similar study by Del et al. (2017b) shows that such individuals are more likely to damage their skeletal muscles during marathons. Another study by Qi et al. (2016) indicates that such individuals are more likely to have non-acute ankle sprains during sports.

A survey conducted by Bray et al. (2009) found 214 genes associated with physical performance and health-related fitness phenotypes. A more recent survey by Ahmetov et al. (2015) found 120 genomic markers associated with elite sports performance.

The ACTN3 gene, known for regulating muscle performance, is a well-known sports gene located from position 66,546,395 to 66,563,329 on chromosome 11. It produces muscle protein alpha-actinin-3, which helps muscles powerfully contract at high speeds. Three genotypes, namely C/C, C/T and T/C, are found at position 66,560,624 on this gene. Research has shown that individuals with the C/C genotype at this location will have better performing muscles and are predisposed to be sprinters whereas individuals with the T/T genotype at this location will have impaired muscle performance and are likely to be endurance athletes (Gineviciene et al., 2016; Yang et al., 2003).

Another prominent sports gene is the ACE gene, which is known for cardiovascular performance and adaptation to physical strain. It is located from position 63,477,061 to 63,498,380 on chromosome 17 and produces the angiotensin I-converting enzyme. At location 63,488,529 on this gene, there could either be insertion or deletion of the ALU repetitive element "ATACAGTCACTTTTTTTTTTTTTTTTGAGACGGAGTCTCGCT CTGTCGCC". Research has shown that individuals with insertion of the repetitive element will have higher strength and power and are predisposed for athletics.

Other examples of sports genes are the FTO gene associated with greater body and appendicular lean mass (Heffernan et al., 2017) and the PPARGC1A gene associated with higher aerobic capacity (Eynon et al., 2010). Some of these sports gene markers are so prominent that many private companies have commercialised them, offering sports genetic tests (Rivard, 2013) for as little as 80 USD. Table 8.2 lists a set of well-known sports genes and Table 8.3 provides some commercial companies offering sports gene testing.

152

Table 8.2 List of sports genes (ordered by observation of commercial use)

Gene	Full name	SNP ID	Alleles	Endurance allele or genotype	Reference for study	Function	Location
ACTN3	lpha actinin 3	rs1815739	C, T	C/C: Better performing muscles. T/T: Impaired muscles	Yang et al. (2003); Gineviciene et al. (2016)	Regulates muscle performance; stabilizes muscle contractile apparatus in fast-twitch muscle fibres	Chr l1, 66560624
ACE	Angiotensin I converting enzyme (peptidyl-dipeptidase A)	rs1799752	Insertion/Deletion of an ALU repetitive element	I/I, I/D	Gineviciene et al. (2016)	Regulates cardiovascular performance and adaptation to physical strain	Chr 17, 63488529
PPARGC1A	Peroxisome proliferator-activated receptor gamma, coactivator 1 alpha	rs8192678	A, C	A	Eynon et al. (2010); Gineviciene et al. (2016)	Aerobic capacity; regulates fatty acid oxidation, glucose utilization, formation of muscle fibres	Chr 4, 23814039
PPARA	Peroxisome proliferator-activated receptor Peroxisome proliferator-activated receptor-alpha	rs4253778	G, C	G/C	Eynon et al. (2010)	Regulates liver, heart and skeletal muscle lipid metabolism, glucose homeostasis, cardiac hypertrophy	Chr 22, 46234737
FTO	Fat mass and obesity associated	rs9939609	A, T	T/T and T/A	Heffernan et al. (2017)	Greater body and appendicular lean mass	Chr 16, 53783615
NFIA-AS2	NFIA antisense RNA 2	rs1572312	C, A	C	Ahmetov et at. (2015)	Maximal oxygen consumption rate (V.O2max)	Chr 1, 60952057
TSHR	Thyroid stimulating hormone receptor	rs7144481	T, C	C	Ahmetov et at. (2015)	Involved in function of the thyroid gland and hormone balance	Chr 14, 81144598
RBFOX1	RNA binding fox-1 homolog 1	rs7191721	G, A	G	Ahmetov et at. (2015)	Oxygen consumption rate, aerobic performance	Chr 16, 7575790

Table 8.3 List of commercial companies offering sports gene testing

Company name and location	Name of test	Price as at April 2018	Genes test for variance	Link (all links accessed 28/11/17)
MyInnerGo Ltd, UK	Sport Gene Test	99 GBP	ACTN3	www.myinnergo.co.uk/products/sport-test
Asper Biogene Estonia, Europe	Athletic Performance Test	80 Euros	ACE, ACTN3	www.asperbio.com/sports-gene-test/asper-wellness/athletic-performance-test
Genomic Express California, USA	Inherited Traits – Athletic Performance tests	99 USD	ACTN3	https://www.genomicexpress.com/genetic-tests/inherited-traits/athletic-performance
Anabolic Genes, France	Fitness DNA Testing: Training and nutrition analysis	134 USD	ACE, ACTN3 and many others	https://anabolicgenes.com/en/entrainement.html
Dr Lal Pathlabs, India	Sports Gene Test	Not known	ACTN3	www.lalpathlabs.com/pathology-test/actn3-sports-gene-genotyping
23andme based in USA, offers test in UK	Health Test	149 GBP	ACTN3 and others	www.23andme.com/en-gb/gen101/variation/speed/
Athletigen Technologies, Canada	Muscular Fitness and other tests	79.99 USD	Not known	https://athletigen.com

STEPS IN ANALYSING GENOMICS DATA FOR SPORTS

The general steps to find SNPs will be explained using an example. Suppose the reference genome of an organism is "TAG A CAT". The first step in the process is to extract DNA from individuals and use a sequencing machine to get raw reads. As an example, the 10 reads from two individuals are as follows.

Reads for individual 1
Read   1 TAGA
Read   2 ACAT
Read   3 AGAC
Read   4 ACAT
Read   5 TAGA
Read   6 ACAT
Read   7 AGAC
Read   8 AGAC
Read   9 TAGA
Read   10 AGAC

Reads for individual 2
Read   1 GAGA
Read   2 ACAT
Read   3 AGAC
Read   4 ACAT
Read   5 GAGA
Read   6 ACAT
Read   7 AGAC
Read   8 AGAC
Read   9 GAGA
Read   10 AGAC

The first task is to align these reads to the reference genome, which is "TAG A CAT". Figures 8.1 and 8.2 show the alignment of these reads for individual 1 and individual 2 respectively. In Figure 8.1, at first position, there are three reads and all have T, so the consensus at position 1 is T. At second position, there are seven reads all having A, so the consensus read at position 2 is A. The more reads supporting a position, the higher the confidence in determining the consensus read. Similarly, the consensus reads at positions 3 to 7 are G, A, C, A and T, respectively. We have the highest confidence in determining the read at position 4, as it is supported

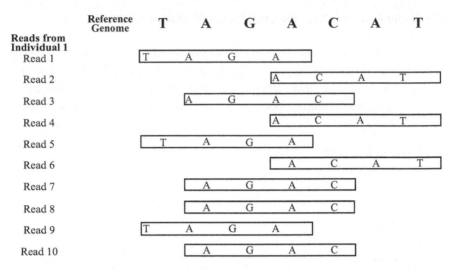

Figure 8.1 Mapping for individual 1

Reference Genome	T	A	G	A	C	A	T
Read 1	G	A	G	A			
Read 2				A	C	A	T
Read 3		A	G	A	C		
Read 4				A	C	A	T
Read 5	G	A	G	A			
Read 6				A	C	A	T
Read 7		A	G	A	C		
Read 8		A	G	A	C		
Read 9			G	A	G	A	
Read 10		A	G	A	C		

Figure 8.2 Mapping for individual 2

by the maximum number of reads, which is 10. So, based on these reads, the genome of individual 1 is "TAG A CAT", which is exactly the same as the reference genome; therefore, individual 1 has no mutation.

Figure 8.2 shows the mapping for individual 2. In this figure at first position, there are only two reads and all of them have G, so the consensus at position

1 is G. At second position, there are seven reads all having A, so the consensus read at position 2 is A. Similarly, the consensus reads at positions 3 to 7 are G, A, C, A and T, respectively. We have the highest confidence in determining the read at position 4, as it is supported by the maximum number of reads, which is 10. Position 5 is unique in the sense that one read at this position supports G and the remaining seven support C. However, as the majority of reads at this position support G, this makes it the consensus read.

Based on these reads, the genome of individual 2 is "GAG A CAT", which is different from the reference genome. Position 1 in the reference genome is T, whereas individual 2 has G. This makes position 1 a promising candidate for any differences, such as higher performing muscles, between individual 1 and individual 2.

Quality control

In the previous example, it seems individual 2 has G at the first position in the genome. However, there is another possibility. What if the sequencing machine has an error and two reads supporting G at first position are incorrect? We are only interested in genuine mutations and not false positives arising out of error in the sequencing process. This brings us to another important step in the process: quality control. Sequencing machines produce FastQ files containing reads and quality scores for each read. This quality score, formally known as a Phred score, indicates the confidence that the base has been correctly identified. A Phred score can generally range from 2 to 40 and a higher value indicates better quality reads. A Phred score of 30 means there is a 1 in 1,000 (which is 10 raised to the power of 3) probability of incorrect base assignment; in other words, the sequence machine is 99.9% sure that the base has been identified correctly. A Phred score of 10 indicates a 1 in 10 probability of incorrect assignment; in other words, the sequence machine is only 90% sure that the base has been identified correctly. Generally, we only include reads with a Phred score of 30 or more for analysis. Formally, the Phred score is -10 times the log to base 10 of the base-calling error probability.

The first step is to check the quality of the raw reads, which can be done using FastQC (Andrews, 2010). Figure 8.3 graphs the quality across all reads in a FastQ file. This FastQ file contains bacterial genome data, which has been generated and published by Jayal et al. (2017). The x-axis in the graph shows the base position and the y-axis shows the

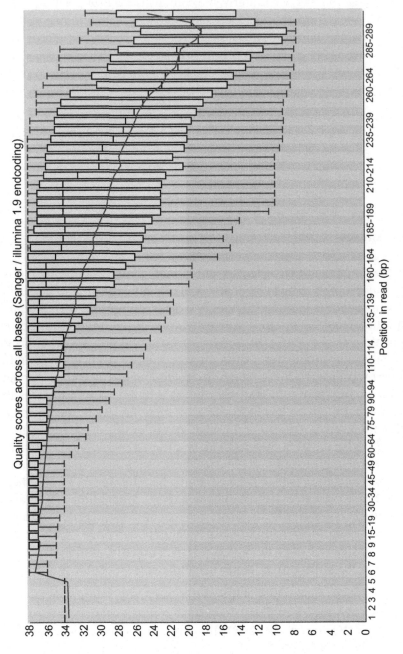

Figure 8.3 Graph for per base sequence quality of raw reads

quality score. A FastQ file has thousands of reads; therefore, the graph takes the average quality score for all reads at each base position and shows them as a box plot. So, in the given example, the first 160 bases are of very high quality with an average score of more than 30 but in the bases towards the end positions, the quality drops to less than 20. Andrews (2010) provides a detailed explanation of graphs generated by FastQC.

In this example, to ensure that only high-quality bases are used for analysis, we can trim the reads to 160 bases. Of course, we will lose many bases by trimming but we can be sure the analysis only contains high-quality reads. Other quality control measures include removing reads less than a certain size or of average quality less than a certain threshold. There is a trade-off between trimming (and other quality control measures) and the number of reads retained for analysis. Analysis using few reads may not be fruitful; therefore, we have to strike a balance between the quality control measures and the reads retained for analysis. The trimming of reads and other quality processing can be done using software such as Trimmomatic (Bolger et al., 2014) and Cutadapt (Martin, 2011). The graph after quality control measures is shown in Figure 8.4. Reads are now

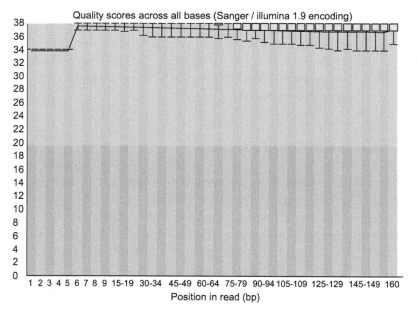

Figure 8.4 Graph showing per base sequence quality of reads post quality control stage

160 bases long and all bases have a quality score over 30, meaning we are 99.9% certain that bases have been identified correctly.

Mapping reads to a reference genome and visualisation

After processing genomics data for quality in the previous step, the reads are then aligned or mapped to a reference genome. There are a number of software programs available for alignment but Bowtie2 (Langmead and Salzberg, 2012) and BWA-Mem (Li and Durbin, 2009) remain two popular choices. An evaluation of various aligning software is available from Thankaswamy et al. (2017) and Pabinger et al. (2014).

The aligned reads can then be visualised using IGV software (Thorvaldsdóttir et al., 2013). Figure 8.5 shows an example of the aligned reads. The top row in this figure shows the base position. As can be seen in Figure 8.5, all reads at position 400 have base "A" but at position 401, some reads have "A" whereas others have "T".

The positions at which aligned reads differ from the reference genome, also known as SNP, can be extracted using variant calling softwares such as Freebayes (Garrison and Marth, 2012) and Varscan (Koboldt et al., 2012). Most SNPs detected are actually false positive and the real aim is to find the few that are indeed true positives. It is beyond the scope of this chapter to go into details but generally it involves hard filtering (such as removing SNPs supported by fewer reads) and running the analysis with multiple samples.

Genome-wide association studies

Having identified promising markers, it is important to test the wider population for any real link between these markers and sports performance. Such studies, known as genome-wide association studies, use genome sequences from large populations to find if a genome variation is linked with sports performance or other traits. Such a study includes two groups: the case group consisting of sports athletes and the control group consisting of individuals without any competitive sports experience. The odds ratio and statistical significance p-value is calculated for the variation in the case group compared to the control group. A p-value less than 5 times 10 to the power -8 (which is equal to .00000005) is

160

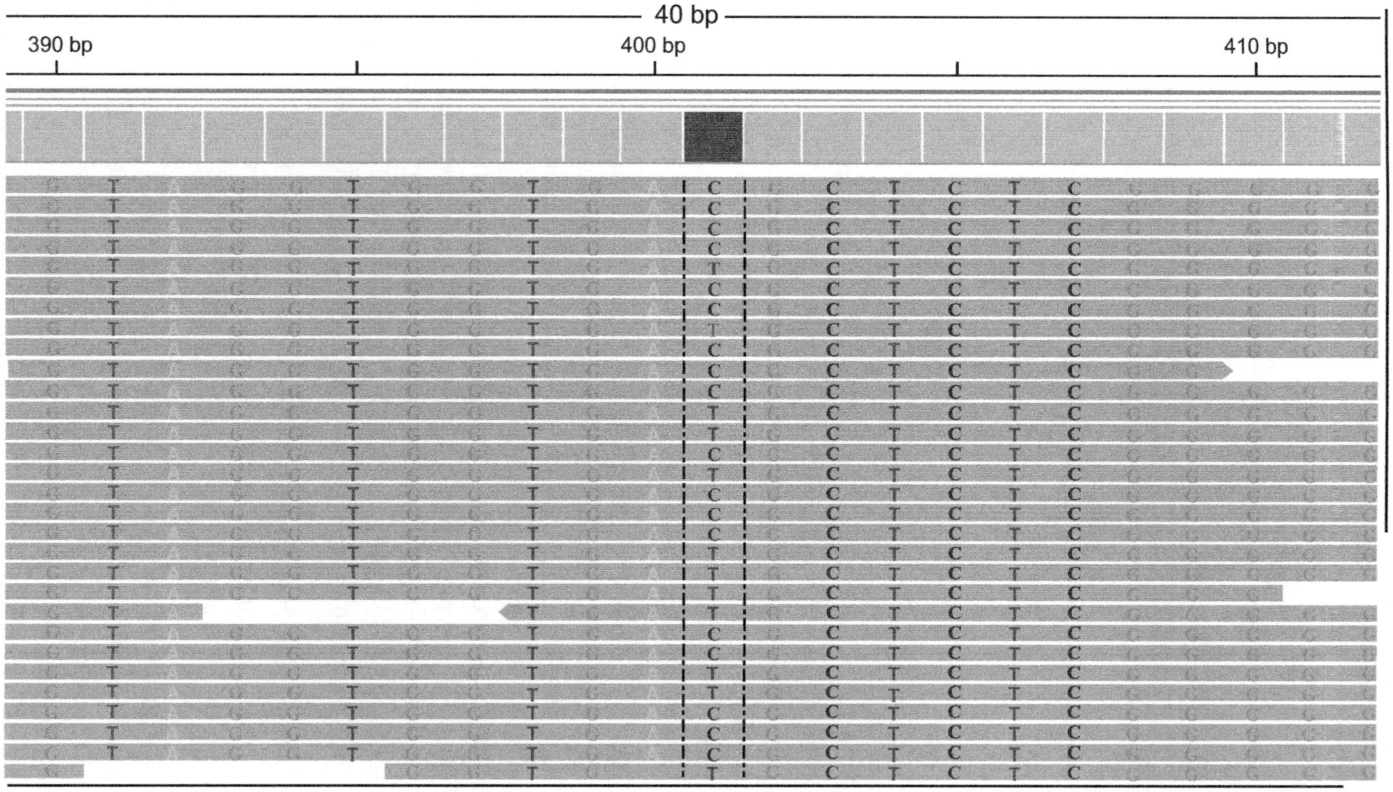

Figure 8.5 Alignment and visualisation of reads

Table 8.4 Genome-wide association data

Genotype count	Cases			
	C/C	C/T	T/T	Total
Athletes	49	52	13	114
Control (Non athletes)	344	475	128	947
Total	393	527	141	1061
Allele count				
	C	T		
Athletes	49 + 49 + 52	52 + 13 + 13		
Control (Non athletes)	344 + 344 + 475	475 + 128 + 128		
Allele count				
	C	T		
Athletes	150	78	228	
Control (Non athletes)	1163	731	1894	
Total	1313	809	2122	2122

generally accepted as a threshold for true association in genome-wide association studies. An odds ratio of 1 means there is no association between the variation and sports performance. An odds ratio of more than 1 means the variation increases the probability of predisposition towards better sports performance whereas an odds ratio of less than 1 means the variation decreases this probability.

Table 8.4 shows a subset of data, collected as part of a study (Gineviciene et al., 2016) from a cohort of European Caucasians from Russia. This subset consists of 1,061 individuals out of which 114 are sports athletes and 947 form the control group. Controls in this study were healthy and unrelated individuals without any competitive sports experience. Genome sequences of all the participants were analysed to find variation in the ACTN3 gene (position 66,560,624 on chromosome 11). Among the sports athletes' genomes, 49 had C/C, 52 had C/T and 52 had T/T. Among the control group's genomes, 344 had C/C, 475 had C/T and 128 had T/T.

Odds that C allele occurs in athletes = 150/1163 = 0.129
Odds that T allele occurs in athletes = 78/731 = 0.107
Odds ratio for C allele over T allele = 0.129/0.107 = 1.206

There have been many genome-wide studies in the area of sports and athletics and a brief summary of six of these have been presented in Table 8.5. Studies S1 through S5 found an association between athletic success and variations in genes such as ACTN3, ACE, FTO and PPARGC1A. However, study S6, which is the largest with 4,250 participants, did not find any

162

Table 8.5 Genome-wide association studies

Study title	Sport type	Total participants	Num athletes	Num control	Gene name	Outcome	Reference
Fat mass and obesity associated (FTO) gene influences skeletal muscle phenotypes in non-resistance trained males and elite rugby playing position	Rubgy	1089	530	559	FTO	Allele T (so genotypes T/T and A/T) are associated with elite athletic success	Heffernan et al. (2017)
ACTN3 genotype is associated with human elite athletic performance	Various sports (judo, cycle, swim)	865	429	436	ACTN3	Allele C associated with better performing muscles and likely sprinter	Yang et al. (2003)
Association analysis of ACE, ACTN3 and PPARGC1A gene polymorphisms in two cohorts of European strength and power athletes	Weightlifter, throwers	1363	161	1202	ACTN3, ACE, PPARGC1A	PPARGC1A and ACE associated with better athletic performance. ACTN3 is not associated	Gineviciene et al. (2016)
Do PPARGC1A and PPARalpha polymorphisms influence sprint or endurance phenotypes?	Endurance athletes	395	155	240	PPARGC1A and PPARA	PPARGC1A is associated with better athletic performance	Eynon et al. (2010)
Genome-wide association study identifies three novel genetic markers associated with elite endurance performance	Athletics	641	449	192	Gene NFIA-AS2, TSHR, RBFOX1	NFIA-AS2, TSHR and RBFOX1 are associated with athletic performance	Ahmetov et al. (2015)
No evidence of a common DNA variant profile specific to world class endurance athletes	Endurance athletes	4280	1520	2760	Many genes including ACTN3 and PPARGC1A	Did not find statistically significant association between any panel of genes and elite endurance athletic performance	Rankinen et al. (2016)

statistically significant association between variations in genomes and athletic success. So there is a need for further studies to confirm association between genomic markers and sports performance in the wider population.

Pathway analysis

To understand the effect of these promising markers, one needs to understand the way they may interact with other genetic information, resulting in a product or change in cell behaviour. This process is known as pathway analysis and it helps to understand the regions of interest. The pathways a gene is involved in can be searched from biological pathway databases such as WikiPathways (Slenter et al., 2017) and Consensus-PathDB (Herwig et al., 2016; Kamburov et al., 2012).

Figure 8.6, generated using the WikiPathways biological pathway database (Slenter et al., 2017), shows the pathway for striated muscle

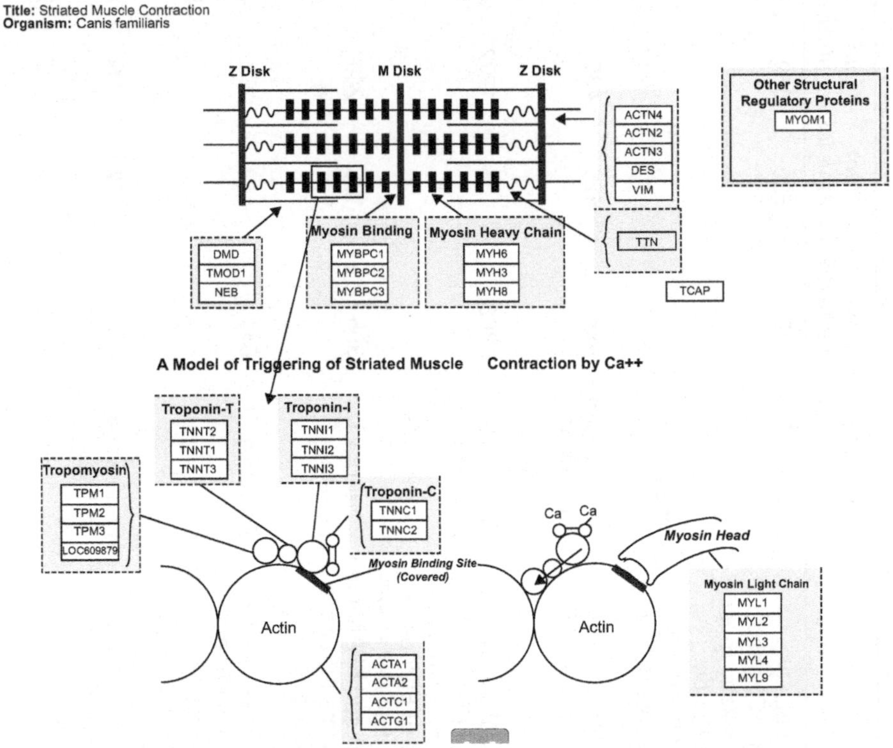

Figure 8.6 Pathway for ACTN3 gene

contraction in humans. As shown in this figure, the ACTN3 gene interacts with other genes such as DES, VIM and TTN. Because ACTN3 has been widely linked with sports performance, the genes with which ACTN3 interacts the most become candidates of interest for further exploration.

ETHICAL IMPLICATIONS

As discussed in the previous section, large-scale studies are still required to fully understand sports genetics. Although use of genetics in sports is a promising area, ethical implications have to be given due consideration. Varley et al. (2018) conducted a survey of UK athletes and support staff to investigate use of genetic testing in sports. Their study found that opinions are divided on using genetics for sports talent identification. However, participants were willing to use genetics for individualising training and reducing injury risk.

HANDS-ON ACTIVITY TO ANALYSE GENOME OF TWO INDIVIDUALS (CODE PLUS DATA)

In this hands-on exercise, we will analyse artificially generated genomic data of two individuals to find the version of the sports gene ACTN3 each carries. The artificial genomic data was generated especially for this chapter using read simulator software for next generation sequencing data wgsim (Li, 2011). The analysis shows that individual 1 is more likely to be an endurance athlete whereas individual 2 is predisposed to being a sprinter.

Recall from previous sections that ACTN3 is a prominent sports gene. Research shows that individuals with "C" at location 66,560,624 on chromosome 11 are predisposed to be sprinters whereas individuals with "T" at the same location are predisposed to be endurance athletes (Gineviciene et al., 2016; Yang et al., 2003).

DOWNLOAD GENOME FILES

a) Download the two FastQ files containing reads for individuals 1 and 2 from the following link. These files are 3.6 MB each.
https://github.com/ambi1999/sportsgenomics
individual1_reads.fq
individual2_reads.fq

Following is the first read from the individual 1 FastQ file. Please note that the first line begins with @ and contains the sequence identifier, the second line contains the raw sequences, the third line contains the plus symbol and the fourth line is the Phred quality score for each raw base in line 2. Each read in individual 1 and 2's FastQ files has 70 bases.

```
@11_12109_12680_1:0:0_2:0:0_0/1
ATGCCCTCCGAGGGCAAGCTGGTCTCTGTGAGCTCTACACA
CATTCCCTAGGTGACCTTGAGGTCCGTAT
+
2222222222222222222222222222222222222222222222222222
222222222222222
```

b) Download the chromosome 11 Fasta file from the following link and save it as chr11.fa in the directory "Chr11Genome". This file will be about 137.8 MB.
www.ncbi.nlm.nih.gov/nuccore/NC_000011.10?report=fasta&from=begin&to=end

SOFTWARE INSTALLATION

Please install the following software and add them to the PATH environment variable. Software and installation instruction are available from the following websites.

1 FastQC:
   www.bioinformatics.babraham.ac.uk/projects/fastqc/
2 Bowtie2:
   http://bowtie-bio.sourceforge.net/bowtie2/index.shtml
3 Samtools
   www.htslib.org/
4 Varscan
   http://varscan.sourceforge.net/
5 Freebayes
   https://github.com/ekg/freebayes
6 IGV
   http://software.broadinstitute.org/software/igv/

166

ANALYSIS FOR INDIVIDUAL 1

Step 1: generating index file for human genome chromosome 11

Change the directory to "Chr11Genome" and run the following command to generate the index files:

bowtie2-build chr11.fa chr11

Step 2: mapping reads to reference genome

a) Generate sam file using the following command:

bowtie2 -x ../Chr11Genome/chr11 -U individual_1_reads.fq -S individual_1_aligned.sam

b) Convert sam to bam file using the following command:

samtools view -b -S -o individual_1_aligned.bam individual_1_aligned.sam

c) Sort the bam file using the following command:

samtools sort individual_1_aligned.bam -o individual_1_aligned.sorted.bam

d) Generate index of bam file using the following command:

samtools index individual_1_aligned.sorted.bam

e) View the bam file:

samtools view individual_1_aligned.sorted.bam

f) Use IGV to view the individual_1_aligned.sorted.bam.

Step 3: variant finding

a) Generate mpileup file:

samtools mpileup -f ../Chr11Genome/chr11 individual_1_aligned.sorted.bam > individual_1_.mpileup

b) Set path to Varscan jar file:

pathVarscan="/home/standalone/genomics/softwares/Varscan/"

c) Generate variants using Varscan. All variants should have a minimum of 40 reads and at least 20 reads should support the variant:

java -jar $pathVarscan/VarScan.v2.4.0.jar mpileup2cns individual_1_.mpileup – min-coverage 40 – min-reads2 20 – output-vcf 1 – variants > individual_1_variants_varscan.vcf

d) Generate variants using Freebayes:

freebayes -f ../Chr11Genome/chr11.fa individual_1_aligned.sorted.bam > individual_1_variants_freebayes.vcf

e) Open the variant file in any spreadsheet software (such as LibreOffice or Microsoft Excel). Figure 8.7 shows the variant file. The fourth entry from the bottom shows "chr11 66,560,624 C T", meaning individual 1 has a C (instead of T) at location 66,560,624 on chromosome 11.

	A	B	C	D	E	F	G	H	I	J	
22	##FORMAT⇨reads2plus)">										
23	##FORMAT⇨reads2minus)">										
24	#CHROM	POS	ID	REF	ALT	QUAL	FILTER	INFO	FORMAT	Sample1	
25	chr11	66546530	.	T	G	.	PASS	ADP=74	WT=0	HET=0	H
26	chr11	66547316	.	C	T	.	PASS	ADP=72	WT=0	HET=1	H
27	chr11	66547892	.	C	G	.	PASS	ADP=62	WT=0	HET=1	H
28	chr11	66548238	.	C	T	.	PASS	ADP=67	WT=0	HET=0	H
29	chr11	66548853	.	C	A	.	PASS	ADP=51	WT=0	HET=0	H
30	chr11	66550424	.	G	C	.	PASS	ADP=58	WT=0	HET=1	H
31	chr11	66550998	.	C	A	.	PASS	ADP=72	WT=0	HET=1	H
32	chr11	66552628	.	A	T	.	PASS	ADP=62	WT=0	HET=1	H
33	chr11	66554886	.	A	C	.	PASS	ADP=71	WT=0	HET=1	H
34	chr11	66556190	.	A	C	.	PASS	ADP=64	WT=0	HET=0	H
35	chr11	66557917	.	CA	C	.	PASS	ADP=75	WT=0	HET=1	H
36	chr11	66560279	.	G	C	.	PASS	ADP=77	WT=0	HET=1	H
37	**chr11**	**66560624**	.	**C**	**T**	.	**PASS**	**ADP=62**	**WT=0**	**HET=0**	H
38	chr11	66560728	.	G	C	.	PASS	ADP=71	WT=0	HET=1	H
39	chr11	66561712	.	G	A	.	PASS	ADP=67	WT=0	HET=0	H
40	chr11	66562932	.	T	A	.	PASS	ADP=88	WT=0	HET=1	H
41											

Figure 8.7 Variants present in genome of individual 1

f) Open the individual_1_aligned.sorted.bam file in IGV and select the Human GRCh38 as reference genome. Select location 66,560,624 and observe the reads. Figure 8.8 shows these aligned reads. Note that location 66,560,624 on this figure (read in the middle) has T for most of the reads, confirming that this individual has T instead of C.

ANALYSIS FOR INDIVIDUAL 2

Repeat steps 1 through 3 for individual_2_reads.fq. Open the individual_2_aligned.sorted.bam in IGV. Figure 8.9 shows aligned reads for individual 2. Note that location 66,560,624 on this figure (read in the middle) has C for most of the reads, confirming that this individual has the "C" version of the ACTN3 gene.

In summary, individual 1 has the "T" version of the ACTN3 gene and individual 2 has the "C" version. So we can infer that individual 1 will have impaired muscle performance and likely be an endurance athlete, whereas individual 2 will have better performing muscles and be predisposed to be a sprinter.

168

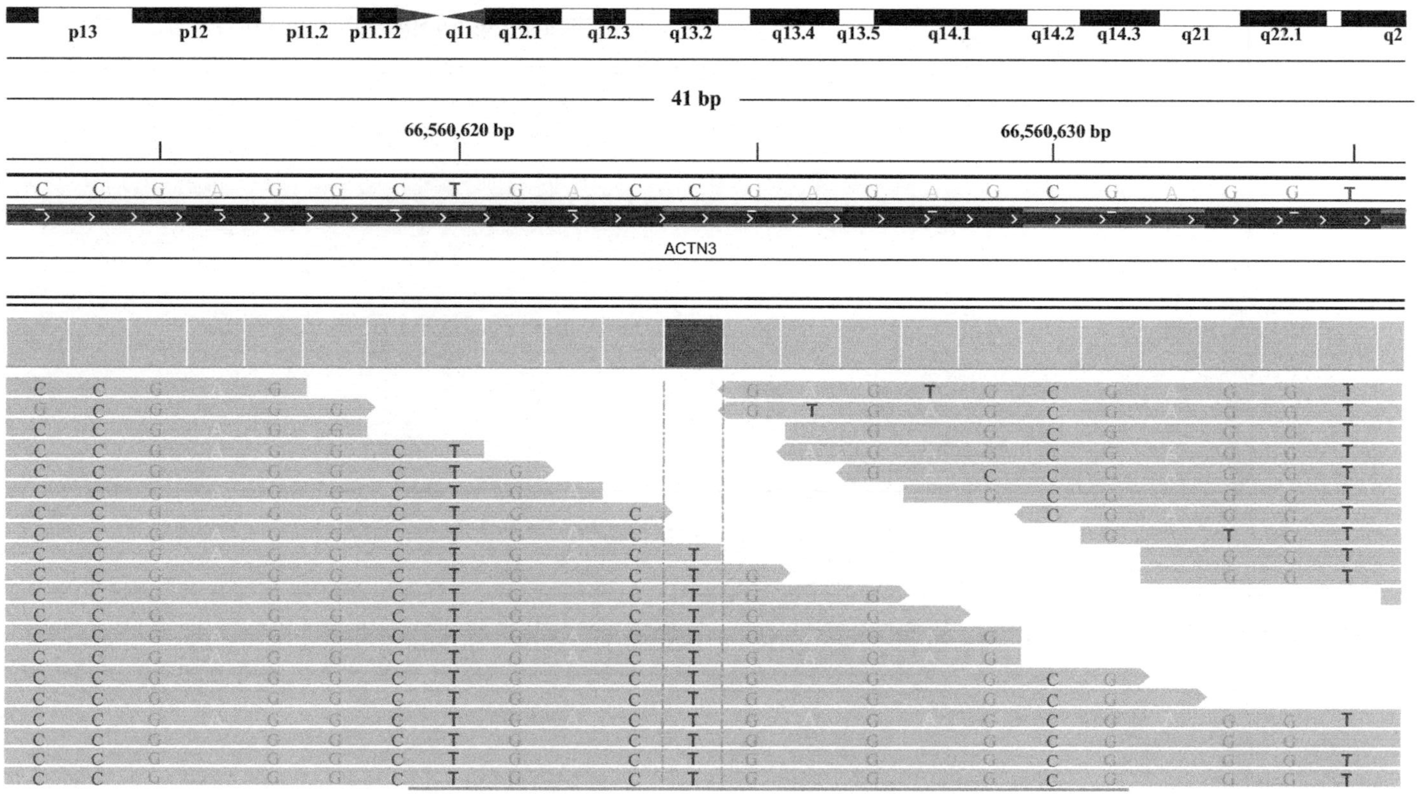

Figure 8.8 Visualising aligned reads for individual 1

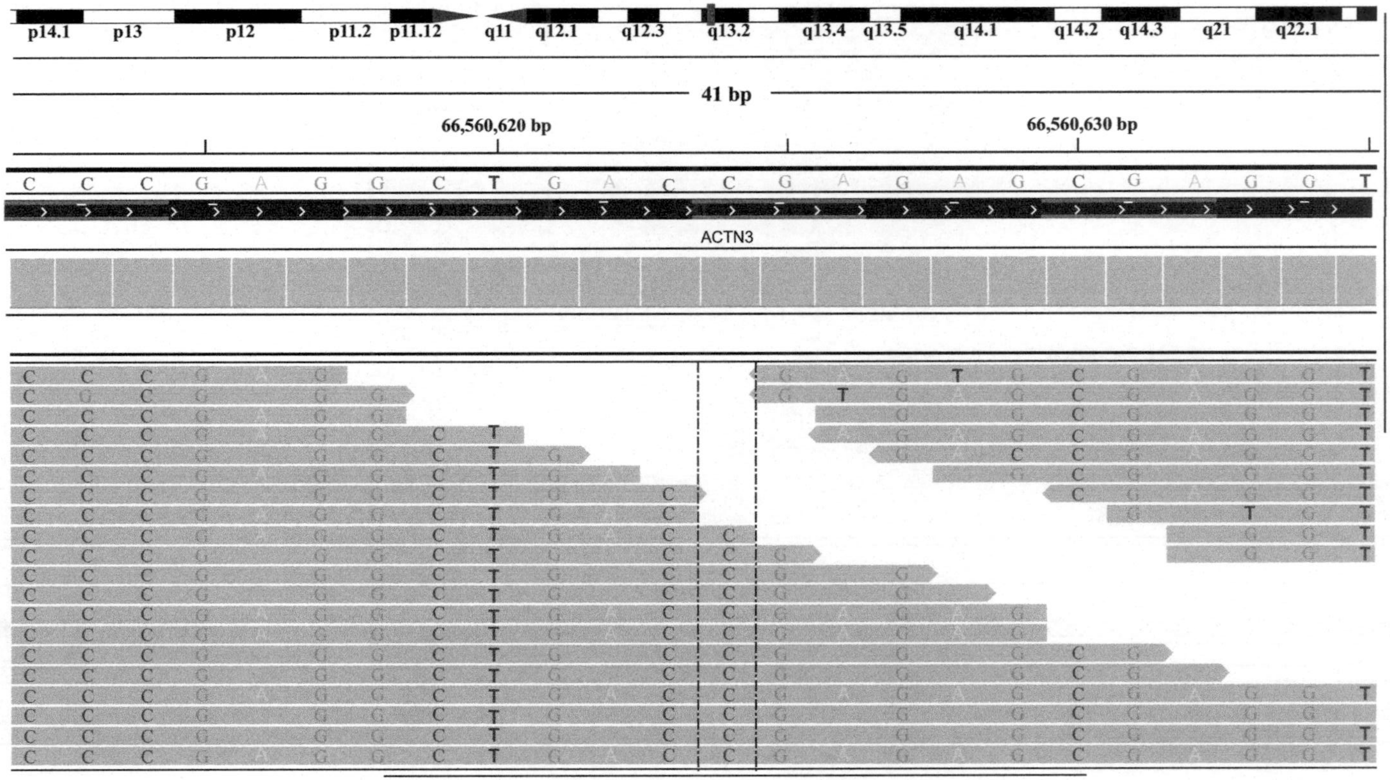

Figure 8.9 Visualising aligned reads for individual 2

REFERENCES

Ahmetov, I.I., Kulemin, N.A., Popov, D.V., Naumov, V.A., Akimov, E.B., Bravy, Y.R., . . . Larin, A.K. (2015) 'Genome-wide association study identifies three novel genetic markers associated with elite endurance performance', *Biology of Sport*, 32(1): 3.

Andrews, S. (2010) 'FastQC: A quality control tool for high throughput sequence data'. www.bioinformatics.babraham.ac.uk/projects/fastqc

Baker, J. and Farrow, D. (2015) *Routledge handbook of sport expertise*, London: Routledge.

Bolger, A.M., Lohse, M. and Usadel, B. (2014) 'Trimmomatic: A flexible trimmer for Illumina sequence data', *Bioinformatics*, 30(15): 2114–2120.

Bray, M.S., Hagberg, J.M., Perusse, L., Rankinen, T., Roth, S.M., Wolfarth, B. and Bouchard, C. (2009) 'The human gene map for performance and health-related fitness phenotypes: The 2006–2007 update', *Medicine & Science in Sports & Exercise*, 41(1): 34–72.

Del Coso, J., Valero, M., Salinero, J.J., Lara, B., Díaz, G., Gallo-Salazar, C., . . . Cacabelos, R. (2017) 'ACTN3 genotype influences exercise-induced muscle damage during a marathon competition', *European Journal of Applied Physiology*, 117(3): 409–416.

Del Coso, J., Valero, M., Salinero, J.J., Lara, B., Gallo-Salazar, C. and Areces, F. (2017b) 'Optimum polygenic profile to resist exertional rhabdomyolysis during a marathon', *PLoS ONE*, 12(3). https://doi.org/10.1371/journal.pone.0172965

Eynon, N., Meckel, Y., Sagiv, M., Yamin, C., Amir, R., Goldhammer, E., . . . Oliveira, J. (2010) 'Do PPARGC1A and PPARα polymorphisms influence sprint or endurance phenotypes?', *Scandinavian Journal of Medicine & Science in Sports*, 20(1). https://doi.org/10.1111/j.1600–0838.2009.00930.x

Garrison, E. and Marth, G. (2012) 'Haplotype-based variant detection from short-read sequencing', arXiv preprint arXiv:1207.3907.

Gineviciene, V., Jakaitiene, A., Aksenov, M.O., Aksenova, A.V., Astratenkova, A.D.I., Egorova, E.S., . . . Utkus, A. (2016) 'Association analysis of ACE, ACTN3 and PPARGC1A gene polymorphisms in two cohorts of European strength and power athletes', *Biology of Sport*, 33(3): 199.

Guilherme, J.P.L.F., Tritto, A.C.C., NORTH, K.N., Lancha Junior, A.H. and Artioli, G.G. (2014) 'Genetics and sport performance: Current challenges and directions to the future', *Revista Brasileira de Educação Física e Esporte*, 28(1): 177–193.

Guth, L.M. and Roth, S.M. (2013) 'Genetic influence on athletic performance', *Current Opinion in Paediatrics*, 25(6): 653.

Heffernan, S.M., Stebbings, G.K., Kilduff, L.P., Erskine, R.M., Day, S.H., Morse, C.I., . . . Raleigh, S.M. (2017) 'Fat Mass and Obesity Associated (FTO) gene influences skeletal muscle phenotypes in non-resistance trained males and elite rugby playing position', *BMC Genetics*, 18(1): 4

Herwig, R., Hardt, C., Lienhard, M. and Kamburov, A. (2016) 'Analyzing and interpreting genome data at the network level with ConsensusPathDB', *Nature Protocols*, 11(10): 1889–1907.

Jayal, A., Johns, B.E., Purdy, K.J., and Maddocks, S.E. (2017). Draft genome sequence of Pseudomonas aeruginosa ATCC 9027, originally isolated from an outer ear infection. Genome Announc 5: e01397-17.

Kamburov, A., Stelzl, U., Lehrach, H. and Herwig, R. (2012) 'The ConsensusPathDB interaction database: 2013 update', *Nucleic Acids Research*, 41(D1): D793–D800.

Koboldt, D.C., Zhang, Q., Larson, D.E., Shen, D., McLellan, M.D., Lin, L., . . . Wilson, R.K. (2012) 'VarScan 2: Somatic mutation and copy number alteration discovery in cancer by exome sequencing', *Genome Research*, 22(3): 568–576.

Langmead, B. and Salzberg, S.L. (2012) 'Fast gapped-read alignment with Bowtie 2', *Nature Methods*, 9(4): 357–359.

Li, H. (2011) 'wgsim-read simulator for next generation sequencing', *Github Repository*. https://github.com/lh3/wgsim.

Li, H. and Durbin, R. (2009) 'Fast and accurate short read alignment with Burrows – Wheeler transform', *Bioinformatics*, 25(14): 1754–1760.

Martin, M. (2011) 'Cutadapt removes adapter sequences from high-throughput sequencing reads', *EMBnet. Journal*, 17(1): 10.

Pabinger, S., Dander, A., Fischer, M., Snajder, R., Sperk, M., Efremova, M., . . . Trajanoski, Z. (2014) 'A survey of tools for variant analysis of next-generation genome sequencing data', *Briefings in Bioinformatics*, 15(2): 256–278.

Pitsiladis, Y.P., Tanaka, M., Eynon, N., Bouchard, C., North, K.N., Williams, A.G., . . . Ashley, E.A. (2016) 'Athlome Project Consortium: A concerted effort to discover genomic and other "omic" markers of athletic performance', *Physiological Genomics*, 48(3): 183–190.

Qi, B., Liu, J.Q. and Liu, G.L. (2016) 'Genetic association between ACTN3 polymorphism and risk of non-acute ankle sprain', *Genetics and Molecular Research: GMR*, 15(4).

Rankinen, T., Fuku, N., Wolfarth, B., Wang, G., Sarzynski, M.A., Alexeev, D.G., . . . Filipenko, M.L. (2016) 'No evidence of a common DNA variant profile specific to world class endurance athletes', *PLoS ONE*, 11(1): e0147330.

Rivard, L. (2013) 'Case study in genetic testing for sports ability' [Web log post]. www.nature.com/scitable/forums/genetics-generation/case-study-in-genetic-testing-for-sports-107403644, accessed 30th November, 2017.

Slenter, D.N., Kutmon, M., Hanspers, K., Riutta, A., Windsor, J., Nunes, N., . . . Ehrhart, F. (2017) 'WikiPathways: A multifaceted pathway database bridging metabolomics to other omics research', *Nucleic Acids Research*, 46(D1): D661–D667.

Thankaswamy-Kosalai, S., Sen, P. and Nookaew, I. (2017) 'Evaluation and assessment of read-mapping by multiple next-generation sequencing aligners based on genome-wide characteristics', *Genomics*, 109(3-4): 186–191.

Thorvaldsdóttir, H., Robinson, J.T. and Mesirov, J.P. (2013) 'Integrative Genomics Viewer (IGV): High-performance genomics data visualization and exploration', *Briefings in Bioinformatics*, 14(2): 178–192.

Varley, I., Patel, S., Williams, A.G. and Hennis, P.J. (2018) 'The current use, and opinions of elite athletes and support staff in relation to genetic testing in elite sport within the UK', *Biology of Sport*, 35: 13–19.

Yang, N., MacArthur, D.G., Gulbin, J.P., Hahn, A.G., Beggs, A.H., Easteal, S. and North, K. (2003) 'ACTN3 genotype is associated with human elite athletic performance', *The American Journal of Human Genetics*, 73(3): 627–631.

172

CHAPTER 9

SOCIAL NETWORK ANALYSIS

INTRODUCTION

Social network analysis uses network graphs to represent social structures, their members and their inter-relationships. The underlying graph theory used in network analysis provides a formal representation of social networks using nodes to represent members of networks and edges to represent their inter-relationships. Social networks can be analysed quantitatively using variables related to the structure of the network and qualitatively by inspecting network graphs. This chapter gives a brief introduction to traditional applications of social network analysis before discussing the use of network graphs in sports and the analysis of sports performance.

SOCIAL NETWORK ANALYSIS

Network analysis can be used in fields where inter-connections, relationships, communication or other links between individuals are important. Social network analysis has been recently applied in areas ranging from emergency services (Houghton et al., 2006), maritime search and rescue (Baber et al., 2013), and cardiac surgical teams (Barth et al., 2015) to the impact of terrorism (Bader and Schuster, 2015) and the detection of money laundering (Dre ewski et al., 2015). Analysing social networks identifies subgroups and cliques, and supports the study of popularity, power and influence as well as marketplace relationships (Miller, 2016: 230–231).

The rise of the Internet and particularly email communication and social media has provided a wealth of data about people's communications, movements and financial transactions (Miller, 2016: 230). This has promoted network analysis research into the Internet and social media (Luo and Zhong, 2015). Network graphs in these application areas are potentially very large and so packages have been developed to allow graphs to be analysed interactively. One such package is Gephi (https://gephi. org/, accessed 22/8/17), which supports real-time visualisation of network graphs and includes the following features:

- Graph-shaping algorithms to improve readability.
- Interactive grouping of nodes.
- Hierarchical structuring of the network allowing groups to be collapsed and expanded.
- Interaction highlighting.
- Ability to apply filter queries to the network to identify and store sub-networks.
- Calculation of network metrics for centrality, closeness, diameter and clustering. The meaning of some of these metrics will be discussed later in the chapter.

Another package is Social Networks Visualizer (SocNetV) (Kalamaras, 2014), which allows network graphs to be created, edited and analysed (http://socnetv.org/, accessed 9/9/17). The package provides metrics for cohesion, density, connectedness, centrality and clustering, algorithms to identify cliques, and visualization options including three-dimensional representations of networks and network graphs superimposed onto geographical maps. Superimposing network graphs in geographical maps is particularly useful in areas such as air traffic analysis (Kirk, 2012: 157).

Measures

Passos (2017) describes metrics used to quantify network properties, including the degree of centrality, network density, network intensity and clustering coefficients. Centralisation metrics quantify the extent to which team members are evenly involved in passing actions. High values indicate that the network may be centralized with a few key players involved in passing much more than others. Lower values reflect a more

174

decentralized structure in which passing activity is distributed more evenly throughout the team. The studies surveyed by Passos (2017) tend to suggest that performance is negatively associated with centralization in team games.

Network density is a metric representing the number of players who are inter-connected by passing relationships. In a sport such as soccer, we may have matches in which passes have been played between every pair of players on a team. In a situation like this, the metric can be adjusted to look at the proportion of player pairs between which three (say) or more passes have been played. Network density has been found to have a positive relationship with performance (Grund, 2012). Network intensity represents passing rate by dividing pass frequencies by a team's possession time.

Clustering coefficients are used to show subgroups or units of teams in which members are strongly connected. High clustering coefficients are often associated with centrality values higher than would be seen for a decentralized network but lower than would be seen for a centralized network. This is due to decentralized sub-networks within clusters but lower interconnectedness between clusters.

ANALYSIS OF PLAYER TRANSFERS

Miller (2016: 230–232) described how network analysis can be used to study player trades in major league baseball. We will use a similar example of player transfers in professional soccer, specifically considering the English FA Championship, which is the second tier of English soccer and a division containing 24 teams. Data for transfers made in the first part of the 2017–2018 season until the end of the first transfer window (31st August 2017) were taken from a publicly available website (www.transfermarkt.co.uk/championship/transfers/wettbewerb/GB2, accessed 9/9/17). These data included the player being transferred, the club they were moving from, the club they were moving to, the player's age, nationality and playing position, whether the move was a transfer or loan and the transfer fee paid. We did not include any players who were free agents before or after the transfers, any players retiring, any players with "unknown" destinations or internal transfers from age group squads to senior first team squads within the same clubs. This left 582 transfers between English FA Championship teams.

The soccer transfer market is truly international with thousands of professional players transferring clubs each season. Network analysis has a role in studying transfers and loan moves within and between countries. Given the volume of transfers each season, it may be necessary to represent the soccer world as a hierarchy with the governing body (FIFA, Fédération Internationale de Football Association) at the top and continental confederations at the next level, followed by national associations, which can be broken down into league and non-league divisions with clubs at the bottom level. This is represented in Figure 9.1, which

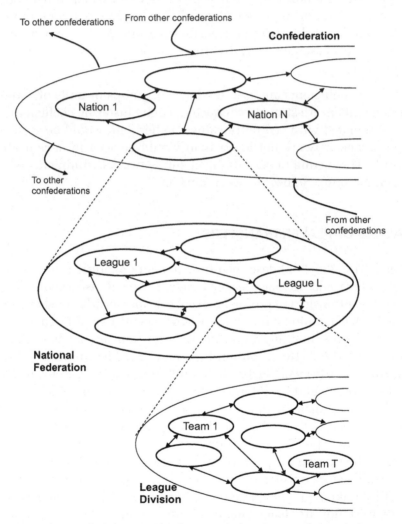

Figure 9.1 Hierarchical network of soccer federations and associations

recognizes that players can move between clubs within the same league or between clubs of different leagues in the same or different countries. Some may feel that a hierarchy based on team value might be better with a top tier containing the world's leading club sides (Miller, 2016: 8).

Given the structure suggested here of representing teams within leagues within countries within continents, we can examine transfers at multiple levels. For example, Figure 9.2 shows transfers within the English Championship highlighting the transfer activity of Cardiff City; this is an example of a radial network or chord diagram (Kirk, 2012: 148–149). The various line widths represent the number of players moving from one club to another; for example, the largest number of players transferring between two clubs in summer 2017 was three players moving from Brentford to Birmingham City. An alternative could be to represent

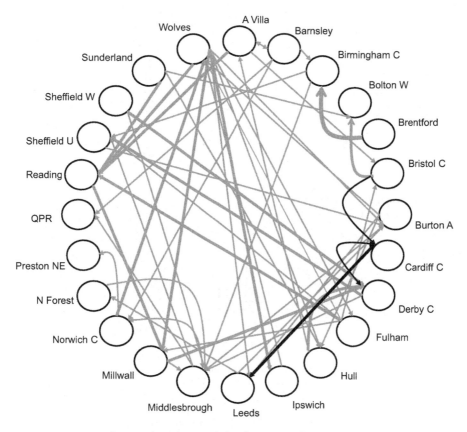

Figure 9.2 Transfers within the English Championship

player values or transfer fees paid by line widths rather than just the volume of players. An interactive analysis of such data could allow us to focus on particular positional roles of interest, loan moves or transfer moves. Given that the data include player age and nationality, there are multiple combinations of criteria that can be used when viewing the data in graphical form.

Figure 9.3 summarises the transfers to and from the English Championship from and to other divisions and other countries. These data could be compared with equivalent data for the English FA Premier League

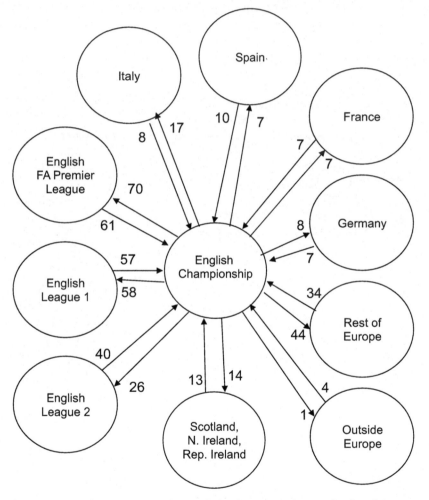

Figure 9.3 Transfers between the English Championship and other leagues and countries

178

to contrast the sources of players transferred in and the destinations of players transferred out. A further contrast that could be examined is the transfer activity of individual teams within the league with the overall pattern of transfers to and from the league. Diagrams like Figures 9.2 and 9.3 could also be used to contrast transfer activity between different seasons, monitoring trends in player transfers. Alternatively, the transfer activity of successful teams promoted to the English FA Premier League could be compared with transfers made by other teams in the league. This could distinguish teams that were promoted or made the play-offs and teams that were relegated to League 1.

RESEARCH INTO PASSING PATTERNS IN TEAM GAMES

Network analysis has been used in sports performance analysis specifically to analyse passing patterns between players (Clemente et al., 2014; Gama et al., 2014; Grund, 2012; Yamamoto and Yokoyama, 2011). It is particularly useful in low-scoring games such as soccer, ice hockey and field hockey in which scoring and creating scoring opportunities on their own do not reflect the quality of overall player performances (Passos, 2017). When network analysis is used to represent passing within a team, the nodes of the network graph represent players and the edges represent passes between players. Traditional analysis of passing performance involves calculating the frequency and success rate percentage of passing by different players in different areas of the playing surface. The use of network analysis goes beyond traditional analyses by also representing players who receive passes so that passing relationships between pairs of players can be analysed.

Clemente et al. (2014) used network analysis to determine the passing network characteristics of successful and unsuccessful teams in the FIFA World Cup 2014. This study found that winning teams within matches had more dense passing networks, more links within the passing networks and a greater clustering coefficient. Further research into soccer performance at the FIFA World Cup 2014 compared passing patterns between teams eliminated in the groups stages with those that proceeded to the knockout stage (Clemente et al., 2015a) and between teams that adopted different tactical formations (Clemente et al., 2015b). Extended network analysis models have incorporated additional variables; for example, Cotta et al. (2013) included timing.

PASSING PATTERNS IN NETBALL

This section uses netball as an example, which is a growing sport but is currently played in mainly Commonwealth countries. Therefore, it is necessary to give a brief introduction to the sport of netball. Netball is played between two teams of seven on a 100 ft by 50 ft court with nets at either end. The game is won by scoring more goals than the opponent, a goal being scored by throwing the ball into the opponent's net. The seven players on a team have specific positional roles and are restricted to particular areas of the court.

- The GK (goal keeper) can only play in the defensive third.
- The GD (goal defence) can play in the defensive third or middle third.
- The WD (wing defence) can play in the defensive or middle thirds except for the shooting circle they are defending.
- The C (centre) can play in all three thirds of the court but not in either shooting circle.
- The WA (wing attack) can play in the middle or attacking third but not in the shooting circle they are attacking.
- The GA (goal attack) can play in the middle and attacking thirds.
- The GS (goal shooter) can only play in the attacking third.

A further restriction is that shots can only be taken from inside the shooting circle, which means the only players who can take shots are the GA and GS. The match is made up of four 15-minute quarters. Play commences with a centre pass, which is also used to restart play after goals are scored. Centre passes are taken by the C and they alternate between the two teams irrespective of who scored the previous goal. Players cannot run with the ball, there is no magical Diego Maradona dribbling, and thus netball is a true team game in which players must pass. Passes cannot be played directly from the defensive third to the attacking third, which means that the GK and GS cannot pass the ball directly to each other.

Network analysis can be used to compare the tactics of different teams or the same teams in different situations. Figures 9.4 and 9.5 show the passing patterns of two international netball teams, Team A and Team B (Butterworth and O'Donoghue, 2016). The complexity of Figures 9.4 and 9.5 is reduced by not showing any passing relationships in which

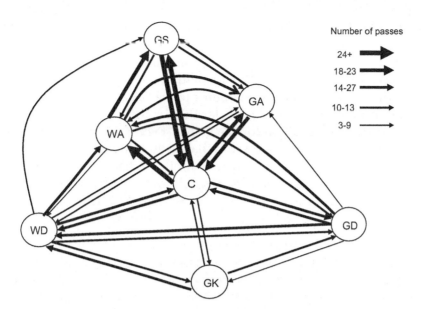

Figure 9.4 Passes made between pairs of players by Team A

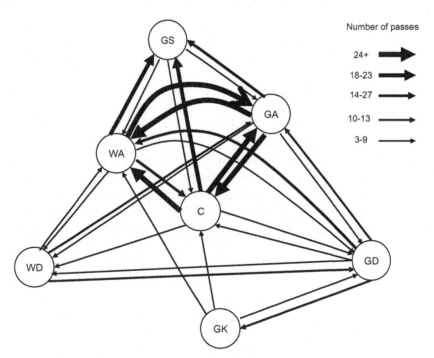

Figure 9.5 Passes made between pairs of players by Team B

the number of passes between a pair of players is fewer than two in the given direction. Figure 9.4 shows that Team A relies heavily on the C to play the ball to the GS and GA, who are the only players allowed to shoot for a goal. The C also plays the ball to the WA more than anyone else with the WA also providing routes to the GA and GS. The C is also the most commonly chosen option for the GA and GS to pass the ball to if they are not in a position to take a shot. Figure 9.5 shows that Team B's GS is a target player who rarely passes to other players; her job is to receive the ball, shoot and score. Team B also has a lower amount of passing among defensive players (GK, GD and WD) than Team A. The C, WA and GA are heavily involved in passing; the GA in particular is utilized much more than her counterpart in Team A.

Figures 9.4 and 9.5 raise a number of issues. First, despite concealing instances in which fewer than three passes have been played between a pair of players, these network graphs are still quite complex. The complexity shown in Figures 9.4 and 9.5 can be further managed through interactive analysis using software packages to focus on particular passers or receivers. For example, we may wish to focus on the passes played to the GA and GS. If we have also recorded the location of these players when they receive each pass, we can isolate the passes they receive when in the shooting circle; these are known as feeds. A second issue is that the raw data recorded for each pass may only identify a recipient for successful passes. If we require the network graph to indicate success levels of passes between particular pairs of players, the coding of unsuccessful passes will need to include the intended recipient. This is not always possible for the analyst to do validly or reliably, which is one reason why such data may not be recorded. If successful and unsuccessful passes are distinguished, the edges of network graphs can be coloured or annotated to indicate the percentage of successful passes. A third issue is that Figures 9.4 and 9.5 do not include important information about passes such as source location, direction, length and trajectory. Filter queries can be applied interactively to focus on players and pass types of interest or to include other criteria such as the match quarter. Network graphs of overall match performance tend to conceal player interactions during periods of interest. Therefore, an alternative approach is to show different passing networks for different time periods within matches (Clemente et al., 2013; Yamamoto and Yokoyama, 2011). A fourth issue regards the shape of the graph. In many application areas, the topology of network graphs can be adjusted

social network analysis

to improve readability. In team games like soccer, team formations may be so well understood that reorganising the graph to reduce lines crossing over might actually reduce the clarity of the chart for a practitioner audience in the given sport.

Inferential comparisons between networks

The lower number of players involved in netball matches than soccer and rugby matches permits chi square tests to compare the frequency of passes between different performances. Consider the passing frequencies shown in Table 9.1. There are 40 pairs of players who can pass the ball between each other when we include both directions between a pair of players and recognize that passes in either direction between the GK and GS are not permitted. Passes between some pairs of players occur infrequently, as we can see in Figures 9.5 and 9.6. The eight player pairs with the highest numbers of passes are shown in Table 9.1 with lower frequency player pairs grouped together under "Other". Team A's performances are not significantly different when playing against Teams B, C and D (χ^2_{16} = 23.2, p = 0.107). Although this is not a statistically significant opposition effect, it is worth considering how we interpret the p value. The p value means that the chance of the differences between the three performances being a result of a sampling error is 0.107. Therefore, there is a reasonably high probability that the differences are down to an actual opposition effect (p = 0.893).

Table 9.1 Touches and pass interactions for Team A and their opponents (Teams B, C and D)

Variable	Team A performances			Opposition performances		
	v Team B	v Team C	v Team D	Team B	Team C	Team D
C > GA	28	22	34	55	48	55
C > GS	37	31	28	18	30	30
WA > GA	19	13	19	46	43	27
C > WA	34	16	27	34	26	25
GA > C	21	8	17	35	23	34
GA > WA	13	8	13	43	25	31
WA > GS	24	28	21	23	18	19
GS > C	30	19	12	9	19	9
Other	286	266	231	192	272	239

The main differences in Team A's performances against these three opponents are:

- The GS plays the ball back to the C far more against Team B.
- The C plays the ball to the WA, GA and GS (together) more against Team B.
- There is a greater variety of pairs of players involved in passes against Team B (Other).
- The WA plays more than twice the number of passes to the GS that she does to the GA against Team C.
- The GA plays fewer passes to the C and WA against Team C.
- The modal pass is from the C to GA against Team D.

Now let us examine the right-most three columns of Table 9.1, which shows significant differences between the performances of Teams B, C and D (χ^2_{16} = 36.7, p = 0.002). This type of analysis can provide evidence of similarity or difference between passing performances. The main similarity between the passing of Teams B, C and D is that passes from players C to GA are the most common for all three teams. The GA to C is the second most frequent pass for Team D compared to the WA to GA for Teams B and C. Team C has the largest variety of passing with more classed as "Other" than the other two teams. This also involves lower frequencies of passes between the GA and C and between the GA and WA than is the case for the other two teams. Team B has the lowest variety of pass types with the highest frequencies for six of the eight most common pass types when we compare the three teams.

Temporal patterns within passing data

Network analysis in volleyball has examined temporal patterns of zones and event types rather than individual player involvement (Hurst et al., 2016). Network diagrams for syntax (Miller, 2016: 217–222) also incorporate semantics. Network analysis of performance in games helps develop an understanding of team cohesion, complex relationships between team members and team structure (Lusher et al., 2010). Another novel use of network analysis has been to compare the success of tennis doubles pairings from different eras (Breznik, 2015). This has been done using a directed graph showing match outcomes between different pairings varying the thickness of edges by how often the pairings played each other and adjusting arrow heads depending on the proportion of matches won by each pairing.

What Figures 9.4 and 9.5 and Table 9.1 do not show us is temporal ordering over more than one pass. Consider Figure 9.4. We can see that the C plays 24 or more passes to the GS and the GS plays more than 24 passes to the C. We can speculate that the C feeds the ball in to the GS who may immediately pass the ball back out to the C to find a better shooting position when the ball is fed in again. However, we cannot be certain from Figure 9.4 that this is actually happening. The GS may not be in the shooting circle when receiving some of these passes from the C. The GS may be passing to the C when they receive passes from other players (WD, WA and GA). We simply cannot tell from Figure 9.4. We may wish to examine sequences of two or more passes that precede goals or missed shots. Passos (2017) describes "individual flow intensity", which is the proportion of possessions a player is involved in that lead to a goal or scoring opportunity. We may wish to examine passing sequences that preceded possession losses. The number of passes per possession is related to this and represented by "ball movement rate" metrics (Passos, 2017). The example we use is passing sequences commencing with the centre pass, which is considered important in netball (Pulling et al., 2016). Consider Figure 9.5; the C plays the centre pass from the centre circle and it must be received by a player within the middle third. Initially, no other players are permitted within the middle third until the centre pass is played. Due to the restrictions on areas the ball can be played to, there are only four players who can receive the centre pass (WD, GD, WA and GA). Once one of these four players receives the centre pass, they could pass the ball to any of the other six players. If the next player to receive the ball is in the middle third, they could also pass the ball to any of the other six players on their team. This means there are 144 (4 × 6 × 6) different sequences of three receivers when passes commence with a centre pass. Research is needed to determine if there are particular sequences that are dominant in international netball. In the absence of such knowledge, the example compares sequences of two passes commencing with the centre pass between Teams A and B. There are 24 possible sequences of two passes commencing with the centre pass; we also need to represent situations where the centre pass or the next pass may fail to reach a teammate. Figure 9.6 shows the observed passing sequences. The nodes represent states in play, which

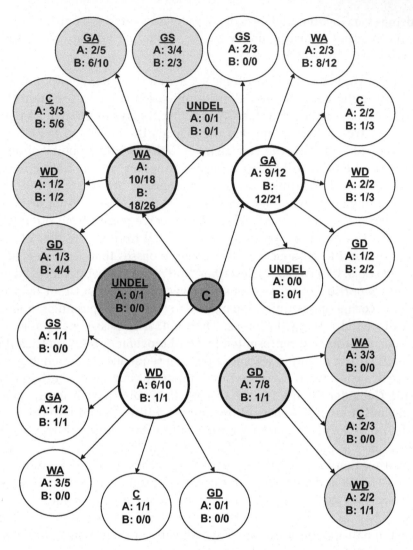

Figure 9.6 Centre pass tactics and effectiveness for two international teams, A and B (fractions represent goals/total number of possessions; UNDEL represents undelivered centre passes)

are effectively who has the ball. The edges not only represent passes but also state transitions; for example, a centre pass played from the C to WA will take the game from a state in which the C is waiting to deliver the centre pass to a state in which the WA has received the ball and is preparing to make the next pass. Within each node, the number of possessions leading to a goal and total number of possessions starting at that state are expressed as a fraction. For example, when the centre pass is played to the WA, Team A scores 10 times from 18 such possessions whereas Team B scores 18 times from 26 such possessions.

Overall, each team has 49 centre passes and they both score from 32 of these. However, the passing patterns they adopt and their relative success using these tactics differ as we can see in Figure 9.6. Team A is prepared to pass the ball backwards from the centre pass to the WD and GD whereas Team B only passes the ball once to these two players. Team A should consider why they do not pass the ball backwards more; they score 13 out of 18 (72.2%) centre passes played backwards compared to 19 out of 30 (63.3%) passed forwards. Team A has a much greater variety of centre pass tactics with no pair of passes used more than five times. Two pass pairs played by Team B (C to WA to GA and C to GA to WA) accounted for 22 of their 49 centre pass possessions. The modal pair of passes (C to GA to WA) is justified by its 66.7% success rate in leading to a goal (8 / 12), which is higher than the 60% (6 / 10) achieved when the centre pass is played to the WA and then the GA.

A further approach for analyzing passing sequences in team games is the use of T-patterns (Borrie et al., 2002; Jonsson et al., 2010; Sarmento et al., 2013). This involves analysis of passing sequences to identify repeated patterns observed within performances. The approach is flexible and sequences that include ordered patterns of events can be recognized even if the patterns are interspersed with other events.

SUMMARY

Network analysis is used to investigate interactions between network members such as organisations and individuals. The approach can be used with a variety of network sizes ranging from very large, such as social media analysis, to very localized, such as passing patterns within team sports performances. This chapter discussed the use of social network analysis to investigate player transfers in professional soccer, describing how network complexity can be managed using hierarchical structures that reflect the organizational structures within sports. A further way of managing complexity within network graphs is by using interactive software packages, such as Gephi and Social Network Visualiser (SocNetV), to flexibly set criteria for the interactions of interest.

Varying line widths and colours can indicate the volume and quality of interactions between network members. There are network metrics for centrality, density, intensity and clustering, which can be used in addition to network graphs to make comparisons between networks. The main application of network analysis within sports performance analysis is to study passing patterns within team games. This chapter described how inferential statistics can be used to compare passing tactic performances within a team as well as between teams. The network graphs on their own illustrate pairs of players who pass the ball to each other. However, temporal patterns of passes are concealed by this representation and need to be analysed by applying alternative approaches to the raw event data from which network graphs are derived.

REFERENCES

Baber, C., Stanton, N.A., Atkinson, J., McMaster, R. and Houghton, R.J. (2013) 'Using social network analysis and agent-based modelling to explore information flow using common operational pictures for maritime search and rescue operations', *Ergonomics*, 56(6): 889–905.

Bader, B. and Schuster, T. (2015) 'Expatriate social networks in terrorism-endangered countries: An empirical analysis in Afghanistan, India, Pakistan, and Saudi Arabia', *Journal of International Management*, 21(1): 63–77.

Barth, S., Schraagen, J.M. and Schmettow, M. (2015) 'Network measures for characterising team adaptation processes', *Ergonomics*, 58(8): 1287–1302.

Borrie, A., Jonsson, G.K. and Magnusson, M.S. (2002) 'Temporal pattern analysis and its applicability in sport: An explanation and exemplar data', *Journal of Sports Sciences*, 20: 845–852.

Breznik, K. (2015) 'Revealing the best doubles teams and players in tennis history', *International Journal of Performance Analysis in Sport*, 15: 1213–1226.

Butterworth, A. and O'Donoghue, P.G. (2016) 'Network analysis of passes in international netball', *World Congress of Performance Analysis in Sport 11*, Alicante, November 2016.

Clemente, F.M., Couceiro, M.S., Martins, F.M.L. and Mendes, R.S. (2014) 'Using network metrics to investigate football team players' connections: A pilot study', *Motriz*, 20(3): 262–271.

Clemente, F.M., Couceiro, M.S., Martins, F.M.L., Mendes, R. and Figueiredo, A.J. (2013) 'Measuring collective behaviour in football teams: Inspecting the impact of each half of the match on ball possession', *International Journal of Performance Analysis in Sport*, 13(3): 678–689.

Clemente, F.M., Martins, F.M.L., Kalamaras, D., Wong, D.P., Mendes, R.S. (2015a) 'General network analysis of national soccer teams in FIFA World Cup 2014', *International Journal of Performance Analysis in Sport*, 15: 80–96.

Clemente, F.M., Martins, F.M.L., Wong, D.P., Kalamaras, D. and Mendes, R.S. (2015b) 'Midfielder as the prominent participant in the building attack: A network analysis of national teams in FIFA World Cup 2014', *International Journal of Performance Analysis in Sport*, 15: 704–722.

Cotta, C., Mora, A.M., Merelo, J.J. and Merelo-Molina, C. (2013) 'A network analysis of the 2010 FIFA World Cup champion team play', *Journal of Systems Science and Complexity*, 26(1): 21–42.

Dreżewski, R., Sepielak, J. and Filipkowski, W. (2015) 'The application of social network analysis algorithms in a system supporting money laundering detection', *Information Sciences*, 295(20): 18–32.

Gama, J., Passos, P., Davids, K., Relvas, H., Ribeiro, J., Vaz, V. and Dias, G. (2014) 'Network analysis and intra-team activity in attacking phases of professional football', *International Journal of Performance Analysis in Sport*, 14: 692–708.

Grund, T.U. (2012) 'Network structure and team performance: The case of English Premier League soccer teams', *Social Networks*, 34(4): 682–690.

Houghton, R.J., Baber, C., McMaster, R., Stanton, N.A., Salmon, P., Stewart, R. and Walker, G. (2006) 'Command and control in emergency services operations: A social network analysis', *Ergonomics*, 49: 12–13.

Hurst, M., Loureiro, M., Valongo, B., Laporta, L., Nikolaidis, P.T. and Afonso, J. (2016) 'Systemic mapping of high-level women's volleyball using social network analysis: The case of serve (K0), side-out (KI), side-out transition (KII) and transition (KIII)', *International Journal of Performance Analysis in Sport*, 16: 696–710.

Jonsson, G.K., Anguera, M.T., Sánchez-Algarra, P., Olivera, C., Campanico, J., Castañer, M. and Chaverri, J. (2010) 'Application of T pattern detection and analysis in sports research', *Open Sports Sciences Journal*, 3: 95–104.

Kalamaras, D. (2014) 'Social Networks Visualizer (SocNetV): Social network analysis and visualization software', *Social Networks Visualizer*. http://socnetv.org/

Kirk, A. (2012) *Data visualisation: A successful design process*, Birmingham, UK: Packt Publishing.

Luo, Q. and Zhong, D. (2015) 'Using social network analysis to explain communication characteristics of travel-related electronic word-of-mouth on social networking sites', *Tourism Management*, 46: 274–282.

Lusher, D., Robins, G. and Kremer, P. (2010) 'The application of social network analysis to team sports, *Measurement in Physical Education and Exercise Science*, 14: 211–224.

Miller, T.W. (2016) *Sport analytics and data science: Winning the game with methods and models*, Old Tappan, NJ: Pearson Education Ltd.

Passos, P. (2017) 'Team member interaction analysis', In P. Passos, A. Duarte and A. Volossovitch (eds.), *Performance analysis in team games* (pp. 74–109), London: Routledge.

Pulling, C., Eldridge, D. and Lomax, J. (2016) 'Centre passes in the UK Netball Super League', *International Journal of Performance Analysis in Sport*, 16: 389–400.

Sarmento, H., Barbosa, A., Anguera, M.T., Campaniço, J. and Leitão, J. (2013) 'Regular patterns of play in the counter-attacks of the FC Barcelona and Manchester United football teams', In D. Peters and P.G. O'Donoghue (eds.), *Performance analysis of sport IX* (pp. 57–64), London: Routledge.

Yamamoto, Y. and Yokoyama, K. (2011) 'Common and unique network dynamics in football games', *PLoS ONE*, 6(12), e29638.

CHAPTER 10

KNOWLEDGE DISCOVERY IN DATABASES AND DATA MINING

INTRODUCTION

Knowledge discovery in databases (KDD) and data mining were mentioned in previous chapters of this book. This chapter distinguishes between KDD and data mining and describes the various stages of the KDD process and how they gradually transform data into knowledge. The chapter mentions the broad disciplines combined within KDD and data mining. However, a full description of specific analysis techniques used within data mining is not provided here as many of these are discussed in more detail during the chapters on machine learning and visualisation. An example of analysing tennis performance data is used to discuss some issues and challenges in KDD and data mining relevant to sports performance.

A wealth of data has been gathered in many application areas thanks to the ever increasing efficiency with which data can be captured and the capacity to store large volumes of data. The data stored in many scientific, business and medical contexts are a valuable resource to support research and inform decision making. There is a need to utilise KDD and data mining to gain actionable knowledge from data resources that cannot be done fully using traditional database querying and transaction processing systems.

Data analysis pre-dates the invention of computers with manual methods, such as regression analysis and Bayes theorem, used for centuries. However, data analysis processes, such as factor analysis, that would have taken many weeks to do manually can now be done efficiently by statistical analysis packages on computers. A further development is the use of databases rather than individual data files to store and maintain data. Data retrieved from databases are still largely analysed using routine methods and such analyses remain quite useful in most application areas. However, the fact that computers and databases are used does not, in itself, mean that processes should be termed "data mining". KDD processes and data mining need to be distinguished from routine data analysis. Most definitions published over the last 25 years are consistent with Frawley et al.'s (1991) description of data mining as non-trivial analysis leading to the extraction of previously unknown knowledge about the given domain.

KDD is a full process of knowledge discovery that includes data mining as a central stage. The stages prior to data mining retrieve task-relevant data, clean them and prepare them for processing by data mining tools. Following data mining, the extracted patterns are communicated and interpreted, often using visualisation, to create new knowledge. Data mining is typically done automatically by computers sifting through data using analysis tools to discover patterns. Although some patterns may be obvious, meaningless or coincidental when examined more closely, data mining can discover "gems" such as important relationships between variables that have not previously been known or hypothesised. We will consider the contrast between KDD and traditional database querying using example analyses of tennis performance data. Database querying is typically goal driven, deductive and answers questions with detailed information whereas KDD is more data driven and inductive, discovering knowledge and generating hypotheses. Consider a tennis performance database including tournament, match, player and ranking details. Examples of routine database querying are:

■ List players who win matches in which they won fewer points than the opponent and players who lost matches in which they won more points than the opponent (Simpson's paradox).
■ List players who reached the quarter-finals of more than one clay court tournament but never reached the last 32 of a grass court tournament.

KDD, on the other hand, seeks to answer questions such as:

■ What, if any, characteristics of players and performances distinguish Simpson paradox matches from other matches?

■ What, if any, characteristics of performances distinguish players who reached the quarter-finals of more than one clay court tournament but never reached the last 32 of grass court tournaments from other players?

This area of work has been referred to as knowledge engineering with those undertaking such work referred to as knowledge engineers. KDD has advantages over developing knowledge using human expertise, which can be slow, subjective and expensive (Fayyad, 1996). KDD is an alternative way of discovering knowledge that uses an array of tools, including statistical, modelling and machine learning techniques. Of course, there are many benefits to using human expertise that should also be recognised, including existing knowledge, intelligence, common sense and experience. The KDD approach generates hypotheses that can be considered by domain experts for further exploration and analysis.

Data mining uses large volumes of low-level data to produce compact, abstract and useful patterns of information (Fayyad, 1996). The general tasks that data mining has been used for are classification, estimation, prediction and profiling (Berry and Linoff, 2004). KDD and data mining have been applied in many specific application domains including clinical medicine, astronomy, analysing remote sensor data, sociology, physics and genetics (Gullo, 2015). A widely cited example in marketing is Walmart's discovery of a link between sales of baby diapers (nappies for UK readers) and beer (Saban, 2001). This knowledge informed Walmart's decision to place beer close to baby diapers within stores, which has been credited with increasing beer sales. Walmart also used data mining techniques to determine when cold and flu remedies should be stocked (Schumaker et al., 2010: 21). Fraud detection is also a commonly cited application area in which KDD has successfully been applied (Schumaker et al., 2010: 21).

KDD and data mining are becoming increasingly important for sports businesses. Marketing activities of sports businesses that can benefit from KDD include ticket sale monitoring, monitoring season ticket usage, up-selling (inducing existing customers to upgrade products or services), customer profiling and customising services (Chen and Lin, 2006). The knowledge created by KDD can be used to combat sports betting fraud (Schumaker et al., 2010: 59–61) with lopsided betting patterns indicating where there may be dishonest practice (Audi and Thompson, 2007).

knowledge discovery in databases and data mining

DISCIPLINES OF KDD AND DATA MINING

KDD and data mining combine database technology, statistics, visualisation, mathematics and high-performance algorithms (Frawley et al., 1991). Since Frawley et al. (1991) provided a description of data mining, database technology has developed further and now data warehousing is used by organisations to manage their data. Organisations have multiple data sources and indeed may have multiple databases. Data warehouses manage these disparate data resources, easing their retrieval (Fried, 2017: 36). There is such a capacity to amass large volumes of data that they are increasingly stored in a non-volatile form; that is, data are never deleted or changed, they are simply added to. Instead of applying a transaction to a customer profile and changing its contents, historical versions of the profile can be retained as well as a full record of transactions. There are various forms of data stored in databases and data warehouses. Databases combine raw low-level data values as well as metadata used by database management systems (DBMS) to represent and manage the structure of the data. Data warehouses contain predominantly metadata, allowing them to manage the collection of databases for the given organisation.

Statistical analyses are applied to data to determine if there are differences between groups or situations, or associations between variables. Different groups of individuals can be compared in terms of numerical variables using analysis of variances tests, supporting post hoc procedures, independent sample t-tests, effect size measures and descriptive statistics such as means and standard deviations. The groups compared could be athletes of differing injury histories, athletes of varying levels of success, or customers from various market sectors. These groups can also be compared in terms of ordinal variables using medians, quartiles, ranges and supporting nonparametric statistical tests. Chi square tests of independence can compare different groups in terms of nominal variables. We may have varying samples of data for the same group of people. These related samples could be data taken at different times or under different circumstances. The same descriptive statistics can be used as when comparing independent groups of people. However, the inferential procedures are different, as the tests are based on related samples; these tests include paired sample t-tests and repeated measure ANOVA tests. Correlation and regression can be used to determine if numerical variables are related and chi square tests can determine if categorical variables are related. Predictive modelling is important in player performance assessment, injury prediction, talent identification and game strategy evaluation (Haghighat et al., 2013). Predictive models of sports performance can be created using data mining techniques and applied to current performance situations. This allows expected performance outcomes for the given opposition and situational factors to be determined. The actual performance can then be evaluated more realistically by comparing it with the expected performance.

Machine learning is covered in detail in Chapter 7. Machine learning is used within KDD (Miller, 2016: 215) as well as other analytics processes and comes in a variety of forms including nonlinear analysis of relationships between variables and artificial neural networks. Machine learning techniques can use supervised learning in which previous cases including dependent outcome indicators are examined to provide predictive models of variables of interest. Alternatively, unsupervised learning techniques can be applied to datasets to allow clusters of cases to be identified without considering a dependent variable from previous cases. The clusters may contain people who are similar with respect to the data stored about them. These clusters may be previously unknown market sectors or performer types and the newly created cluster variable can be used the same way as any other grouping variable to discover factors associated with cluster membership.

Visualisation allows exploratory patterns discovered through data mining to be presented in effective abstract ways that are naturally understood by decision makers (Zhu and Chen, 2005). It is not sufficient for data mining to discover patterns if this new information is not acted upon because decision makers were unable to understand it. The presentation of findings from data mining needs to be appropriate for the given application domain and audience. For example, sports-specific representations can be used within scouting tools (Schumaker et al., 2010: 56–58). Further detail about visualisation can be found in Chapter 3.

Mathematical techniques can be used during the pre-processing of data prior to data mining, during the data mining stage or to post-process resulting patterns. Geospatial data can be pre-processed using geometry and trigonometry. Pattern recognition can use matrix processing and graph mining can be used in social network analysis. Mathematical methods often depend on the nature of the data that KDD approaches are

knowledge discovery in databases and data mining

applied to. For example, different mathematical methods could be used with engineering and genealogical data.

High-performance algorithms have been deemed important in data mining (Frawley et al., 1991). There are some KDD applications in which it is more important to thoroughly mine the data and carefully interpret any patterns that emerge. Indeed, hypotheses generated in this way may lead to further research that is time consuming but important. The use of high-performance algorithms in such situations is not so important, as decision makers will be prepared to wait for quality information rather than using information produced rapidly but not as rigorously. Rather, high-performance algorithms are important when decision makers are dealing with exploratory patterns using interactive visualisation. Experimental analyses may involve changing parameter settings and query types as data are explored. Personnel involved in such analyses may be important individuals whose time is valuable; bringing several such individuals together at the same time is difficult. Therefore, when they are required to discuss information displayed using interactive visualisation, the systems need to be highly efficient to allow discussions to run smoothly.

MINING TENNIS PERFORMANCE DATA

This chapter uses tennis performance data mining to illustrate the various stages of the KDD process. There is a wealth of tennis performance data provided by the official websites of the four Grand Slam tournaments. These data can be analysed to gain knowledge about tennis performances. O'Donoghue and Holmes (2015: 50–54) described the point-by-point data provided by the "Slam Tracker" facility and how text pre-processing is needed to extract variables from the point records. These data have been found sufficiently reliable for research purposes based on a comparison of data for 10 matches with data derived from independent video observation of the same matches (Moss and O'Donoghue, 2015). Moss and O'Donoghue's (2015) momentum study is a good example of where data mining approaches can be advantageous. Moss and O'Donoghue (2015) gathered data from official Internet sites of Grand Slam tennis tournaments and pre-processed them in spreadsheet files before executive summary data were loaded into statistical analysis packages. A data mining environment with a proper infrastructure for retrieving and processing relevant tennis performance information could have saved multiple versions of the data being processed by multiple packages. A database would have allowed full performance data to be stored independently of individual research aims. The data model shown in Figure 10.1 is not a full entity-relationship model but a more abstract model used early during the design phase. The database needs to support a variety of querying related to point, game, set and match patterns; tournament and individual player analyses; player cluster identification and more reductive approaches about tennis performances in general.

The boxes of Figure 10.1 are candidate entities and lines between boxes indicate likely relationships between the entities represented. Container relations are common in this example, as points are played within games that, in turn, are played within sets. Sets are played within matches that are played within tournaments. Matches are played between players; this could be represented in a number of ways. We could have separate relations to represent the winning and losing player within a match or we could simply have a "played in" relation linking each match to two players and linking each player to many matches. If doubles matches are to be included, we might need additional entities to represent doubles pairings and matches between various doubles pairings. There may be

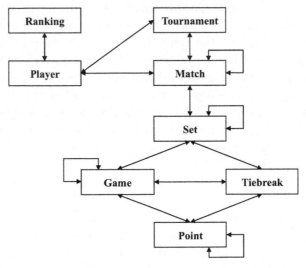

Figure 10.1 Data model for tennis performance

196   knowledge discovery in databases and data mining

temporal relationships between instances of entities of the same class. For example, we may wish to show a relation between consecutively played points, games or sets. There is also a temporal relationship between a tiebreak and the game that preceded it. There are more efficient alternatives whereby any points, games or sets played in a given match can be retrieved from the database and then sorted into time order based on the score at the beginning of the point. This avoids having a multitude of relations between point instances when we may be interested in consecutively played sequences of two, three or more points.

Most of the data will be stored within point instances. The basic attributes of a point are:

- Score at the start of the point (sets, games and points).
- Serving player.
- Whether the point required a second serve.
- The speed of the serve(s).
- The number of shots played.
- The type of point (ace, double fault, net point, baseline rally).
- Player who won the point.
- Method of point ending.

Far greater detail could be included about points. In fact, we could go right down to the shot level, recording where each shot was played from and to, and the type of stroke used including spin and pace.

Because normal games and tiebreaks are made up of points, we do not need to repeat the point details although some summary information about these game types could be stored. For example, we could store the score in sets and games at the start of the game, who the serving player was, who won the game (or tiebreak) and what the overall score in points was at the end of the game (or tiebreak). Similarly, a set instance may include the score in sets at the start of the set, the player who served first in the set, who won the set and what the score in games was for the set. There are various match types that need to be distinguished. This can be done by including an attribute within a match that dictates whether it is the best of three or five sets. A further attribute can state whether tiebreaks are played in the final set. There are Tiebreak 10 matches, Fast4 matches as well as traditional tennis matches. The round within the given tournament a match is played in could be part of the relationship between a match and the tournament or included as an attribute of the match.

The match instances can also include whether it is a women's singles, men's singles, women's doubles, men's doubles or mixed doubles match. Around the time this chapter was written, John McEnroe speculated that Serena Williams would rank 700th on the men's tour (Guardian, 2017). Perhaps Serena Williams and the 700th ranked male player should play! If that were to happen, database designers would probably decide it was a one-off match not worth enhancing the database model for.

Important information to include in the tournament entity is the court surface, whether matches are played indoors or outdoors and the grading of the tournament. The representation of player rankings needs to be considered carefully. Player rankings change regularly and certain queries and data mining explorations will need to know the player rankings at the times at which they play matches. There may be some players with ranking points who have not participated in any of the tournaments included in the database but who may participate in matches to be added to the database at some future date. It is important to store ranking information as completely as possible in case any data mining tasks look at trends in rankings and their association with success in matches and tournaments.

STAGES OF THE KDD PROCESS

Database and data warehouse creation

Figure 10.2 shows the main stages of the KDD process and how they gradually derive knowledge from data. Data capturing is technically not a stage of the KDD process but Figure 10.2 recognises that databases, data warehousing and KDD environments need to first be established and databases need to be populated and kept up-to-date. Establishing a KDD/data mining environment requires creating a data warehouse. The data warehouse may use existing databases or newly created ones. Database design requires knowledge of the application domain and the types of query and data mining tasks that might be applied to the data. Databases are not just for data storage but also have a business role within organisations (Mathew, 2017: 56). There is a choice of database management systems (DBMS) that could be used, which depends on the nature of the data, how often they are updated, and the type of retrieval queries commonly used. The database could be relational (Codd, 1970) or object-oriented (Hughes, 1991), for example.

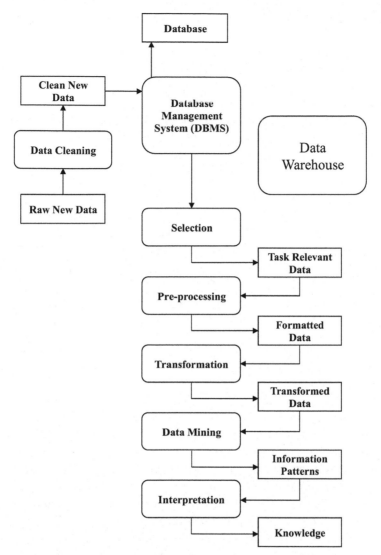

Figure 10.2 Stages of the KDD process.

There are decisions about the entities, attributes and relationships of the data model, and often time versus space trade-offs to consider. For example, we could have relationships to show that a tennis player competed in a match and that the match occurred within a particular tournament. An additional relationship between a player and a tournament they have entered is redundant in that this can be determined from the player competing in a match that was within the given tournament. However, if we do not include an "entered" relationship between player and tournament, the query requiring knowledge of the players who entered tournaments will need two steps to determine this intermediate data from the database instead of one. The biggest issue with storing redundant data is not the use of additional storage space but the risk that data may become inconsistent when updates are made. This is not such an issue in the tennis example used here because the match and historical ranking data are non-volatile.

A database could be designed to more efficiently process certain query types that may be common within KDD processes. This might involve storing intermediate forms of data and maintaining these as new players, matches, tournaments and ranking data are added to the database. However, databases cannot be expected to store every possible intermediate data structure for every possible query. Therefore, database structures tend to be as general as possible for knowledge engineers to understand them and to support any query that might be applied to the data.

A database design not only allows us to structure the data but also consider their semantic constraints and how these can be used to develop data quality checks. These checks help ensure the data's integrity and consistency and can be applied at the point new data are added to the database. There are other data cleaning tasks specific to data mining that cannot be made at the point of data capture; rather, they need to be applied during the KDD pre-processing stage. Data capture processes exist within systems that operate independently of the KDD process. Tennis match data are routinely gathered to provide match statistics on the websites of major tennis tournaments; world rankings are maintained by the ATP (Association of Tennis Professionals) and WTA (Women's Tennis Association). A data warehouse run by these governing bodies could have access to official tournament, match, player and ranking databases. When independent research organisations are developing such a KDD environment, they need to have means of gathering and storing relevant publicly available data provided by the official websites in a way that does not violate the terms and conditions of these sources. Data presented on official tournament websites will need to be captured in a form suitable for database entry and checked to ensure the data are consistent and satisfy any constraints required within and between database records.

200

Selection

Once a KDD environment exists, KDD activities can commence. The first stage of the KDD process is "Selection". The selection stage commences with the knowledge engineers setting knowledge discovery goals. This is informed by application domain knowledge and understanding knowledge gaps. The data relevant to the knowledge discovery goals need to be identified; therefore, database querying is used to extract these data from the data warehouse. The selection of features to include in the data mining stage can be done using a variety of approaches including expert opinion (Haghighat et al., 2013). Consider a knowledge discovery task that seeks to explore tennis player behaviour on game points when serving (40–0, 40–15, 40–30 and advantage for), break points against (0–40, 15–40, 30–40 and advantage against) and any other points. This almost sounds like we are specifying a null hypothesis that there will be no difference between these score-line states for any of the variables we will be looking at. However, in our KDD approach, we do not restrict confirming or refuting such a hypothesis. It could be that the score-line and/or sets have an impact on score-line effects within games. There may be some players who play all the points the same way and others who exhibit score-line specific tactical behaviour; performance quality could also be effected by the score-line. Perhaps player ranking, gender, nationality, involvement in doubles games, age, experience or some other factors combine with the game score-line to impact behaviour. Furthermore, dependent variables might be influenced by the score-line. Thus, the selection of data to include within data mining tasks is not as straightforward as one might imagine.

Pre-processing

Data pre-processing cleans the data by removing "noise" and handling missing data (Gullo, 2015). During pre-processing, selected data may be removed to make data mining more efficient and valid. For example, if we are interested in differences in play between game points for the server, break points and other points, we will need to remove some matches in which one or both players did not play enough break points. If a player in a match only plays four break points and the data mining tools explore the percentage of points in which certain tactics were applied, the value is going to be 0, 25, 50, 75 or 100. These are large steps caused by single points that might have an undue influence on the knowledge discovered, which we would usually prefer not to be heavily influenced by individual performances. Pre-processing also needs to deal with missing data. Some variables may be missing for particular cases. For example, in Grand Slam tennis matches, variables about winners, unforced errors, net points and serve directions are only recorded for matches played on certain courts, such as "show courts". If the missing variables are essential to the given KDD task, match records without these variables should be excluded. Another form of missing data may occur when a match is not completed. We may have a full record of the points played and the incomplete match may have still been longer than many completed matches. There may be situations in which we can justify the inclusion of the match – for example, if there are sufficient break points played and match outcome might be irrelevant to the KDD task.

Transformation

The data transformation stage reduces the selected data to a form suitable for data mining tools. In our example of comparing game points, break points and other points, we do not need any tiebreak points. Indeed, we may decide to apply data mining tools at a match level rather than an individual point level. This would involve transforming individual point data (categorical) into percentages of point types in which different tactics were applied. This avoids lengthy matches having an undue influence on the knowledge produced. Similarly, some players may play more matches than others and therefore we may wish to aggregate multiple performances for a single player together. The argument in favour of this transformation is it avoids some players having an undue influence on the knowledge discovered because they played more matches than others. One argument against aggregating a player's matches together into a single player record is that the performances of players who reach the latter tournament stages are more representative of the nature of tennis played at those tournaments. A further argument against aggregating a player's matches is it artificially removes player variability with respect to tactics applied in different score-lines.

Data can be overlaid with demographic information to make data mining processes more effective. This is typically done in market research KDD tasks. The data warehouse may have separate databases for different features included in the KDD task, such as transactions and customer demographic data. In our tennis example, the match data and ranking data are stored in different databases. The issue this raises for our KDD process is that although we can aggregate a player's matches together into a single record, we need to represent the quality of the player using their world ranking, which varies between tournaments. Solutions could be to apply an average or categorised subrange of world ranking.

Data mining

The central data mining task of the KDD process is applied to the transformed data. During this stage, data mining tools extract interesting patterns from the data. These patterns may be clusters, rules or associations that are derived by artificial intelligence, machine learning or statistical methods. The main artificial intelligence tools used are artificial neural networks. These can be trained using previous case data to predict categorical information from data patterns. Within a KDD environment, multiple categorical variables can be explored in this way. When neural network models can be cross-validated using a subset of the data, the trained neural networks can be used to predict missing values.

Decision trees (Chen et al., 2004) are a classification technique that comes from the machine learning realm. Decision trees are hierarchical structures used in classification problems allowing potential class predictions to be narrowed down as different variables are considered. The trees are constructed and refined using training data. Other methods of classification used in data mining are nearest neighbour analysis and support vector machines (SVM).

Statistical methods allow the wealth of data stored in databases to be summarised using descriptive and inferential procedures. There is an overlap with machine learning and classification techniques, as some statistical procedures predict group membership based on data values. Statistical techniques supporting such classification are cluster analysis, logistic regression and discriminant function analysis. Regression analysis has also been used within data mining to model more continuous variables (Schumaker et al., 2010: 18).

Anomaly detection looks for data patterns that occur infrequently and are noticeably different than the bulk of the data stored. For example, we may discover different score-line effects on performance and clusters of players associated with each effect. There may be individual players who have unique score-line effects once serving games, receiving games and tiebreakers are all considered together. Rules are typically expressed in the form "IF X THEN Y". Association rules link data items and also include the level of supporting evidence for these links. For example, we may discover some players who only serve to an opponent's backhand side on critical points such as break and game points. There may be variations on this based on first serve, second serve, serving to the deuce court and serving to the advantage court.

Social network analysis represents people, groups and organisations as nodes within a graph in which the edges represent communication links between people. The frequency and nature of communications are examined to determine the probability of individuals being linked. Exploring matches between pairs of players may identify that some players have "bogie" opponents who they underperform against when we consider the players' relative world rankings. Social network analysis is covered in more detail in Chapter 9.

Other techniques used in data mining include collaborative filtering, market basket and survival analyses (Chen and Lin, 2006), automatic interaction detection (Kotler, 2003: 54), Bayesian methods (Haghighat et al., 2013), fuzzy systems (Haghighat et al., 2013), rule-based heuristics (Schumaker et al., 2010: 19) and genetic algorithms (Schumaker et al., 2010: 19, 67).

Interpretation

The mined patterns are considered by experts who attempt to explain them and, in so doing, extract new knowledge. The interpretation of mined patterns is often assisted by visualisation tools and other post-processing techniques to highlight characteristics within the patterns that can be exploited by organisations. The new knowledge produced can then be utilised by decision makers. Patterns found about score-line effects could be used to help players improve their own performances or understand opposition tendencies. When a player is not as successful in some score-line states as others, there may be a role for coaching or sport psychology interventions to help reduce the negative impact of being in certain score-lines during tennis games. The data mining stage

204

may also show certain opponents to have score-line specific tactics; this knowledge is potentially useful in preparing for matches against these opponents to help anticipate factors such as serve direction.

SUMMARY

The main challenge for KDD processes is that they deal with large volumes of data of differing types and sources. These sources may be distributed across different application systems with data streaming into various systems in parallel. In addition to the large number of cases, there are many entities represented within databases, meaning there are also multiple variables. Data are dynamically evolving and can be noisy, unreliable or even missing. The large number of variables used means there are numerous variable combinations that could be potentially explored using various data mining tools. Indeed, KDD not only explores combinations of variables but can also use combinations of analysis methods during the data mining stage. Therefore, it is not possible to have an automatic KDD system that sifts through every possible combination of method and variable pairing. The selection stage is necessary and requires human expertise, as does the interpretation stage. The time frame for generating knowledge is also a challenge for KDD processes and depends on the application area and the purpose of the KDD tasks. When data are mined interactively, high-performance algorithms are necessary to ensure patterns are presented to decisions makers in a timely manner. The patterns provided need to be presented in a way that enhances interpretation by experts. This is especially true in interactive mining, in which decision making may occur under greater time pressure. Therefore, KDD environments need an infrastructure to allow use of multiple techniques through interfaces with efficient communications between computers managing the various databases in which interactive mining tasks are controlled.

A further challenge to data mining activity is that data must be used legally and ethically. Those who provide data to organisations should do so with an understanding of how the data are to be used. Data handlers need to comply with data protection legislation and prevent excessive and unnecessary use of data that violate such legislation. There are also social impacts of data mining in many domain areas; an example in sports is in talent development, in which knowledge generated by a KDD process could be used inappropriately to make decisions regarding sports recruitment, sponsorship, selection and deselection. The knowledge provided by data mining include patterns that have limitations, just as any other scientific results are evidence rather than conclusive proof. The patterns provided and the knowledge generated by interpreting these need to be considered together with any inherent limitations of KDD processes.

REFERENCES

Audi, T. and Thompson, A. (2007) 'Oddsmakers in Vegas play new sports role', *The Wall Street Journal*, A1.

Berry, M.J.A. and Linoff, G.S. (2004) *Data mining techniques: For marketing, sales and customer relationship management*, 2nd edn., Indianapolis, IN: Wiley Publishing, Inc.

Chen, S.-C., Shyu, M.-L., Chen, M. and Zhang, C. (2004) 'A decision tree-based multimodal data mining framework for soccer goal detection', *IEEE International Conference on Multimedia and Expo, 2004, ICME'04* (Vol. 1, pp. 265–268).

Chen-Yueh Chen, C.-Y. and Lin, Y-H. (2006) 'Market research approach for sports data mining', *The Sport Journal*, 9(3): unpaginated.

Codd, E.F. (1970) 'A relational model for data of large shared data banks', *Communications of the ACM*, 13: 377–387.

Fayyad, U. (1996) *Advances in knowledge discovery and data mining*, Menlo Park, CA: AAAI Press.

Frawley, W.J., Piatetsky-Shapiro, G. and Matheus, C.J. (1991) 'Knowledge discovery in databases: An overview', In G. Piatetsky-Shapiro and W. Frawley (eds.), *Knowledge discovery in databases*, Cambridge, MA: AAAI/MIT Press.

Fried, G. (2017) 'The data ecosystem', In G. Fried and C. Mumcu (eds.), *Sport analytics: A data-driven approach to sport business and management* (pp. 33–46), London: Routledge.

Guardian (2017) www.theguardian.com/sport/video/2017/jun/27/john-mcenroe-serena-williams-ranked-700th-mens-tour-tennis, accessed 11th July 2017.

Gullo, F. (2015) 'From patterns in data to knowledge discovery: What data mining can do', *Proceedings of the 3rd International Conference Frontiers in Diagnostic Technologies, ICFDT3 2013* (pp. 18–22), Elsevier.

Haghighat, M., Rastegari, H. and Nourafza, N. (2013) 'A review of data mining techniques for result prediction in sports', *ACSIJ Advances in Computer Science: An International Journal*, 2(5): 7–12.

Hughes, J.G. (1991) *Object-oriented databases*, Hemel Hemstead, Hertfordshire, UK: Prentice Hall International.

Kotler, P. (2003) *Marketing management*, 11th edn., Upper Saddle River, NJ: Pearson, Education Inc.

Mathew, R. (2017) 'Customer relationship management and fan engagement analytics', In C.K. Harrison and S. Bukstein (eds.), *Sports business analytics: Using data to increase revenue and improve operational efficiency* (pp. 53–68), London: Routledge.

Miller, T.W. (2016) *Sports analytics and data science: Winning the game with methods and models*, Old Tappan, NJ: Pearson.

Moss, B. and O'Donoghue, P.G. (2015) 'Momentum in US Open men's singles tennis', *International Journal of Performance Analysis in Sport*, 15(3): 884–896.

O'Donoghue, P.G. and Holmes, L.A. (2015) *Data analysis in sport*, London: Routledge.

Saban, K.A. (2001) 'The data mining process: At a critical crossroads in development', *Journal of Database Marketing*, 8(2): 157–167.

Schumaker, R., Solieman, O. and Chen, H. (2010) *Sports data mining*, New York, NY: Springer.

Zhu, B. and Chen, H. (2005) 'Information visualization', *Annual Review of Information Science and Technology (ARIST)*, 39: 139–178.

CHAPTER 11

DATA MANAGEMENT AND INFRASTRUCTURE

INTRODUCTION

As technology develops, products tend to integrate features and services together that may have previously been provided separately. In the early days of computing, programs were written in separate environments to the mainframe computers that compiled and executed them. With the advent of the microcomputer, integrated programming support environments (IPSEs) brought together program editing, checking, debugging, execution features, help facilities and version control support. In recent years, the term *integrated development environment* (IDE) has been used instead of IPSE (Miller, 2016: 267).

One only has to consider the capabilities available on one's mobile phone to see how communications and multimedia technologies are integrated together providing benefits to phone owners. The integration of general tools within phone and tablet devices for recording and transmitting data has provided hardware/firmware platforms promoting the development of specific integrated systems in many application areas. Common video codecs and protocols for data transfer between devices have helped application developers produce systems that run on multiple platforms. For example, Sportscode (HUDL, Lincoln, NE) transfers data in Extensible Markup Language (XML) between devices over a wireless network. This permits multiple operators to enter various data using iPads into a common timeline associated with a video recorded onto a central Apple Mac computer. This level of integration is smoother and more immediate than what was possible during the early days of multimedia computing. Consider the Match Analysis Video Integrated

System (MAVIS) prototype developed in the mid-1990s (O'Donoghue et al., 1996). The computer used to develop the system required a special video capture card so the match video could be transferred from the video camera that recorded it onto the computer. Nonetheless, this was an early example of general multimedia integration exploited by a specific application need. Indeed, the Borland Delphi programming language used to develop MAVIS included a library of video access procedures developed with multimedia applications in mind.

This chapter provides a rationale for integrating multiple data streams and analysis functions by discussing challenges that occurred during the analysis of the decathlon (Chapter 3). The chapter then reviews the integration of different data types within sports performance analysis systems and processes. Finally, the chapter examines high-performance management in sports, its use of multiple data types and how analytics support should be fully integrated with the strategic goals of sports organisations.

RATIONALE FOR DATA MANAGEMENT INFRASTRUCTURE

Let us consider the example of the decathlon used in Chapter 3 to discuss interactive visualisation and decision making. The data were gathered and analysed by an author of this book (O'Donoghue) who describes some issues he had during the exercise due to the lack of infrastructure. The data were initially entered into Microsoft Excel to complete the initial checking and data cleaning processes described in Chapter 3. The first issue was that there were five sets of performances analysed for different purposes:

- The 211 performances, including more than one performance for some athletes.
- The best performance for each of the 100 decathletes included in the dataset.
- The 65 pairs of performances done by the same athletes in consecutive years. Table 3.2 shows there were 10 subsets of these data representing the 27 to 42 athletes who improved their performance in a discipline from one year to the next.
- The nine performances of Thomas Van der Plaetsen.
- The data for athletes finishing in the places shown in Figure 3.3 for various athletic championships (Gold, Silver, Bronze, 5th, 10th, 15th, 20th).

A second issue was that some analyses needed to be done in SPSS (SPSS, an IBM company, Armonk, NY) rather than in Microsoft Excel (Microsoft, Redmond, WA). Excel is an excellent package for data management and pre-processing of data but SPSS was needed to undertake some multivariate analyses applied to the data.

A third issue was that the same dataset needed to be arranged in two different ways so it could be used to produce a box and whiskers plot (Figure 3.2), and undertake the principle components (Figure 3.4) and cluster analyses (Figure 3.5). The data needed to be arranged using 10 rows for each performance so the 10 events were treated as a grouping variable when producing the box and whiskers plot. However, the 10 events needed to remain in separate columns to apply the principle components and cluster analyses.

The fourth issue was that the data needed to go from Microsoft Excel to SPSS back to Microsoft Excel to produce the loading plots shown in Figure 3.4. The data were loaded into SPSS to complete the principle components analysis, producing several outputs. One was the table of correlations between the five rotated principle components and the points earned in the 10 decathlon disciplines, which was required to produce the loading plots. This actually formed a sixth set of data in which the discipline was the unit of analysis and the variables of interest were the correlation coefficients with the five principle components. These were placed back into Microsoft Excel to convert the loading plots to scatter plots. Even if this had been done in SPSS, the correlations would need to be taken from an SPSS output viewer file and placed in a new SPSS data sheet to apply the SPSS graph plotting tool.

The target setting stage of the process involved correlation of points improvements with initial scores for events, inspection of relationships, modelling of variances to apply for each event given the ability of the athlete of interest, exploration of event combinations and analysis of the points increases that could be achieved by improving in these events. Furthermore, it was necessary to superimpose the output of an individual athlete analysis on top of an analysis of the wider population of athletes who acted as a reference (Figure 3.8). It should also demonstrate the difficulty of developing any sports analytics infrastructure that is all things to all sports. If you consider some specialities of your own sports and the data involved, whether your sport is cricket, martial arts, a team game or some other sport, you should realise that most sports have data analysis and presentation issues specific to the given sport. Therefore, we recommend that any data management infrastructure specialises in the given sport. Hopefully, this example of the decathlon has highlighted the difficulties that arise when we do not have a data management infrastructure that will support all the analyses we wish to apply to the data. Developing such an infrastructure is not straightforward.

Successful sports organisations are able to use their data for many purposes. A good example of this is a case study of New Jersey Youth Soccer (Mumcu, 2017) in which data analytics were applied to investigations of diverse areas such as hooliganism, supporter relations and team travel. A database of decathlon performer and performance data is central to such an infrastructure. We need to store as much information as we legally and ethically can about performers and performances to support many analysis forms. For example, Chapter 3 did not consider the age of athletes when investigating feasible improvements in various disciplines. We may be interested in improvements that can be made by athletes of a particular age in a period of two to three years leading up to a major championship. A further set of variables that could be stored about decathlon athletes is their performances in track and field competitions outside decathlon events. There may be associations between performances within and outside decathlons. Indeed, decathletes may compete in 200m races, a distance not included in the decathlon but that may be associated with performance in its disciplines.

The data management infrastructure also needs efficient and effective capabilities to add new data and retrieve data from the database. The database querying language needs to allow various subsets of data to be extracted, preferably using a flexible and interactive interface to set criteria of interest. In our decathlon example, we would wish to access the subsets of data listed previously and store these as intermediate data structures within data mining processes or more applied target setting activities.

Once the required data have been extracted, they need to be structured to support any analyses applied to them. Therefore, the data management infrastructure needs ways of partitioning data, switching rows and columns, sorting data, etc without the data having to be processed in packages outside the data management infrastructure.

INTEGRATION OF DATA STREAMS IN SPORTS PERFORMANCE ANALYSIS

Computerised sports analysis systems

Within sports performance analysis, there has been an increase in integration of sports performance data as technology has developed. During the pioneering days of notational analysis, manual notation involved a clear separation of match videos and quantitative information recorded using sequential systems and tally charts. The CABER (Capture and Analysis of Behavioural Events in Real-time) system (Patrick and McKenna, 1986) was one of the first to integrate video and quantitative event data. The videos were recorded on VHS tape and a computer controlled the forward-winding and rewinding of tapes to show the video sequences of interest. The computer was connected to the video cassette player using an RS232 interface cable. As data storage capacities improved, multimedia computers allowed video data to be stored on random access disks, which made video sequence retrieval more efficient than when serial access tapes were used. MAVIS (Match Analysis Video Integrated System) was an academic prototype that allowed video sequences satisfying criteria entered by coaches to be displayed in a flexible manner (O'Donoghue et al., 1996). Both CABER and MAVIS involved match event criteria entered so a database could be searched to retrieve the video times of events satisfying the criteria of interest. Today, this integration of match event database and match video is an essential feature of all commercial sports analysis systems, such as Focus X2/X3 (Elite Sports Analysis, Delgaty Bay, Scotland), Dartfish (Dartfish, Fribourg, Switzerland), Sportscode (HUDL, Lincoln, NE) and Nacsport (Nacsport, Gran Canaria, Spain). These commercial products made many advances on the MAVIS system; most importantly, they are generic systems in which analysts can define their sport event types, allowing the packages to be used for any sport in which events could be tagged during video analysis. The automated integration of quantitative and unstructured forms of data within a centralised system improves the efficiency with which information can be used by decision makers (Alamar, 2013: 41–43). Indeed, although coaches today may still rely on analysts to tag videos during match observation, the coaches themselves are able to use commercial video analysis packages to examine match statistics, identify areas requiring attention, preview relevant video sequences and produce highlights

212

movies for use in team debriefings. Examination of match statistics is greatly helped by further integration of analysis features within commercial packages. For example, Sportscode has an output window in which summary statistics can be updated live with colour coding of outputs for interpretation. For example, traffic light colours (green, amber and red) can be used to indicate the quality of performance based on success statistics (good, average and poor, respectively). The output window can be wirelessly transmitted live to an iPad or iPhone used by the coaches on the bench to support real-time decision making. Nacsport produces information dashboards that summarise data automatically and present them visually in a manner that aids coach decision making.

In addition to video and structured match event data, some packages also allow event locations to be entered into images of the playing surfaces. For example, Prozone's MatchViewer system (Prozone Sports Ltd, Leeds, UK) allows soccer event locations to be recorded. This information can then be presented for sets of events meeting criteria of interest; for example, we may be interested in seeing the locations of passes made by players of interest in the first half of a match.

Coaching support environments

Coaching support environments such as Team Performance Exchange (Team Performance Exchange, Best, Holland) and CoachLogic (www. coach-logic.com/, accessed 21/9/17) are used to enhance communication between players and coaches. These systems allow video sequences to be uploaded and viewed within a password-protected Internet-based system. The videos may be tagged using video analysis packages and the clips can also be viewed using mobile apps. CoachLogic stores the tagged video, allowing video sequences to be selected based on criteria of interest in a similar interactive way to that provided by video analysis packages. Discussion forums allow coach and player comments about highlighted areas of performance to be added and recorded as well as the use of task lists. This is a flexible approach allowing squad discussion to occur in an asynchronous fashion and without requiring busy squad members to be located in the same room. This allows training sessions to devote more time to physical, technical and tactical training, as much of the coaching discussion will have already taken place. This is a decentralised approach in the sense that it integrates the computerised match analysis package and the web-based coaching support environment. Some may regard this as a centralised approach, as the data streams emanating from the computerised match analysis system are integrated with other coaching data within the coaching support environment. The integration is stronger and more centralised when the same producer has created the video analysis package as well as its web-based support environment. For example, the Dartfish package can be used with Dartfish TV to provide statistical and related video sequence information over a web-based password-protected interface. These integrated coaching support environments can be used throughout the season, including preparation and competition periods. For example, Nibali (2017) describes a case study from the Singapore Sports Institute's preparation for the South East Asia games in which a video ecosystem integrates the capture, storing and sharing of performance videos. This allows athletes and coaches to access relevant video sequences using a Dartfish mobile app.

There are still further developments that can be made to add further integration within sports performance analysis and coaching environments. Sports performance data are no longer restricted to events that are observed and tagged by system operators. Sports performance analysis now uses automatically gathered data such as GPS data and other ball and player tracking data, with potential for further data to be gathered using wearable devices for physiological monitoring (Miller, 2016: 170), smart clothing and optical tracking devices (Nibali, 2017). As has already been mentioned, the commercial packages available today integrate match videos with a more structured database of match information. Nonetheless, these two types of information are still examined separately with quantitative statistics, focussing qualitative analysis on more complex, richer video information. Further integration could be the inclusion of key quantitative results within video sequences to reinforce why the particular sequences are shown. A further area of integration of video and statistical information is the development of multimedia profiles (Butterworth, 2018). Profiles in sports performance analysis have traditionally included quantitative information only presented in graphical form (James et al., 2005; O'Donoghue, 2005). Multimedia profiles present quantitative information about performers derived from multiple matches showing typical performances. This allows areas of performance that are executed well, not so well, consistently and not so consistently to be easily recognised. A key feature of multimedia profiles

data management and infrastructure

is the ability to display video sequences associated with different levels of performance with respect to each indicator included in the profile. Multimedia profiles can also include annotated images, audio information, pitch or court maps and virtual reality output. Virtual reality can be used interactively, allowing views relevant to individual players that are not possible from video (Wiemeyer and Mueller, 2015). The use of data from multiple matches is a welcome development, as match analysis packages have typically been used to analyse single matches at a time. Future developments in the integration of match videos and quantitative match information are in accessing quantitative information related to video content; this is essentially moving in the opposite direction from how these data have been used to date. In other application areas such as product marketing, video hotspots allow viewers to access quantitative information about the products shown in the video (www.videoclix. com, accessed 17/9/17). This type of approach would be beneficial in sports performance analysis in which players or events shown in video sequences could be clicked on to display additional details.

INTEGRATED SPORTS ANALYTICS SYSTEMS

Sports business analytics

So far, the chapter has discussed integration of data streams and functions within commercial video analysis packages and coaching support environments. Analytics combines the management of data with analysis, modelling and visualisation processes, serving a wider business context in which there are more diverse data streams and processing needs. The main sports business analytics textbooks (Alamar, 2013; Fried and Mumcu, 2017; Harrison and Bukstein, 2017: ix) discuss the benefits of integrating data streams within sports businesses. The integration of data streams helps streamline business processes, giving sports organisations a competitive advantage. Sports organisations maintain data used in multiple areas; these data include medical reports, financial plans and performance videos. Centralising an organisation's data improves efficiency by providing "one version of the truth" (Alamar, 2013: 7, 29). An integrated analytics environment allows decision makers to access any of the organisation's data in an interactive and flexible manner when making decisions. Integrated data streams are more powerful than the sum of the equivalent data streams when segregated because integration promotes synergies among the various data streams and allows decision makers to consider information derived from combined data streams in a rich organisational context, improving the quality of decisions (Alamar, 2013: 38).

There are challenges to establishing an integrated analytics approach within organisations. Moving from a culture in which an organisation's data streams are segregated to the use of an integrated analytics environment involves change, which some staff may feel threatened by and resist. Therefore, leadership is essential to promote the development and uptake of integrated analytics environments (Alamar, 2013: 102). Plans for developing integrated analytics environments need to consider the roles and responsibilities of organisation staff within data collection, analysis and decision making. In marketing applications, integrated analytics environments need to provide multiple data views to sports organisations, their suppliers and customers (Miller, 2016: 80–81, 129). Analytics systems also need to implement appropriate security mechanisms to prevent unauthorised access to data and functions (Fried, 2017).

High-performance management systems

The wealth of complex data within high-performance sports needs to be reduced to key markers relating to organisational targets. The objectives for the athletes or governing body may be to win or improve performance. The analytics systems used by high-performance managers not only need to integrate heterogeneous datasets but be fully integrated with, if not designed around, the strategic plan and targets of the sports organisation. Integrating analytic systems with organisational targets ensures that the data stored and analysed, as well as the information produced, are relevant to organisational success and we avoid analysing data for its own sake. Strategic management involves target setting and monitoring performance in relation to these targets. The data streams to be managed within an integrated analytics environment need to be designed in a way that reflects the business functions of the data (Miller, 2016: 121). Organisational performance is represented in a high-level abstract form using key performance indicators as well as more detailed information that contributes to and is aligned with organisational performance within a high-performance environment. Wiltshire (2013) discussed the various

216

data types used by high-performance managers during planning, monitoring and evaluation of performances. The aspects of interest include athlete lifestyle, talent screening, tactical and technical performance, strength and conditioning, training plans, psychological assessments (for individual players, teams and coaches), injury surveillance, cardiac screening, muscular-skeletal screening and anti-doping. Miller (2016: 194) added scouting reports and coach input among the data types to be included.

Pervasive and ubiquitous computing has enhanced the quantity and accuracy of data that can be recorded during training and competition. Recently developed technologies applied in sports performance analysis include accelerometers, strain gages, force sensors and inertial sensors (Baca, 2015). Wiltshire (2013) identifies several benefits of using interdisciplinary multiple data types within high-performance management systems:

- Cohesive and coherent use of data, avoiding disjointed data management by various support services.
- The ability to set targets based on fused data.
- Reduced redundancy.
- Improved data security.
- Balanced use of various datasets based on their relative importance to organisational goals.
- Improved monitoring of player performance and injury risk using automatic alerts.

The rationale for using detailed information about sports performance within high-performance management systems is similar to the rationale for coaches using objective sports performance data (Franks and Miller, 1991): to avoid inaccurate, biased and incomplete assessment of athlete performance. The data stored within high-performance management systems need to be used ethically, fairly and transparently. The use of medical data needs to be legal and compliant with ethical standards of medical professions. Indeed, the storage and use of all data need to comply with data protection laws. Performance data need to be used fairly with respect to talent development, performance reviews and selection.

The information used within high-performance management systems needs to be presented in a way that enhances understanding, improving the accuracy and speed of decisions. This requires an effective dashboard interface to provide a concise set of the most critical information presented with visual impact. Therefore, the most common queries that can be anticipated during the development of integrated sports analytics environments should be associated with a dashboard interface that provides a concise yet reasonably complete view of the information required. A further consideration in the design of the interface is that various levels of users need to be provided with data views that support the types of information they are privileged to see and the decisions they make.

SUMMARY

As computing and communication technology has developed, there has been an increase in the integration of various technologies. The integration of hardware capabilities has been exploited by software systems that have progressed from individual programs to systems that integrate multiple processes within consistent environments. Sports performance analysis has progressed from notation systems that separated manual notation from video resources to the computerised video analysis packages we use today that integrate match videos with structured event data. Further integration within sports performance analysis has combined event location data, heart rate data and dashboards of summary analyses with match event data and videos. Coaching support environments integrate sports performance analysis, feedback and discussion forums, enhancing communication between coaches and players. High-performance management systems integrate analytics processes with strategic directions of sports organisations. The benefits of integrating data streams include reduced data duplication, streamlined analysis processes and enhanced security. High-performance managers are able to use multiple data resources within context when monitoring performance and making decisions.

REFERENCES

Alamar, B.C. (2013) *Sports analytics: A guide for coaches, managers and other decision makers*, New York, NY: Columbia University Press.
Baca (2015) 'Data acquisition and processing', In A. Baca (ed.), *Computer science in sport: Research and practice* (pp. 46–81), London: Routledge.

218

Butterworth, A. (2018) 'Multimedia performance profiling', Ph.D. Thesis, Cardiff, UK: Cardiff Metropolitan University, UK.

Franks, I.M. and Miller, G. (1991) 'Training coaches to observe and remember', *Journal of Sports Sciences*, 9: 285–297.

Fried, G. (2017) 'The data ecosystem', In G. Fried and C. Mumcu (eds.), *Sport analytics: A data-driven approach to sport business and management* (pp. 33–46), London: Routledge.

Fried, G. and Mumcu, C. (2017) *Sport analytics: A data-driven approach to sport business and management*, London: Routledge.

Harrison, C.K. and Bukstein, S. (2017) *Sport business analytics: Using data to increase revenue and improve operational efficiency*, Boca Raton, FL: CRC Press.

James, N., Mellalieu, S.D. and Jones, N.M.P. (2005) 'The development of position-specific performance indicators in professional rugby union', *Journal of Sports Sciences*, 23: 63–72.

Miller, T.W. (2016) *Sports analytics and data science: Winning the game with methods and models*, Old Tappan, NJ: Pearson Education Inc.

Mumcu, C. (2017) 'An introduction to analytics and data', In G. Fried and C. Mumcu (eds.), *Sport analytics: A data-driven approach to sport business and management* (pp. 17–32), London: Routledge.

Nibali, M. (2017) 'Analysing our way to better sport performance', In G. Fried and C. Mumcu (eds.), *Sport analytics: A data-driven approach to sport business and management* (pp. 49–75), London: Routledge.

O'Donoghue, P.G. (2005) 'Normative profiles of sports performance', *International Journal of Performance Analysis of Sport*, 5(1): 104–119.

O'Donoghue, P.G., Robinson, J. and Murphy, M.H. (1996) 'A database system to support immediate video feedback for coaching', *Proceedings of the 14th Applied Informatics Conference* (pp. 258–261), Innsbruck, Austria, February 1996.

Patrick, J.D. and McKenna, M.J. (1986) 'A generalised system for sports analysis', *Australian Journal of Science and Medicine in Sport*, September 1986: 19–23.

Wiemeyer, J. and Mueller, F. (2015) 'Information and communication technology-enhanced learning and training', In A. Baca (ed.), *Computer science in sport: Research and practice* (pp. 187–213), London: Routledge.

Wiltshire, H.D. (2013) 'Sports performance analysis for high performance managers', In T. McGarry, P.G. O'Donoghue and J. Sampaio (eds.), *Routledge handbook of sports performance analysis* (pp. 176–186), London: Routledge.

CHAPTER 12

SPORTS ANALYTICS APPLICATIONS IN SOCCER

INTRODUCTION

Over the past two decades, there has been considerable growth in the use of performance analysis within team sports due to developments in modern performance analysis software, making it more accessible to coaches, clubs and organisations. The integration of digital video footage and computer technology has led to systems that are easy to use; therefore, a degree in computer science or statistics is not required to be a competent user (James, 2006). Licensed and subscription-based self-coding performance analysis software such as Sportscode (www.hudl.com/elite/sportscode), Nacsport (www.nacsport.com/en/), Dartfish (www.dartfish.com) and the LongoMatch open-source project (https://longomatch.com/en/open-source/) are cost-effective or free platforms that have increased the integration of performance analysis into the coach-athlete-sport science relationship (Drust, 2010; Lago, 2009) and have become an integral part of the coaching process (Hughes and Franks, 2007).

Prior to this, the traditional approach to analysing technical and tactical performance in team games was exclusively through coach observations. These observations were often qualitative; therefore, they could be less objective and systematic (e.g. structure and comprehensive), used the observers' subjective impressions, slowed the analysis process, and often needed to take advantage or rely on the experiences and expertise of the coach. In contrast, quantitative game observations are more objective due to the systematic categorisation of behaviours used to collect data (Memmert et al., 2016). From these data, individual player and team performance can be analysed.

More recently, with the development of valid and reliable semi-automated computer tracking systems and global positioning systems (GPS) that log event data and monitor player position, velocity and movement patterns (Bradley et al., 2007; Cummins et al., 2013; Valter et al., 2006), there are large volumes of data collected on technical, tactical and physical aspects of performance. For example, positional tracking of 22 players and the ball using x- and y-coordinates at 25 frames per second would amount to around 3,100,000 total positions (data points) during the game (Memmert et al., 2016). Performance analysis companies such as STATS (www.stats.com), Opta (www.optasportspro.com) and ChyronHego (http://chyronhego.com) provide services in which games are coded and analysed during and after the match on behalf of the club, league or governing body, whereas GPS companies like Catapult (www.catapultsports.com/uk/) and STATsports (http://statsports.com) allow sports scientists to monitor players' data during training and the game.

The availability of performance analysis systems, services and research, especially in soccer, means it is integrated into the workflow when possible and the majority of professional soccer clubs employ performance analysts and/or have access to performance analysis data. Performance analysts are often responsible for pre-match analysis, live feedback, post-match analysis and feedback, scouting analysis and trend data analysis (Wright et al., 2013). However, a critical review, comment on this critical review and a systematic review (Carling et al., 2013; Mackenzie and Cushion, 2012; Sarmento et al., 2014) in performance analysis highlight a frequent disconnect between research and application due to a lack of context (e.g. opposition's style of play, home advantage, current score-line, officiating decisions) and situation-specific information (e.g. the pitch location where actions took place, quality of the pass or ball control, quality of the players' decision making and skill) on measured variables. This is because the research paradigm often adopts a positivist approach concerned with identifying a cause-and-effect relationship between these variables (often referred to as performance indicators) and outcomes.

In contrast, coaches and performance analysts use simple frequency counts of technical and tactical performance indicators to segment the game for a more interpretive (i.e. qualitative) analysis of the video footage in the applied setting, so it can form part of the feedback process to players (Wright et al., 2014). For example, a survey of 46 elite coaches reported that the selection of performance indicators was influenced by their coaching philosophy (91%) and "gut instinct" (43%) and that only some performance indicators remained constant whereas others fluctuated from game to game (Wright et al., 2012).

Therefore, this chapter initially reviews previous historical research in soccer and defines strategy, playing styles and tactics, so these concepts can be used as frameworks to develop more sensitive and specific performance indicators that measure these aspects of the game. In addition, some examples of approaches and techniques used to measure playing styles and tactics are provided. The chapter concludes with a team case study using the recently released STATS playing styles framework.

PERFORMANCE INDICATORS IN SOCCER

Soccer is an example of an invasion game with a primary objective of scoring goals, while not conceding goals. Moreover, it is a goal-striking game that requires teams to legally direct the ball at a target so it crosses the goal line between two posts 7.32m apart and below a crossbar 2.44m above the ground. Therefore, to achieve this objective, attacking teams coordinate actions that maintain possession of the ball so it can invade space directly in front of the target (i.e. scoring zone) to attempt a goal, whereas defending teams coordinate actions to reduce available space and attempt to regain possession.

Performance indicators are a selection, or combination, of action variables that describe some or all aspects of performance and should relate to successful performance or outcomes (Bartlett, 2002). Previously in soccer, indicators were classified based on the quality of performance (e.g. passes per possession) and scoring indicators (e.g. goals scored). Performance indicators such as goals, number of shots, passes or passing accuracy are examples used to assess team and individual player performance. For example, researchers have attempted to identify key performance indicators associated with successful outcomes in competitions such as the World Cup (Franks, 2005; Liu et al., 2015; Ruiz-Ruiz et al., 2013; Scoulding et al., 2004), Euro Cup (Yiannakos and Armatas, 2006), Champions League (Almeida et al., 2014; Lago-Peñas et al., 2011), English Premier League (Adams et al., 2013; Bradley et al., 2013; Bush et al., 2015), Spanish League (Castellano et al., 2013; Lago-Peñas and Dellal, 2010) and Bundesliga (Hiller, 2014; Vogelbein et al., 2014; Yue et al., 2014) to predict team performance. Performance analysis research

222

in soccer has mostly focused on key performance indicators such as goals, shots, possession and passing patterns prior to scoring a goal as an attempt to predict future outcomes (Franks, 2005; Jones et al., 2004; Taylor et al., 2005).

Since Reep and Benjamin's (1968) seminal work demonstrating that approximately 80% of goals were from passing sequences of three passes or fewer, with a goal scored every 10 shots, there has been debate on whether longer or shorter passing sequences are more effective, with the literature reporting mixed findings. More recently, studies demonstrate that more goals are scored from shorter passing sequences, which are more frequent than longer passing sequences; however, once the data are normalised, longer passing sequences are more efficient (Franks, 2005; Tenga et al., 2010b). In addition to passing sequences, longer possession durations are typically associated with successful teams; however, differences in the length of passing sequence durations have been reported between international teams and the English Premier League (Carling et al., 2007; Jones et al., 2004; Tenga and Sigmundstad, 2011). Furthermore, it has been reported that more goals are scored in the second half of games and that midfielders and forwards score more goals than any other position (Acar et al., 2009; Barreira et al., 2013; Grant et al., 1998; Partridge et al., 1993; Taylor et al., 2005; Yiannakos and Armatas, 2006). Goal scoring and variables associated with scoring are easily measured to determine some degree of performance efficiency. However, the prevalence of goals compared to other invasion games is low; therefore, additional behaviour patterns and event data need to be considered and analysed.

Goal shots have been measured to analyse attacking performance and include performance indicators such as pitch location of the shot, shot outcome (i.e. goal, on-target, off-target, goalkeeper save) and shot frequency (Bate, 1988; Collet, 2013; Corbellini et al., 2013; Chervenjakov, 1988; Ensum et al., 2005; Garganta et al., 1997; Hughes and Churchill, 2005; Hughes and Franks, 2005; Hughes et al., 1988; Lago-Ballesteros and Lago-Peñas, 2010; Lago-Peñas et al., 2011; Pollard et al., 2004). It was found that shots taken closer to the goal and in central positions are more likely to produce a goal. Due to the importance of invading this central position close to the goal, researchers, analysts and coaches have focused on attacking third entries and penalty area entries, and factors that might influence goal scoring opportunities. Ruiz-Ruiz et al. (2013) analysed teams that were winning, drawing and losing during games in the Germany World Cup 2006 and found that winning teams made more penalty area entries, and there was a moderate correlation between the number of entries and the likelihood of scoring a goal. Similarly, Tenga et al. (2010c) reported a 1% scoring probability based on an average of three goals and 280 possessions per match in the Norwegian league 2004 season; therefore, they examined the relationship between broader measures such as scoring opportunities and score box entries. A score box possession was defined as an entry into the score box with a high degree of control (i.e. space and time for the attacking team to perform intended actions). In addition, they examined possession type and defensive stability and reported counterattacks as more effective than elaborate possessions when playing against an imbalanced defence (Tenga et al., 2010a, 2010b; Tenga et al., 2010c). Furthermore, regaining the ball closer to the opponent's goal increases the chance of scoring and scoring opportunities, probably due to the proximity of the goal and an imbalanced defence (Garganta et al., 1997; Hughes and Churchill, 2005; Wright et al., 2011).

It is worth noting that of the 1,688 team possessions from open play included in the analysis by Tenga et al. (2010c), 80 (4.7%) led to scoring opportunities and 167 (9.9%) to score box possessions, whereas the remaining 1,441 (85.4%) team possessions had other outcomes (i.e. no score box possession, or possession lost in the defensive, middle or attacking third). This is a significantly large proportion and it would be useful to better define, describe and understand what happens during these possessions or phases of play. Previous researchers have focused on ball possession during competitions and its association with successful performance (Bell-Walker et al., 2006; Breen et al., 2006; Duarte et al., 2013; Hughes and Franks, 2005; Jones et al., 2004; Lago-Ballesteros and Lago-Peñas, 2010; Lago-Peñas et al., 2011; Oberstone, 2009; Williams, 2003), areas of the pitch where teams maintain possession (Ridgewell, 2011; Tenga and Sigmunstad, 2011), and maintenance of possession close to the opponent's goal as an indicator of a successful attack (Bartlett et al., 2012). Conversely, having more ball possessions than your opponent does not always lead to the production of scoring opportunities and goals (Bate, 1988; Wright et al., 2011). Moreover, like other performance indicators, possession is influenced by contextual factors such as match location (i.e. home or away), match status (i.e. winning, drawing or losing) and quality of the opposition (Lago-Peñas, 2009; Lago-Peñas and Dellal, 2010; Lago-Penas and Lago-Ballesteros, 2011;

Taylor et al., 2008) and once these factors are accounted for, possession becomes a poor predictor of performance (Collet, 2013).

Attempting to identify performance indicators to predict performance has generated mixed results, often due to interpretation of performance indicator definitions and the difficulty in including contextual and situational variables. Researchers have also: 1) relied on a classic approach of linear causality whereby an explanation or success assumption is based on a naive chain of cause and effect; 2) been constrained to use performance indicators based on availability rather than an attempt to develop a deeper understanding of performance; 3) been confounded by the availability of large datasets required for predictive modelling in which the number of predictive variables are exponentially related to the number of observations/games; and 4) discovered the possibility that information will start to lose relevance once datasets overlap multiple seasons (Carling et al., 2013; Mackenzie and Cushion, 2012). Therefore, analysts have adopted a reductionist approach in which performance indicators are used to segment the video into critical moments from the game that can provide feedback to the coach and players. Advancements in technology and techniques have resulted in additional data; however, to connect the researcher and practitioners (i.e. analysts and coaches), we need to improve our understanding of strategy, tactics, playing styles and transitions within the game to develop more specific and sensitive performance indicators and metrics.

SOCCER STRATEGY, PLAYING STYLE AND TACTICS

Team sports such as soccer require the players of two opposing teams to interact directly and concurrently to achieve an objective (i.e. score a goal); therefore, the actions of the players and teams are influenced by the organisation of the opposition and cooperation of teammates, the huge degree of freedom and variability, and the skill of a player to act in specific conditions (Garganta, 2009). Gréhaigne et al. (1995, 1997) identified space and time, information and organisation as the three main challenges in invasion team sports that can be contested with appropriate strategy and tactics. Therefore, tactical match performance depends on the quality of individual players or team actions in space and time during match play to be successful (Memmert et al., 2016). Moreover, tactical modelling can be useful for coaches, players, analysts and researchers in identifying regular or random game features during attacking and defensive play, providing information on player and team efficacy, and providing benchmarks for training.

Strategy and tactics are important factors that influence the outcome of the game and are fundamental to successful performance in soccer (Carling et al., 2007; Yiannakos and Armatas, 2006). Strategy has been defined as the plans, principles of play or action guidelines decided on prior to a match that inform how the players and team will interact during the game (Hewitt, 2016). For example, attacking strategies might involve moving players to field positions where they can receive the ball or score, overlap their teammate and defensive player in the direction of the goal to exploit space, or increase the width and depth of the team's surface area to create space in critical areas and/or a player numerical advantage (i.e. unbalanced defence). In contrast, defensive strategies might involve the immediate delaying of the opposition's attacking play once it regains possession through the restriction of passing options and time to make the pass, and/or the increase of player density and structure (i.e. defensive shape) in defensive areas.

In addition, strategies are influenced by the playing style, defined as the team's general behaviour to achieve attacking and defensive objectives. Playing styles are often based on the coaching philosophy. Previous literature and the football community have defined attacking and defending playing styles. Attacking playing styles include direct, possession or elaborate, counterattacking, total soccer and crossing, whereas defending playing styles include low pressure and high pressure (Bangsbo and Peitersen, 2000; Garganta et al., 1997; Pollard et al., 1988; Wright et al., 2011). The team's strategy and specific playing styles inform the subsidiary units (i.e. defending back four) and individual player position roles and responsibilities so agreed instructions known as tactics can be provided by the coaching staff.

Tactics, or tactical decision making, are defined as the specific attacking and defensive voluntary actions that are executed as a solution to the immediate or future anticipated situations, which are influenced by the opposition. In addition, changes to tactics might occur based on team and player attributes, player injury/substitution, quality of opposition, current match status (i.e. winning, drawing or losing) and/or match location (i.e. home or away). Tactics determine how the team plans to manage space and time, and individual (i.e. one-on-one attacking and defending events

226

with or without the ball) and group (i.e. the cooperation between subsidiary units to achieve objectives) actions (Fradua et al., 2013; Garganta, 2009). Tactics are often changed to gain an advantage during competition, influenced by contextual and situational factors and the interaction between and within the two teams (Rein and Memmert, 2016). Therefore, pre-match strategy and tactics are important, as they inform team, subsidiary unit and individual player tactical decision making prior to the game but also during the competition as it evolves across time.

Furthermore, during the game, one team will be in a phase of play that directly impacts the opposition's phase of play, and vice versa. The theory of dynamical systems has been used to describe the interaction between the two teams and how perturbations change the rhythmic flow of attacking and defending (Gréhaigne et al., 1997; McGarry et al., 2002). For example, an attacking phase of play may influence the opposition's tactics used in the defensive phase based on the position of each team's players on the field in relation to the ball during a possession transition. However, to describe the playing style and tactics used during these phases of play, a framework to segment the game is required. Hewitt (2016) stated that phases of play can be categorised as one of the following: Established Attack, Transition from Attack to Defence, Established Defence, Transition from Defence to Attack and Set Plays (see Figure 12.1). For further simplicity, moments of play were grouped into three phases: 1) Established Offense and Defence; 2) Transitional Play; 3) and Set Plays. The terminology used to describe these three phases is familiar and used by coaches, players and analysts to describe strategy, playing styles and tactics in soccer. It is vital to create a common language between researchers and practitioners so we can develop more appropriate questions to understand performance, which should lead to the identification of indicators that better capture aspects of performance.

Measuring playing styles and tactics

Traditionally, analyses of playing styles and tactics have been conducted using notation to categorise events or actions and generate frequency counts and average statistics (Bartlett, 2002). Therefore, previous studies have measured attacking performance indicators like passing variables and possessions (Collet, 2013; Franks, 2005; Lago-Peñas and Dellal, 2010; Liu et al., 2015), and defensive performance indicators like ball regain

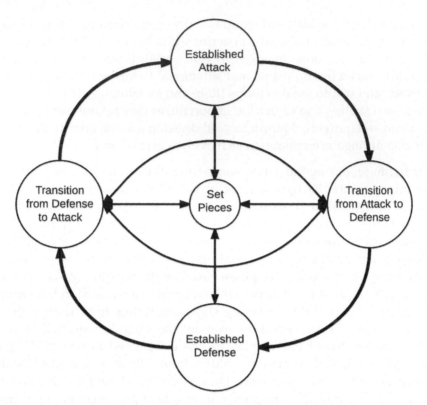

Figure 12.1 Moments of play (from Hewitt, 2016)

location and recovery time (Bell-Walker et al., 2006; Vogelbein et al., 2014) often in isolation and used them to make inferences about attacking and defensive playing styles and tactics. For example, a direct playing style includes short passing sequences of four or less passes and counter attacks that include a long pass or maximum of two passes that transition quickly through the midfield zone, whereas a possession playing style involves a high number of consecutive passes and includes elaborate attacks of five or more short passes that progress more slowly through midfield (Olsen and Larsen, 1997; Franks, 2005; Tenga et al., 2010b). In addition, other styles such as counter attack, total football, crossing, low press and high press have been described in the literature; however, they are often poorly defined or provide little or no information about associated performance indicators. More recently, researchers have used multiple performance indicators to create behaviour indexes, multivariate statistical approaches and spatiotemporal analyses to identify playing styles and tactics.

Kempe et al. (2014) developed the Index of Game Control (IGC) and Index of Offensive Behaviour (IOB), which combine multiple variables of offensive actions to evaluate tactical behaviour, rather than one or two variables such as possession and number of passes. IGC was calculated using several passing and passing success parameters (passes per action, passing direction, target player passes, passing success rate, and passing success rate in forward direction) to provide information on game control, specifically how accurate an attacking sequence was performed. To assess a team's playing style and distinguish between direct and possession play, the IOB was calculated by combining IGC with parameters that measured the duration and distance covered by the offensive actions and the overall game speed (i.e. mean passes per attack, game speed, mean time of attack, gain of possession, distance per attack and relative ball possession rate). The IOB differentiated between direct and possession playing style and enabled fine distinctions between offensive tactical approaches used by various teams. For example, IOB scores for Germany (7.35) and Spain (16.13) indicated they used the possession style to varying degrees, whereas Honduras (-8.45) and Italy (2.19) used a direct style. In addition, the most successful teams (i.e. top four teams in the 2009–2010 and 2010–2011 Bundesliga and quarter-finalists in the 2010 FIFA World Cup) preferred the possession style of play and had a higher index score for game control, mainly due to more possessions, accurate passing and increased game speed. Moreover, the indexes are sensitive in differentiating tactical behaviour and therefore could be integrated to review performance across the game.

Fernandez-Navarro et al. (2016) employed exploratory factor analysis using principle component analysis (PCA) on 19 performance indicators to define different playing styles and identify associated performance indicators. Factor analysis is a statistical method for identifying clusters of variables that enable data to be reduced into sets of factors. In addition, for each factor, the performance indicators with the highest factor loading (i.e. the correlation between the performance indicator and factor) were identified. Six factors extracted accounted for 88% of the cumulative variance and defined 12 playing styles, split into eight attacking (i.e. direct vs. possession, crossing vs. no crossing, wide vs. narrow possession, fast vs. slow progression) and four defending (i.e. pressure on wide vs. central areas, low vs. high pressure) styles. Using these factors, a specific team's reliance on one or a combination of these styles can be identified to create a playing styles profile (see Table 12.1). For example, in season 2006–2007, Everton had a direct, no crossing,

Table 12.1 Team styles of play from season 2006–2007

Teams	Attacking styles of play								Defensive styles of play			
	1	2	3	4	5	6	7	8	1	2	3	4
1. Atletico de Madrid	•	•	•			••	•		•	•		•
2. Barcelona	••	••		•••		••	••		•	•	•	•
3. Betis				••	••••		•••	•	•			•
4. Bilbao	••			••				•		••		••
5. Celta	•••			••	••		•	•	•	•		•••
6. Deportivo				•••								••
7. Espanyol			•••	•••	••			•	•••	•		•••
8. Mallorca									•			••••
9. Osasuna				•								••••
10. Real Madrid		••			••	••	•	•	•	•	•	•
11. Real Sociedad	•		•						•		•	
12. Sevilla		••		••	••	••	•	•	••		•	
13. Valencia									•			
14. Zaragoza		•		•••	•	••	•	•	•••	•		
15. Arsenal	••	••	•••			••		•		••		
16. Aston Villa	••					••				•••		
17. Bolton	••							••		••		
18. Chelsea	•		•••	•		••	••			•	•	
19. Everton	•									•		
20. Liverpool		•	•••			••	••		•	•		
21. Manchester City	••		•••				•				•	
22. Manchester United				•						•		
23. Portsmouth	•			•				••				
24. Tottenham		•			••			•		••	•	
25. West Ham			••							••		••
26. Wigan	•		•		•		•			••		•

Note: The number of dots indicates the degree of utilisation of the style of play by the team; more dots indicate a higher utilisation.

• Score between 0 and ±1.   •• Score between ±1 and ±2.   ••• Score between ±2 and ±3.   •••• Score between ±3 and ±4.

Table 12.2 Team styles of play from season 2010–2011

Teams	Attacking styles of play								Defensive styles of play			
	1	2	3	4	5	6	7	8	1	2	3	4
27. Atletico de Madrid	•			•	•			•				•
28. Barcelona		••••	•		••			•		••		••
29. Bilbao	•		•	•								••
30. Getafe		•		•	•			•	••		••	
31. Levante	•			••	•••			•••	•			
32. Osasuna	••		••					•				
33. Real Madrid		•	••		•	••	•		•			•
34. Real Sociedad	•		••		•		•	•	•			•
35. Valencia		•	••		•			•	•		•	
36. Villareal		••	••			•			•			••
37. Zaragoza	•				•	•		•	•			

Note: The number of dots indicates the degree of utilisation of the style of play by the team; more dots indicate a higher utilisation.

• Score between 0 and ±1. •• Score between ±1 and ±2. ••• Score between ±2 and ±3. •••• Score between ±3 and ±4.

narrow possession, fast progression, low and central areas pressure playing style profile, whereas Barcelona had a possession, no crossing, narrow possession, fast progression, high and central areas pressure profile. Therefore, when reviewing the associated performance indicators, Everton had a higher percentage of forward passes, lower percentage of sideways passes and possessions, and regained the ball closer to their own goal. Barcelona's performance indicators scores were in the opposite direction; moreover, during the 2010–2011 season, their playing style profile changed to adopt alternative styles (i.e. crossing, wide and slow progression) and intensify the use of previous styles such as possession and pressure in high and central areas. This change was the result of a new manager and players; therefore, the ability to detect change when other factors alter could influence the tactical plans when preparing for an opponent to perturb or disrupt their playing style.

Due to the availability of player and ball positional tracking data in soccer, spatiotemporal approaches such as Voronoi diagrams and centroid analysis (see Chapter 6 for further details) have been used to analyse tactical behaviour and develop insights on tactics during attacking and defensive phases, transitions and critical moments such as goals (Fonseca et al., 2013; Frencken et al., 2011). Centroid analysis can provide characteristics on the centroid position and surface area of a team. The centroid position is the average position of the team's outfield players for one team, whereas surface area is the total space covered by the team's outfield players. Tracking the centroid position will provide information on how a team moves as a unit across the pitch, whereas increases and decreases in surface area provide information on how a team creates or reduces space when attacking and defending. Frencken et al. (2012) used this approach to examine if inter-team distance dynamics correspond to match events in elite soccer matches (UEFA Champions League quarter-final 2008–2009). They identified 242 critical match events; 51 were dead ball situations (i.e. throw-ins, goal kicks, corner kicks and free kicks) but 93% of critical events selected using longitudinal rate and inter-team distance related to the ball being passed longitudinally and/ or players moving forwards and backwards and 87% of critical events selected using lateral rate and inter-team distance related to the team in possession passing sideways or the defending team changing position laterally. Moreover, in a 3s window prior to one of two goals and two out of 14 goal attempts, there were periods of high variability across the measures. Although this was only one match, inter-team distances provide new tactical performance indicators to measure tactical behaviour.

Fonseca et al. (2012) used Voronoi diagrams to characterise spatial interaction dynamics of players in a team to better understand how opposite teams coordinate player locations on the field to define and adjust their dominate regions during a game. Specifically, they used the minimum interpersonal distance between teammates ($Dist_{NT}$) and the area of the dominant region for each player ($Area_{DR}$) to characterise individual and collective player behaviour. For example, the variables identified that players from the team with the ball are further apart from each other, whereas defending players are closer to each other. Moreover, $Dist_{NT}$ and $Area_{DR}$ over time were lower in regularity for the defending team, suggesting more unpredictable defending behaviours likely due to the constant spatial reorganisation of players to protect the goal in response to the attacking team.

Playing styles analysis case study

The small sample of examples from current studies presented in the previous section demonstrates the field's current research direction. More importantly, some of the data analytics approaches described and validated can be integrated into the coaching process and provide meaningful insights on playing styles and tactics that can impact performance. However, these larger datasets use analytical approaches and techniques and programme software that are often beyond the capability of the practitioners working directly with the team. Therefore, the challenge is to integrate these approaches into intuitive, user-friendly software packages. More importantly, the data need to be effectively visualised to help the user analyse and interpret them. Finally, it is important that the software used to categorise and segment playing styles and tactics can be linked back to the relevant qualitative video so coaches, analysts and players can review game events.

Recently, STATS developed a framework that analyses playing styles objectively from ball event data (e.g. touches, passes, crosses), location of that event on the pitch and the player involved in the event captured during the game. Moreover, to develop the playing styles framework, they engaged analysts and coaches from the English Premier League and other European leagues to identify and define eight playing styles. Each of the eight playing style definitions are calculated independently using algorithms and applied to every team possession during the game. Each team possession is then given a membership value (between 0–100%)

that represents the strength of the playing style during that specific possession. An important thing to note is that multiple playing styles can be active during a possession. For additional information on the playing styles analysis, visit these website links: www.stats.com/industry-analysis-articles/stats-playing-styles-introduction/ (accessed 28/11/17) and www.stats.com/webinars/advanced-analytics-in-soccerfootball-playing-styles-analysis/ (accessed 28/11/17). The eight playing styles follow:

1   Direct Play (DP): DP captures the instances of play in which teams attempt to move the ball quickly towards the opposition's goal using passes. The distance of the passing event (i.e. pass, direct free kick pass, indirect free kick pass, cross, direct free kick cross, indirect free kick cross, goal kick, goalkeeper throw, goalkeeper kick, throw in and clearance) is the parameter measured to provide the membership value. Forward distance gained from these passing events must be greater than 20m to qualify as DP and reaches 100% at 40 metres.

2   Counter Attack (CA): CA occurs once a team regains possession and moves the ball into attacking areas via passes, dribbles or a combination of both. To qualify as a CA, the ball must reach a target location within the opponent's half. This target location varies based on the regain location, with the speed of transition from the regain location to the target location as the parameter for the membership value. The quicker the ball is moved up the pitch, the higher the membership percentage value.

3   Maintenance (MA): This is the first of three styles calculated in a very similar way. MA captures possessions in which a team secures and maintains possession of the ball in the defensive area of the pitch. The time spent in possession directly relates to the membership value. To qualify, possession must last for more than 10s and membership value increases linearly up until 30s, when it reaches 100%.

4   Build Up (BU): BU captures controlled ball possessions during which a team looks for opportunities to attack. Like MA, BU membership is calculated based on time spent in a zone between the halfway line and opposition's penalty area. To qualify, possession must last more than 8s and membership value increases linearly up until 25s, when it reaches 100%.

5   Sustained Threat (ST): Again, similar to MA and BU, but with the focus on time spent in the attacking third of the pitch. To qualify as ST, time spent in possession must be more than 6s and membership value increases linearly up until 20s, when it reaches 100%.

234

6   Fast Tempo (FT): This style is used to capture when a team moves the ball quickly to increase the tempo and speed of the game. FT calculates sequences of consecutive individual "fast possessions" that occur in the opponent's half. Individual fast possession is when the player releases the ball to a teammate in less than 2s or dribbles at a high tempo.

7   Crossing (Cr): All other styles have a continuous score to establish membership, whereas Cr membership is based on a binary score, so all crosses are assigned as 100%. Cr occurs when a ball is delivered from a wide area of the pitch with the intention of finding a teammate.

8   High Press (HP): HP captures how high up the pitch teams regain possession from events such as interceptions, header, tackles and blocks. The first parameter taken into consideration is the location in which the team regains possession. HP regains are those higher than 5m prior to the halfway line. The membership value increases linearly up until 15m into the opponent's half, when it reaches 100%. To retain the full membership value, the opposition must be in possession for a minimum of 10s.

To better understand how England would fare in the Euro 2016 championships, STATS produced a report titled "Analysing England ahead of Euro 2016" that included playing styles analysis to better understand the technical and tactical nature of the team (www.stats.com/publications/analysing-england-ahead-euro-2016/, accessed 28/11/17). The initial phase was to review England's playing styles from the World Cup 2014 in Brazil by comparing them to the tournament average (Figure 12.2a). England had a tendency to cross the ball frequently (+21% the tournament average) and keep possession in attacking areas to achieve sustained threat (+28%). The significance of crossing for England was probably due to the selection of creative players in wide areas, such as Danny Welbeck and Raheem Sterling as wide attackers with additional support in attacks from full-backs Glen Johnson and Leighton Baines making forward runs. Furthermore, their above average values for maintenance (+18%) and sustained threat (+28%) was due to the dominance of possession during their three group D games.

The second phase involved a comparison between Germany and France, who at the time were favourites to win Euro 2016. Germany and France demonstrated significantly higher levels of the fast tempo (+132% and

+76%, respectively) in comparison to England's -3% score. In addition, Germany developed their possession-based playing styles further by increasing their scores for fast tempo (+279%), sustained threat (+195%) and build up (+202%) during the Euro 2016 qualifiers (Figure 12.2b). Some caution is required with interpretation, as the quality of the opposition (based on an average FIFA ranking of 86.2) was lower during the qualifiers; however, it does suggest an evolving tactical approach and refinement of their playing style.

The final phase was a review of England's playing styles during the Euro 2016 qualifiers to identify any changes since the World Cup 2014 (Figure 12.2c). Their undefeated qualification campaign demonstrated a major increase in fast tempo (+124%) and sustained threat (+115%) compared to previous scores (-3% and +28%, respectively). As previously, caution is required due to weaker opposition (average FIFA ranking of 96); however, playing styles analysis reveals a change in tactical behaviour. The challenge for England is the sustainability of this playing style profile during the tournament and an ability to impose their style on the opposition so they can progress further in the tournament.

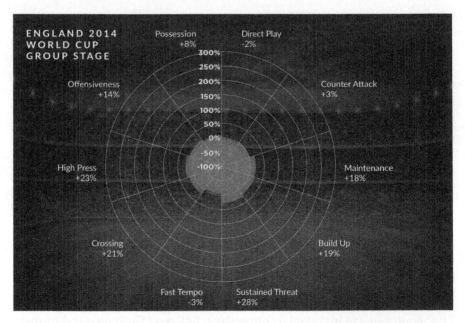

Figure 12.2 (a) England 2014 World Cup groups stages; (b) Germany 2016 Euro qualifying; (c) England 2015 Euro qualifying (courtesy of STATS)

sports analytics applications in soccer

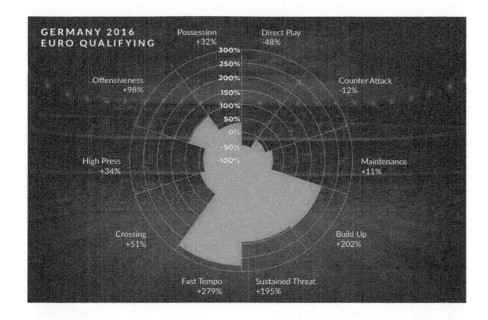

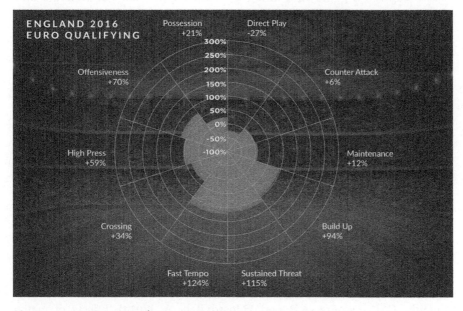

Figure 12.2 (Continued)

STATS playing styles framework is a useful tool that can objectively capture the eight styles so the teams' playing styles profile can be described for various situations (e.g. tournament type, match location, match status, quality of opposition). In addition, a team's playing style profile can be tracked over time to examine the impact of the manager/coaching staff attempts to adapt their playing philosophy or determine if during an individual game, tactics have been successfully delivered by the team, subsidiary units and individual players.

SUMMARY

In summary, this chapter provided an overview of previous studies in soccer, definitions of strategy, playing styles and tactics and examples of measuring them, and a team case study using STATS playing styles. Previous studies on performance indicators have produced mixed results in predicting performance, which is often due to differences in definitions and interpretation of performance indicators and the difficulty in including contextual and situational variables. Therefore, one approach is to develop a better understanding of strategy, playing styles and tactics to capture a game in a language familiar to coaches, analysts and players. Researchers have used behaviour indexes, multivariate statistical approaches and spatiotemporal analysis to identify playing styles and tactics; however, there still appears to be a disconnect between the research and practitioners. Finally, the STATS playing styles analysis framework is an example of how analysts and coaches can be engaged to develop products that can develop objective measures for the analysis of subjective tactical behaviour.

REFERENCES

Acar, M.F., Yapicioglu, B., Arikan, N., Yalcin, S., Ates, N. and Ergun, M. (2009) 'Analysis of goals scored in the 2006 World Cup', In T. Reilly and F. Korkusuz (eds.), *Science and football VI* (pp. 235–242). London: Routledge.

Adams, D., Morgans, R., Sacramento, J., Morgan, S. and Williams, M.D. (2013) 'Successful short passing frequency of defenders differentiates between top and bottom four English Premier League teams', *International Journal of Performance Analysis in Sport*, 13(3): 653–668.

Almeida, C.H., Ferreira, A.P. and Volossovitch, A. (2014) 'Effects of match location, match status and quality of opposition on regaining possession in

UEFA Champions League', *Journal of Human Kinetics*, 41(1): 1–12. http://doi. org/10.2478/hukin-2014-0048

Bangsbo, J. and Peitersen, B. (2000) *Soccer systems and strategies*, Champaign, IL: Human Kinetics.

Barreira, D., Garganta, J., Pinto, T., Valente, J. and Anguera, M.T. (2013) 'Do attacking game patterns differ between first and second halves of soccer matches in the 2010 FIFA World Cup?' In H. Nunome, B. Drust and B. Dawson (eds.), *Science and football VII* (pp. 193–198). London: Routledge.

Bartlett, R.M. (2002) 'The use of performance indicators in performance analysis', *Journal of Sports Sciences*, 20(10): 739–754.

Bartlett, R.M., Button, C., Robins, M., Dutt-Mazumder, A. and Kennedy, G. (2012) 'Analysing team coordination patterns from player movement trajectories in soccer: Methodological considerations', *International Journal of Performance Analysis in Sport*, 12(2): 398–424.

Bate, R. (1988) 'Football chance: Tactics and strategy', In T. Reilly, A. Lees, K. Davids and W.J. Murphy (eds.), *Science and football* (pp. 293–301), London: E & FN Spon.

Bell-Walker, J., McRobert, A., Ford, P. and Williams, A.M. (2006) 'A quantitative analysis of successful teams at the 2006 World Cup finals', *Insight: The F.A. Coaches Association Journal*, Autumn/Winter: 36–43.

Bradley, P.S., Lago-Peñas, C., Rey, E. and Gomez Diaz, A. (2013) 'The effect of high and low percentage ball possession on physical and technical profiles in English FA Premier League soccer matches', *Journal of Sports Sciences*, 31(12): 1261–1270. http://doi.org/10.1080/02640414.2013.786185

Bradley, P.S., O'Donoghue, P., Wooster, B. and Tordoff, P. (2007) 'The reliability of ProZone MatchViewer: A video-based technical performance analysis system', *International Journal of Performance Analysis in Sport*, 7(3): 117–129.

Breen, A., Iga, J., Ford, P. and Williams, A.M. (2006) 'World Cup 2006 – Germany. A quantitative analysis of goals scored', *Insight: The F.A. Coaches Association Journal*, Autumn/Winter: 44–53.

Bush, M., Barnes, C., Archer, D.T., Hogg, B. and Bradley, P.S. (2015) 'Evolution of match performance parameters for various playing positions in the English Premier League', *Human Movement Science*, 39: 1–11. http://doi. org/10.1016/j.humov.2014.10.003

Carling, C., Williams, A.M. and Reilly, T. (2007) *Handbook of soccer match analysis*, London: Routledge.

Carling, C., Wright, C., Nelson, L. and Bradley, P. (2013) 'Comment on "Performance analysis in football: A critical review and implications for future research"', *Journal of Sports Sciences*, 32: 1–6. http://doi.org/10.1080/02640 414.2013.807352

Castellano, J., Alvarez, D., Figueira, B., Coutinho, D. and Sampaio, J. (2013) 'Identifying the effects from the quality of opposition in a Football team positioning strategy', *International Journal of Performance Analysis in Sport*, 13(3): 822–832.

Chervenjakov, M. (1988) 'Assessment of the playing effectiveness of soccer players', In T. Reilly, A. Lees, K. Davids and W.J. Murphy (eds.), *Science and football* (pp. 288–292), London: E & FN Spon.

Collet, C. (2013) 'The possession game? A comparative analysis of ball retention and team success in European and international football, 2007–2010', *Journal of Sports Sciences*, 31(2): 123–136. http://doi.org/10.1080/02640414.2012.72 7455

Corbellini, F., Volossovitch, A., Andrade, C., Fernandes, O. and Ferreira, A.P. (2013) 'Contextual effects on the free kick performance: A case study with a Portuguese professional soccer team', In H. Nunome, B. Drust and B. Dawson (eds.), *Science and football VII* (pp. 217–222), London: Routledge.

Cummins, C., Orr, R., O'Connor, H. and West, C. (2013) 'Global Positioning Systems (GPS) and microtechnology sensors in team sports: A systematic review', *Sports Medicine*, 43(10): 1025–1042. http://doi.org/10.1007/s40279-013-0069-2

Drust, B. (2010) 'Performance analysis research: Meeting the challenge', *Journal of Sports Sciences*, 28(9): 921–922. http://doi.org/10.1080/02640411003740769

Duarte, R., Araujo, D., Folgado, H., Esteves, P.T., Marques, P. and Davids, K. (2013) 'Capturing complex, non-linear team behaviours during competitive football performance', *Journal of Systems Science and Complexity*, 26(1): 62–72.

Ensum, J., Pollard, R. and Taylor, S. (2005) 'Applications of logistic regression to shots at goal in association football. In T. Reilly, J. Cabri and D. Araujo (eds.), *Science and football V* (pp. 211–218). London: Routledge.

Fernandez-Navarro, J., Fradua, L., Zubillaga, A., Ford, P.R. and McRobert, A.P. (2016) 'Attacking and defensive styles of play in soccer: Analysis of Spanish and English elite teams', *Journal of Sports Sciences*, 34(24): 1–10. http://doi.org/10.1080/02640414.2016.1169309

Fonseca, S., Milho, J., Travassos, B. and Araújo, D. (2012) 'Spatial dynamics of team sports exposed by Voronoi diagrams', *Human Movement Science*, 31(6): 1652–1659. http://doi.org/10.1016/j.humov.2012.04.006

Fonseca, S., Milho, J., Travassos, B., Araújo, D. and Lopes, A. (2013) 'Measuring spatial interaction behavior in team sports using superimposed Voronoi diagrams', *International Journal of Performance Analysis in Sport*, 13(1): 179–189.

Fradua, L., Zubillaga, A., Caro, Ó., Iván Fernández-García, Á., Ruiz-Ruiz, C. and Tenga, A. (2013) 'Designing small-sided games for training tactical aspects in soccer: Extrapolating pitch sizes from full-size professional matches', *Journal of Sports Sciences*, 31(6): 573–581. http://doi.org/10.1080/02640414.2012.74 6722

Franks, I.M. (2005) 'Analysis of passing sequences, shots and goals in soccer', *Journal of Sports Sciences*, 23(5): 509–514. http://doi.org/10.1080/02640410 410001716779

Frencken, W., de Poel, H., Visscher, C. and Lemmink, K. (2012) 'Variability of inter-team distances associated with match events in elite-standard soccer', *Journal of Sports Sciences*, 30(12): 1207–1213. http://doi.org/10.1080/02640 414.2012.703783

Frencken, W., Lemmink, K., Delleman, N. and Visscher, C. (2011) 'Oscillations of centroid position and surface area of soccer teams in small-sided games', *European Journal of Sport Science*, 11(4): 215–223. http://doi.org/10.1080/1 7461391.2010.499967

Garganta, J. (2009) 'Trends of tactical performance analysis in team sports: Bridging the gap between research, training and competition', *Revista Portuguesa De Ciências Do Desporto*, 9(1): 81–89. http://doi.org/10.5628/rpcd. 09.01.81

Garganta, J., Maia, J. and Basto, F. (1997) 'Analysis of goal-scoring patterns in European top level soccer teams', In J. Bangsbo, T. Reilly and A.M. Williams (eds.), *Science and football III* (pp. 246–250), London: E & FN Spon.

Grant, A., Reilly, T., Williams, A.M. and Borrie, A. (1998) 'Analysis of the goals scored in the 1998 World Cup', *Insight: The F.A. Coaches Association Journal*, 2(1): 18–20.

Gréhaigne, J.-F., Bouthier, D. and David, B. (1997) 'Dynamic-system analysis of opponent relationships in collective actions in soccer', *Journal of Sports Sciences*, 15(2): 137–149. http://doi.org/10.1080/026404197367416

Gréhaigne, J.-F. and Godbout, P. (1995) 'Tactical knowledge in team sports from a constructivist and cognitivist perspective', *Quest*, 47(4): 490–505. http://doi. org/10.1080/00336297.1995.10484171

Hewitt, A. (2016) 'Game style in soccer: What is it and can we quantify it?', *International Journal of Performance Analysis in Sport*, 16(1): 1–19.

Hiller, T. (2014) 'The importance of players in teams of the German Bundesliga in the season 2012/2013 – A cooperative game theory approach', *Applied Economics Letters*, 22(4): 324–329. http://doi.org/10.1080/13504851.2014.941527

Hughes, M.D. and Churchill, S. (2005) 'Attacking profiles of successful and unsuccessful teams in Copa America 2001', In T. Reilly, J. Cabri and D. Araujo (eds.), *Science and football V* (pp. 221–224), London: Routledge.

Hughes, M.D. and Franks, I.M. (2005) 'Analysis of passing sequences, shots and goals in soccer', *Journal of Sports Sciences*, 23(5): 509–514.

Hughes, M.D. and Franks, I.M. (2007) *The essentials of performance analysis: An introduction*, London: Routledge.

Hughes, M.D., Robertson, K. and Nicholson, A. (1988) 'Comparison of patterns of play of successful and unsuccessful teams in the 1986 World Cup for soccer', In T. Reilly, A. Lees, K. Davids and W.J. Murphy (eds.), *Science and football* (pp. 363–367), London: E & FN Spon.

James, N. (2006) 'Notational analysis in soccer: Past, present and future', *International Journal of Performance Analysis in Sport*, 6(2): 67–81.

Jones, P.D., James, N. and Mellalieu, S.D. (2004) 'Possession as a performance indicator in soccer', *International Journal of Performance Analysis in Sport*, 4(1): 98–102.

Kempe, M., Vogelbein, M., Memmert, D. and Nopp, S. (2014) 'Possession vs. direct play: Evaluating tactical behavior in elite soccer', *International Journal of Sports Science*, 4(6A): 35–41. http://doi.org/10.5923/s.sports. 201401.05

Lago, C. (2009) 'The influence of match location, quality of opposition, and match status on possession strategies in professional association football', *Journal of Sports Sciences*, 27(13): 1463–1469. http://doi.org/10.1080/ 02640410903131681

Lago-Ballesteros, J. and Lago-Peñas, C. (2010) 'Performance in team sports: Identifying the keys to success in soccer', *Journal of Human Kinetics*, 25: 85–91.

Lago-Peñas, C. (2009) 'The influence of match location, quality of opposition, and match status on possession strategies in professional association football', *Journal of Sports Sciences*, 27(13): 1463–1469.

Lago-Peñas, C. and Dellal, A. (2010) 'Ball possession strategies in elite soccer according to the evolution of the match-score: The influence of situational variables', *Journal of Human Kinetics*, 25(1): 293–8. http://doi.org/10.2478/v10078-010-0036-z

Lago-Peñas, C. and Lago-Ballesteros, J. (2011) 'Game location and team quality effects on performance profiles in professional soccer', *Journal of Sports Science and Medicine*, 10(3): 465–471.

Lago-Peñas, C., Lago-Ballesteros, J. and Rey, E. (2011) 'Differences in performance indicators between winning and losing teams in the UEFA Champions League', *Journal of Human Kinetics*, 27(1): 1–12. http://doi.org/10.2478/v10078-011-0011-3

Liu, H., Gomez, M.-Á., Lago-Peñas, C. and Sampaio, J. (2015) 'Match statistics related to winning in the group stage of 2014 Brazil FIFA World Cup', *Journal of Sports Sciences*, *33*(12): 1205–1213. http://doi.org/10.1080/02640414.2015.1022578

Mackenzie, R. and Cushion, C. (2012) 'Performance analysis in football: A critical review and implications for future research', *Journal of Sports Sciences*, 31(6): 639–676. http://doi.org/10.1080/02640414.2012.746720

McGarry, T., Anderson, D.I., Wallace, S.A., Hughes, M.D. and Franks, I.M. (2002) 'Sport competition as a dynamical self-organizing system', *Journal of Sports Sciences*, 20(10): 771–781. http://doi.org/10.1080/026404102320675620

Memmert, D., Lemmink, K.A.P.M. and Sampaio, J. (2016) 'Current approaches to tactical performance analyses in soccer using position data', *Sports Medicine*, 47(1): 1–10. http://doi.org/10.1007/s40279-016-0562-5

Oberstone, J. (2009) 'Differentiating the top English Premier League football clubs from the rest of the pack: Identifying the keys to success', *Journal of Quantitative Analysis in Sports*, 5(3): Article 10.

Olsen, E. and Larsen, O. (1997) 'Use of match analysis by coaches', In J. Bangsbo, T. Reilly and A.M. Williams (eds.), *Science and football III* (pp. 209–220), London: E & FN Spon.

Partridge, D., Mosher, R.E. and Franks, I. (1993) 'A computer assisted analysis of technical performance – A comparison of the 1990 World Cup and intercollegiate soccer', In T. Reilly, J. Clarys and A. Stibbe (eds.), *Science and football II* (pp. 221–231). London: E & FN Spon.

Pollard, R., Ensum, J. and Taylor, S. (2004) 'Estimating the probability of a shot resulting in a goal: The effects of distance, angle and space', *International Journal of Soccer and Science*, 2(1): 50–55.

Pollard, R., Reep, C. and Hartley, S. (1988) 'The quantitative comparison of playing styles in soccer', In T. Reilly, A. Lees, K. Davids and W. J. Murphy (eds.), *Science and Football* (pp. 309–315). London: E & FN Spon.

Reep, C. and Benjamin, B. (1968) 'Skill and chance in association football', *Journal of the Royal Statistical Society*, 131(4): 581–585. http://doi.org/10.2307/2343726

Rein, R. and Memmert, D. (2016) 'Big data and tactical analysis in elite soccer: Future challenges and opportunities for sports science', *SpringerPlus*, 5(1): 1–13. http://doi.org/10.1186/s40064-016-3108-2

Ridgewell, A. (2011) 'Passing patterns before and after scoring in the 2010 FIFA World Cup', *International Journal of Performance Analysis in Sport,* 11(3), 562–574.

Ruiz-Ruiz, C., Fradua, L., Fernández-García, Á. and Zubillaga, A. (2013) 'Analysis of entries into the penalty area as a performance indicator in soccer', *European Journal of Sport Science*, 13(3): 241–248. http://doi.org/10.1080/1 7461391.2011.606834

Sarmento, H., Marcelino, R., Anguera, M.T., Campanico, J., Matos, N. and Leitão, J.C. (2014) 'Match analysis in football: A systematic review', *Journal of Sports Sciences*, 32(20): 1831–1843. http://doi.org/10.1080/02640414.2014.898852

Scoulding, A., James, N. and Taylor, J. (2004) 'Passing in the Soccer World Cup 2002', *International Journal of Performance Analysis in Sport*, 4(2): 36–41.

Taylor, J.B., Mellalieu, S.D. and James, N. (2005) 'A comparison of individual and unit tactical behaviour and team strategy in professional soccer', *International Journal of Performance Analysis in Sport*, 5(2): 87–101.

Taylor, J.B., Mellalieu, S.D., James, N. and Shearer, D.A. (2008) 'The influence of match location, quality of opposition, and match status on technical performance in professional association football', *Journal of Sports Sciences*, 26(9): 885–895.

Tenga, A., Holme, I., Ronglan, L.T. and Bahr, R. (2010a) 'Effect of playing tactics on achieving score-box possessions in a random series of team possessions from Norwegian professional soccer matches', *Journal of Sports Sciences*, 28(3): 245–255. http://doi.org/10.1080/02640410903502766

Tenga, A., Holme, I., Ronglan, L.T. and Bahr, R. (2010b) 'Effect of playing tactics on goal scoring in Norwegian professional soccer', *Journal of Sports Sciences*, 28(3): 237–244. http://doi.org/10.1080/02640410903502774

Tenga, A., Ronglan, L.T. and Bahr, R. (2010c) 'Measuring the effectiveness of offensive match-play in professional soccer', *European Journal of Sport Science*, 10(4): 269–277. http://doi.org/10.1080/17461390903515170

Tenga, A. and Sigmundstad, E. (2011) 'Characteristics of goal-scoring possessions in open play: Comparing the top, in-between and bottom teams from professional soccer league', *International Journal of Performance Analysis in Sport*, 11(3): 545–552. http://doi.org/10.1080/24748668.2011.11868572

Valter, D., Adam, C., Barry, M. and Marco, C. (2006) 'Validation of Prozone: A new video-based performance analysis system', *International Journal of Performance Analysis in Sport*, 6(1): 108–119.

Vogelbein, M., Nopp, S. and Hökelmann, A. (2014) 'Defensive transition in soccer – are prompt possession regains a measure of success? A quantitative analysis of German Fußball-Bundesliga 2010/2011', *Journal of Sports Sciences*, 32(11): 1076–1083. http://doi.org/10.1080/02640414.2013.879671

Williams, A.M. (2003) 'What does Quantitative Match Analysis tell us about successful attacking football?', *Insight: The F.A. Coaches Association Journal*, 6(3): 33–35

Wright, C., Atkins, S. and Jones, B. (2012) 'An analysis of elite coaches' engagement with performance analysis services (match, notational analysis and technique analysis)', *International Journal of Performance in Sport*, 12(2): 436–451. http://doi.org/10.1080/24748668.2012.11868609

Wright, C., Atkins, S., Jones, B. and Todd, J. (2013) 'The role of performance analysts within the coaching process: Performance Analysts Survey', *International Journal of Performance in Sport*, 13(1): 240–261.

Wright, C., Atkins, S., Polman, R., Jones, B. and Sargeson, L. (2011) 'Factors associated with goals and goal scoring opportunities in professional soccer', *International Journal of Performance Analysis in Sport*, 11(3): 438–449.

Wright, C., Carling, C. and Collins, D. (2014) 'The wider context of performance analysis and it application in the football coaching process', *International Journal of Performance Analysis in Sport*, 14(3): 709–733. http://doi.org/10.1080/24748668.2014.11868753

Yiannakos, A. and Armatas, V. (2006) 'Evaluation of the goal scoring patterns in European Championship in Portugal 2004', *International Journal of Performance Analysis in Sport*, 6(1): 178–188.

Yue, Z., Broich, H. and Mester, J. (2014) 'Statistical analysis for the soccer matches of the first Bundesliga', *International Journal of Sports Science & Coaching*, 9(3): 553–560. http://doi.org/10.1260/1747-9541.9.3.553

INDEX

246

248

254